D1416886

The Many Worlds
of Man

JACK CONRAD

The Many Worlds

of Man

Drawings by Stephen Rogers Peck

Thomas Y. Crowell Company

New York / Established 1834

ACKNOWLEDGMENT is made to the following for permission to quote from copyrighted sources:

Appleton-Century, Affiliate of Meredith Press, *Primitive Man as Philosopher,* by Paul Radin, copyright © 1927, 1955 by D. Appleton & Co.; reprinted by permission. *Crashing Thunder,* by Paul Radin, copyright 1926 by D. Appleton & Co., reprinted by permission.

Doubleday & Company, Inc., *The Heathens,* by William Howells, copyright 1948 by William Howells; reprinted by permission of the publisher.

Holt, Rinehart and Winston, Inc., *Cultural Anthropology,* by Felix M. Keesing, New York, 1958; by permission of the publishers.

McGraw-Hill Book Company, *Mirror for Man,* by Clyde Kluckhohn, copyright © 1949; by permission of the publishers.

The Macmillan Company, *Our Primitive Contemporaries,* by George Murdock; reprinted with permission of the publisher.

National Association of Educational Broadcasters, *Ways of Mankind,* a series of twenty-six radio programs produced by the NAEB; used with permission of the NAEB.

The Ronald Press Company, *Race and Nationality—As Factors in American Life,* by Henry Pratt Fairchild, copyright 1947 by The Ronald Press Company; by permission of the publishers.

The University of Chicago Press, *The Human Animal,* by Weston La Barre, copyright 1954; by permission. *Hopi Ethics: A Theoretical Analysis,* by Richard Brandt, copyright 1954; by permission.

ENDPAPER CREDITS:
Front, left; back, left and right: American Museum of Natural History, New York.
Front, right: University Museum, Philadelphia.

For my wife, Madelyn,
and the different women
that she is

Contents

Illustrations

Illustrations

Illustrations

The kinds and ways of men are many,
and in this diversity is found
the key to human survival
and development.

CHAPTER 1

The Chosen People

. . . human institutions and motives are legion,
on every plane of cultural simplicity or complexity,
and . . . wisdom consists in a greatly increased
tolerance toward their divergencies.

RUTH BENEDICT

HUMAN DIFFERENCES

Modern man is acutely aware of the differences between himself
and other people. A great many differences are real; they can be seen
or smelled or heard. Others, while not physically "there," are equally
real to the person who imagines them. Physiological and cultural differences stand out when an African Negro encounters a European
white. Coloration, clothing, food habits, odor, language—all announce
sharply and dramatically that here is a different type of being. From
these immediate observations each man draws additional conclusions.
To the European, lack of clothes may indicate lack of morals; little
technology, an inferior mind; and a cow-dung hairdressing, the absence of aesthetic sensibilities. The African, on the other hand, may
be convinced that only the depraved eat eggs, the stupid boast, and
the insensitive bathe with perfumed soap. In each case, obvious and
inferred differences have effectively obscured the common ground
these men share. Neither knows nor cares enough about the other to
seek a factual explanation for the differences that offend him.

Their ancestors apparently did no better. In early times as now, man found his own people more pleasingly formed, endowed with higher intelligence, and blessed with better morals than foreigners. Unusual appearance and manner were interpreted as signs of inferiority or malevolence. The familiar face and form, the traditional custom and object, were to be trusted; the stranger, the new belief and practice, were usually suspect.

Feeling that members of one's own society are somehow more human than outsiders has been and is one of man's most pervasive delusions. This ethnocentric attitude stands out with special clarity among those peoples of the world who are convinced that they alone are true men. They describe other peoples in quite unflattering terms.

The Carib Indians, for example, have stated with no equivocation, "We alone are people." Similarly, the ancient Egyptians used the word *romet* (men) only among themselves and in no case for strangers. The Lapps of Scandinavia reserve the term "human being" for those of their own kind, while the Cherokee Indians call themselves *Ani-Yunwiya*, which means "principal people." The Kiowa Indians of the Southwest are willing to accept other peoples as human, but the very name, *Kiowa*, meaning "real people," shows their true feeling.

If you were shown photographs of contemporary primitive peoples and asked to choose the specimens least attractive by Western standards, you would probably point to the Hottentots of the Kalahari Desert in South Africa. These people, with their sparse peppercorn hair, prematurely wrinkled faces, and enormous posteriors, are physically grotesque from our point of view. Yet to themselves they are a superior breed, apart from other men. They are, in their own terms, "the men of men."

Other groups, somewhat more physically attractive but equally "backward" in our eyes, also heap superlatives upon themselves and abuse upon others. The Alaskan Eskimos of the Norton Sound area call themselves *yu'-pik* which means "fine people." Their term for the neighboring Indians, whom they greatly dislike, is "louse eggs." Greenland Eskimos also appear to be well satisfied with themselves but unimpressed with others. For some time following their first contact with the white man, they believed that Europeans had been sent to Greenland for the express purpose of learning good manners and proper behavior. Their highest compliment for a foreigner was, "He is almost as well-bred as we."

The Koryaks of Siberia live a simple, unadorned life in a harsh environment. They exist through their skill in fishing and in herding

2

reindeer. Despite their lack of luxuries and leisure, they refuse to believe that other peoples are better off. A typical reply to a visitor who boasts of his own country is, "If you could enjoy these advantages at home, what made you take so much trouble to come to us?" The reader will recall an American variation: "If you don't like it over here, why don't you go back where you came from?" But if the Koryaks are smug about what little they have, their neighbors, the Chuckchee, are even less discerning. Participating in the same general way of life, they ridicule the Koryaks as old women capable only of tending flocks.

Less remote examples of ethnocentrism are not hard to find. We in America use many terms that enable us to establish ourselves as superior to other Americans: kike, wop, nigger, greaser, mick, goy, dago, and so on. Other terms announce our imagined superiority over peoples outside of our nation: frog, heathen, kraut, savage, limey, yellow-belly, gook, and the like. These terms of derision have come to mean many things, but at bottom they all say, "He is different. Therefore he is certainly inferior, and probably not to be trusted."

The high regard that peoples have for themselves, and their low esteem for foreigners, are threads running through virtually every area of man's social and cultural life. Each group loudly proclaims itself the most advanced race, having developed the best food and the proper clothing, the superior tongue, the most desirable courtship and marital customs, an obviously superior economic system, the most satisfactory laws, and the loveliest arts. And, of course, each enjoys the protection of the highest god, who chose this group as the one people in all of creation deserving his blessings.

Such reasoning has produced a fantastic human comedy in which each member of the global troupe has cast himself in the role of the hero. A modern play attempting to operate under these conditions would probably not get past the first act, if indeed it were ever staged at all. Mankind's ethnocentric drama has already had a relatively long run, but until now the stage has been so large that the actors only competed with their nearest, strong-voiced rivals. Those with weak lungs were never taken seriously anyway. Today, however, the entire theater has become quite small, and technology has allowed the weak voices to be heard. Consequently, an excellent show may yet have to fold, not because the story is bad, but because each actor believes himself to be a hero in the only part that matters. If the show is to go on—if man is to survive—he must look clearly at his differences to see what they mean, and what they do not mean.

3

SOME OF MAN'S ATTITUDES
TOWARD HIMSELF AND OTHERS

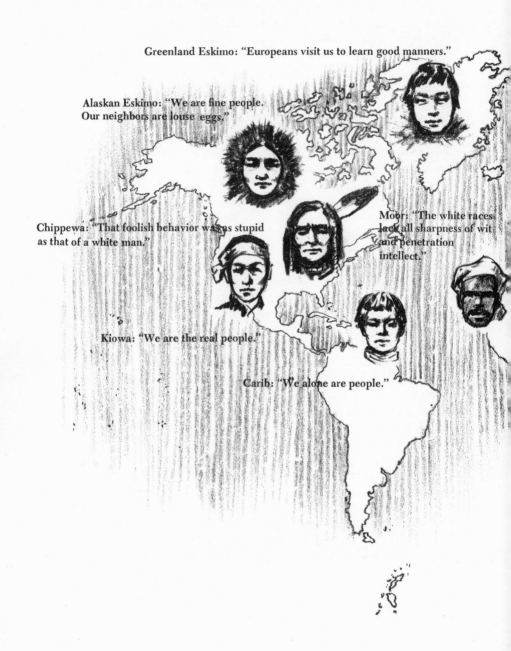

Greenland Eskimo: "Europeans visit us to learn good manners."

Alaskan Eskimo: "We are fine people. Our neighbors are louse eggs."

Chippewa: "That foolish behavior was as stupid as that of a white man."

Moor: "The white races lack all sharpness of wit and penetration intellect."

Kiowa: "We are the real people."

Carib: "We alone are people."

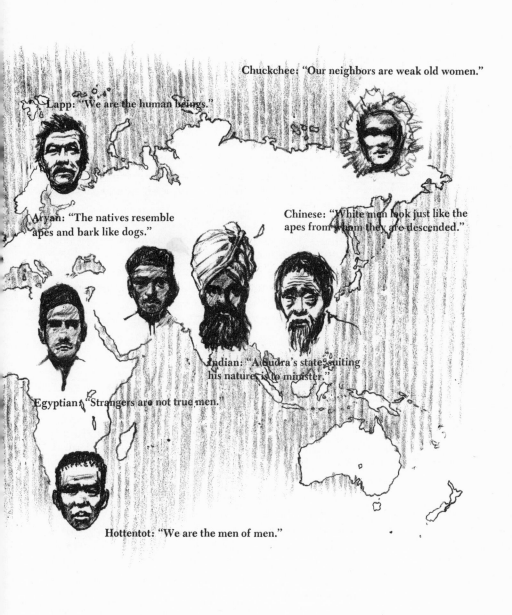

Chuckchee: "Our neighbors are weak old women."

Lapp: "We are the human beings."

Aryan: "The natives resemble apes and bark like dogs."

Chinese: "White men look just like the apes from whom they are descended."

Indian: "A Sudra's state, suiting his nature, is to minister."

Egyptian: "Strangers are not true men."

Hottentot: "We are the men of men."

MEN ARE BOTH SIMILAR
AND DIFFERENT

For a number of years now a great mass of evidence has been building up, incontestable evidence that the physiology and psychology of all men are basically alike. Equally conclusive is the knowledge that the differences between men have occurred for sound reasons. Each variation in appearance or behavior demonstrates human adaptation to various conditions of life.

The implications of this knowledge of ourselves—for international peace, for human achievement, for the future of man—are clear. Yet in the world of power politics these facts have been either unknown or disregarded. Nations have conducted their affairs as if the only human beings in creation lived within their boundaries and no place else. Scholars have gone to the other extreme by overstressing the unity of man and telling us that differences do not matter. The truth is that they do matter. They are of enormous importance because they are often more obvious than similarities. The problem is to understand them. Not as man has done for millennia, always equating human variation with inferiority, and not with blind naiveté of the one-world, we-are-all-God's-children idealist. Neither approach does justice to the highly variable nature of man. The first errs because it misinterprets, the second because it minimizes, man's countless differences.

HUMAN VALUES AND
THE FREEDOM TO VARY

This book appraises the problem of human differences from a point of view. It makes four basic value judgments:

1. *Human life is valuable.* No one has the right to abuse other men by duress, torture, or slavery. Only under exceptional circumstances, as when individuals jeopardize the lives of others, does society have the right to destroy human life.
2. *Biological variation is valuable.* Through long-term genetic variation man evolved from lower forms of life to dominate the world. All living men belong to a single species, but vary significantly within this classification. These variations give man an enormous capacity to prevail regardless of his environment.
3. *Cultural variation is valuable.* The customs and things that man has produced represent the creative human response to problems.

6

They show clearly that man has never passively accepted his situation but has questioned, probed, and experimented. His varied answers reflect the richness of his greatest capacity—the ability to create. In the absence of objective guidelines by which culture may be evaluated, any custom should be accepted as both right and valuable for a specific society unless it violates the first assumption, or until the society itself decides to change.

4. *Individual variation is valuable.* People should be free to pursue their own goals within the basic framework of their society if these activities do not interfere with the freedom of others.

This point of view does not accept all human differences uncritically, to be judged only in relation to a particular individual or society. Neither does it evaluate differences rigidly, against a detailed set of absolute standards. It emphasizes the value of the *freedom to be different* within a framework of rules. So long as the rules that regulate behavior do not violate the basic individual right to live with dignity, societies should be free to formulate their own customs. And so long as individuals respect the bulk of these rules and the freedom of others, their own freedoms should remain intact.

The assumptions concerning the value of human life and individual variation are taken for granted in this book, since I believe that psychologists and philosophers have amply defended them elsewhere. My efforts are aimed at presenting the case for the value of biological and cultural variations. To do this I have first traced man's evolution from lower forms of life and his development into biologically different races. Then I have described how human beings came to live in groups and how it is that their social behavior varies so markedly. Throughout, I have tried to show that human variations exist for sound and understandable reasons—that difference does not automatically mean inferiority. More than this, I have taken the position that *the human capacity to vary is man's most precious asset, that human differences are the best possible evidence of man's greatness.*

Ultimately, man must accept human variation for what it is— a testament to the triumph of human physiology, reason, and imagination in the face of stupendous difficulties—or he will perish. Somehow he must learn to live with two great clusters of human differences that have disturbed him throughout his history, differences in appearances and differences in behavior. Man's misunderstanding of the significance of these variations has caused much of his historical inhumanity toward his fellow men. It is now leading him toward the destruction not only of these differences but of himself as well.

7

CHAPTER 2

Creation and Evolution

... any being, if it vary however slightly in
any manner profitable to itself, under the complex
and sometimes varying conditions of life,
will have a better chance of surviving. . . .

CHARLES DARWIN

IN THE BEGINNING

Life on earth appears to have begun more than two billion years
ago with single-celled protozoa. Whether all life has evolved from a
single organism is not known. Several units may have appeared simultaneously in the same area, or at widely scattered places about the
earth. Neither do we know whether this momentous debut was part
of a divine plan that represents the expressed will of God, or whether
it was a fortuitous fusion of chemicals under extraordinary conditions. As far as current objective knowledge is concerned, a belief
that the first life was a "natural accident" is as much a myth as is a
belief that it was divinely willed. Indeed, the distinguished French
philosopher-scientist Lecomte du Noüy has demonstrated that it is
virtually a mathematical impossibility for life on earth to have occurred by chance alone. He estimates that the time necessary to form
by chance a single complex protein molecule as found in protoplasm
would be about twenty-seven times longer than the earth has existed. And since multitudes of these molecules would be necessary
before even the simplest organism could have life, du Noüy dismisses

the belief in a chance beginning for life as "an act of faith and not a scientific explanation."

On the other hand, as gamblers, statisticians, and various scientists point out, even the most unlikely events are mathematical possibilities. Where chance-produced life was concerned, this remote possibility simply may have happened quite early within its mathematical system of odds. In a crap game the chances of throwing one's number four times in a row are 1,296 to 1, yet many men have done this shortly after opening the game rather than after a thousand or so tosses. A chance of $10^{1,000}$ (or 1 followed by 1,000 zeros) to 1 is not exactly a sure thing, but it may occur during the first second of its possibility as well as the last. Dr. du Noüy acknowledges this but does not take it seriously. Biochemist George Wald has more recently shown that the odds for the spontaneous generation of life are not nearly so high as du Noüy and others had supposed. Drawing on the work of Harold Urey, Nobel laureate in chemistry, who experimentally synthesized some of the basic amino acids found in all protein molecules, Wald makes a strong case for the natural origin of life not only on our own planet, but on many of the probable ten million million planets in the universe that are like ours.

Of course no one can compute the mathematical odds for and against the existence of a god or the odds for and against such a being creating life. It is useless to try to prove anything of this nature through odds; life was produced either by chance or by design, and at this time we cannot say with any degree of objectivity or confidence which actually did occur.

MYTHS OF MAN'S CREATION

As soon as living things appeared on earth with the capacity to reproduce themselves and to become modified through environmental forces, the possibility of human life existed. Indeed, looking backward from the fact of our existence, we can say that man was inevitable. But this is hindsight, and scientific hindsight at that. In a casual glance backward there is nothing very obvious that suggests that man developed from lower forms of life. Consequently, few people in history have suspected the lengthy and complex fact of evolution. Although man has asked himself endless questions about his origins, his answers have varied enormously, since, for the most part, they have been imaginatively rather than empirically derived. Virtually every known society, past and present, has produced one or more theories on the subject. Most of the ancient theories had to do with some sort of original creation; others postulated an evolutionary sequence. Some came surprisingly close to the generally accepted theories of today; others were nowhere near the truth as we know it. But their correctness or incorrectness should not obscure the fact that, without exception, they were all guesses, and it is as meaningless to praise a society for a right hunch as to ridicule a society for a wrong one. The important fact is that all people have raised profound questions relating to their origins and have demonstrated an amazing suppleness of imagination and intellect in grappling with them. The creation myths clearly show this. In spite of the bizarre nature of many of these accounts, it must be remembered that they are not merely idle stories. They have served the important function of explaining many unknown aspects of life to man. They have been believed in with conviction and with fervor.

The biblical story of creation is well known in Western society, although there are great differences of opinion about its interpretation. To some, Genesis gives a literal, step-by-step, day-by-day account, and that is that. Martin Luther was quite outspoken about this. "The world with all its creatures was created in six days," he said, and the biblical account speaks "neither allegorically nor figuratively." More recently biblical scholars have become aware of the antiquity of the universe and concede that a day in the eyes of God may have actually been a million years or so. College sophomores and other iconoclasts never tire of reminding us that it is rather silly to believe in an account which describes the appearance of light three full days (or three million years, if you prefer) before the creation of the sun. More mature thinkers are prone to acknowledge the conceptual grandeur of this account of creation, although they are quite sure that it is simply a prescientific myth. At least, one must admire the shrewdness of the guesswork involved in a step-by-step creation with man appearing in good evolutionary fashion very late on the program.

An old Winnebago Indian creation myth, which appeared in *Crashing Thunder*, edited by Paul Radin, is as majestic in scope as the Old Testament account, and its creator-god, Earthmaker, is much less remote than the God of Genesis. In the beginning, Earthmaker was alone, and in his loneliness he cried. Thus did creation begin.

Earthmaker was sitting in space when he came to consciousness. Nothing was to be found anywhere. He began to think of what he was to do and finally he cried. Tears flowed from his eyes and fell below where he was sitting. After a while he looked below and saw something bright. The bright objects were tears, of which he had not been aware and, which falling below, had formed the present waters. They became the seas of today.

Then Earthmaker began to think again. He thought, "Thus it is whenever I wish anything. Everything will become the water of the seas." So he wished for light and it became light. Then he thought, "It is as I have supposed; the things that I wished for, come into existence as I desired." Then he again thought and wished for this earth and this earth came into existence. Earthmaker looked at the earth and he liked it, but it was not quiet. It moved about as do the waves of the seas. Then he made the trees and he saw that they were good. But even these did not make the earth quiet. It was however almost quiet. Then he created the four cardinal points and the four winds. At the four corners of the earth he placed them as four great and powerful spirits, to act as weights holding down this island earth of ours. Yet still the earth was not quiet. Then he made four large beings and threw them down toward the earth and they were pierced through the earth with their heads eastward. They were really snake-beings. Then it was that the earth became still and quiet. Now he looked upon the earth and he liked it.

Again he thought of how things came into existence just as he desired. Then it was that he first spoke and said, "As everything happens just as I wish it, I shall make a man like myself in appearance." So he took a piece of earth and made it like himself. Then he talked to what he had created but it did not answer. He looked at it and he saw that it had no mind or thought. So he made a mind for it. Again he talked to it but it did not answer. So he looked at it again and he saw that it had no tongue. Then he made it a tongue. Then he talked to it again but it did not answer. So he looked at it and he saw that it had no soul. So he made it a soul. He talked to it again and then it very nearly said something but could not make itself intelligible. So Earthmaker breathed into its mouth and talked to it and it answered.

Like the Genesis account, this is a fine story, but it also contains some unsatisfactory elements. The actual creation of man seems rather sophisticated with its stress on a mind, a tongue, and a soul as prerequisites for humanness. But what of the four compass points and the four winds? And what are we to do with the snakes? Snakes were not involved in holding the earth still during its creation any more than they were in recommending a forbidden apple sometime later, and most of us know it. But myths, like snakes, do not die an easy death.

One of the most detailed descriptions of man's creation is found in a myth of the Boonoorong of Southern Australia. In the beginning Pundjel, like Earthmaker and God, decided to make man out of clay. With unmatched self-assurance, however, he began the construction of two men at the same time.

11

With his big knife he cut three large sheets of bark. On one of these he placed a quantity of clay, and worked it into a proper consistency with his knife. When the clay was soft, he carried a portion to one of the other pieces of bark, and he commenced to form the clay into a man, beginning at the feet; then he made the legs, then he formed the trunk and the arms and the head. He made a man on each of the two pieces of bark. He was well pleased with his work, and looked at the men a long time, and he danced round about them. He next took stringybark from a tree, . . . made hair of it, and placed it on their heads—on one straight hair and on the other curled hair. Pundjel again looked at his work, much pleased . . . and once more he danced round about them. . . . After again smoothing with his hands their bodies, from the feet upwards to their heads, he lay upon each of them, and blew his breath into their mouths, into their noses, and into their navels; and breathing very hard, they stirred. He danced round about them a third time. He then made them speak, and caused them to get up, and they rose up, and appeared as full-grown young men.

Again we find a combination of good and bad guesses. Modern biologists agree with the Boonoorong that the head was the last part of the human anatomy to be smooth, that is, to reach its present form, but the initial major step in man's development was not taken by the feet. Instead, the upper body was the first area to resemble its approximate present form, followed by the pelvis and lower limbs, and finally the skull.

The foregoing accounts of the creation of man are imaginatively drab in comparison with those of some other societies. Clay is a good substance for your god to make a man from only if he and his people know about clay and pottery and that sort of thing. Even then, clay may be too mundane or too inert to catch his fancy. Consider, for example, the following creation stories.

In the beginning, according to the Samoans, the great god Tangaloa first covered the earth with a giant vine. This vine decomposed into worms, and the worms developed into men and women. In African Bushongo mythology, Bumba, the creator-god, vomited up all creation, beginning with the sun, moon, and stars, followed by various animals and, finally, man. A Society Islands account declares that man was first a ball, out of which his arms, legs, and head were subsequently pulled. The ancient Scandinavian *Edda* tells that a divine cow carved the first man out of ice with her tongue, and then suckled him to give him strength. Many Micronesian and Melanesian peoples relate blood to original creation. Thus, in an Admiralty Island myth, the first man and woman were hatched from two eggs which were previously generated by a quantity of blood. Even more

MATERIALS USED IN THE CREATION OF MAN

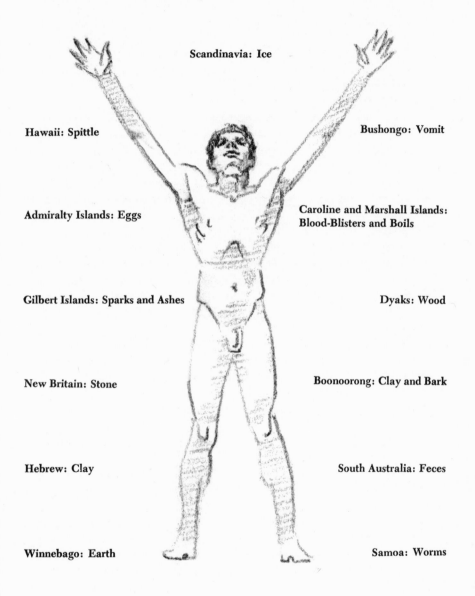

Scandinavia: Ice

Hawaii: Spittle

Bushongo: Vomit

Admiralty Islands: Eggs

Caroline and Marshall Islands:
Blood-Blisters and Boils

Gilbert Islands: Sparks and Ashes

Dyaks: Wood

New Britain: Stone

Boonoorong: Clay and Bark

Hebrew: Clay

South Australia: Feces

Winnebago: Earth

Samoa: Worms

dramatic is the belief of peoples in the Caroline and Marshall islands that the first men burst forth from divine blood-blisters and boils. The Baganda of Africa say that man descended from heaven, while the Zulus say that he came up from the earth through the mouth of a cave. The natives of New Britain see man as originally formed from stone, the Dyaks of Borneo say that he was carved from the strong-fibered Kumpong tree, and the Gilbert Islanders believe that he was generated from the sparks and ashes of a divinely ignited tree.

In addition there are numerous myths, somewhat less attractive by Western standards but obviously quite acceptable to their creators. An interesting example is the Hawaiian myth that the gods simply spat on the ground to form man. Another is the ancient Egyptian belief that man was first created by a god who impregnated himself through oral-phallic masturbation. A South Australian myth holds that god created man by molding his own excrement and then making it laugh and become alive by tickling it.

In the face of such outlandish creation myths, the reader may well have difficulty in remaining objective about them. It is natural for us of the Western world to find that the Genesis story is superior to most, if not all, of the others. We learned it so early in life and in such a sacrosanct context that it is almost a part of us. Yet we cannot demonstrate that the belief that man was formed from clay on the sixth day of creation is better than the belief that he erupted from a festering boil on the skin of a divine being. Our dislike of boils and blood blisters has nothing to do with the value of the story. Nor can we reject the spittle-clay creation idea in favor of the water-clay story simply on aesthetic grounds. If in the beginning we had actually been formed from a god's waste products, this would be fact whether or not we liked it, regardless of the shock to our aesthetic sensibilities.

Myths simply cannot be evaluated on the basis of which is better and which is worse. The sweep and color of the prose may be judged, as may the relative complexity of the concepts involved, but it is quite impossible to say which of two wrong answers is best. This is where the scientist can clear up a great deal of confusion. Rather than belaboring such impossible questions as, Which is the superior idea: man from rock, man from wood, or man from clay? he asks an old question in a new way, "What can we say about the origin of man in the light of all known objective evidence?" Those who can accept their mythologies for the rich, imaginative guesses that they are can find in the science of anthropology a true history of man in broad outline. They will not find a complete history, because gaps exist in our present knowledge. They will not find a history correct in every detail, since scientists do not always agree on specific interpretations. But they will find a myth-free, generally nonsubjective history of the origin and development of man.

EVIDENCES OF EVOLUTION

Man was not "created by the Trinity on October 23, 4004 B.C., at nine o'clock in the morning," as supposed by Dr. John Lightfoot, a seventeenth-century vice-chancellor of Cambridge University. Nor was he thrown up by an ailing Bumba long ago in the wilds of Africa. He evolved from lower forms of life which originated more than two billion years ago on an earth which was already several billion years old. Near-men probably walked the earth a million years ago. The evidence for these facts is as varied as it is conclusive. No longer does the idea of evolution rest solely on Charles Darwin's *Origin of Species,* although his was a beautifully documented and closely reasoned case. Several major bodies of evidence now stand behind the fact of evolution, evidence that has been painstakingly gathered, sifted, and integrated by paleontologists and biologists.

Fossils / Paleontology is the science devoted to the study of fossil animal forms. It is closely allied with geology. In fact, were it not for a number of geological conditions and processes, there would be few old bones around for paleontologists to analyze in the first place. Most dead land creatures simply decompose under the combined attacks of weather, oxygen, and bacteria. Throughout history, however, a few have undergone some sort of quick burial which has removed them from the normal disintegration process. They have been drowned, frozen, trapped in mud and asphalt deposits, and in more recent times deliberately buried. Once buried, some remains have been preserved by underground water. The water has occasionally deposited mineral matter in the interstices of the bones and produced durable stonelike fossils. In other cases, the original bones have been entirely replaced with minerals from ground water. Occasionally, water dissolved all the bone and left a space, called a natural mold, from which specialists may produce a cast of the original form.

The age of a given fossil is not necessarily fixed by its depth below the surface of the earth, because the layers accumulate at different rates. As a general rule, however, the more ancient the specimen, the deeper it lies. Analysis of the strata tells a dramatic story of the se-

15

quential development of life upon earth. The deeper we dig, the fewer varieties of fossil bones we find. This clearly indicates that there were far fewer different species of animals on earth in very early times than now. It follows that many new and varied forms of life must have evolved from older forms. Moreover, if we dig to depths where there are no bones, we often find evidence of marine life—fossil shells, seaweed, and the like. Paleontologists are agreed that this points to the ancient evolution of all land creatures from very ancient sea creatures. By measuring the comparative radioactivity of the minerals in which these old remains are embedded, developmental dates have been worked out, with an error of less than 10 percent, for the enormous period of time from about 30 million to 500 million years back. The British biologist J. B. S. Haldane comments in *Genetics, Paleontology, and Evolution* about several dates thus established: "We know that somewhere around 350 million years ago our ancestors were fish, 270 million years ago amphibians somewhat like salamanders, 200 million years ago reptiles not very like any living forms, and 70 million years ago, mammals something like shrews."

Vestigial Remains / The fact of evolution is further supported by vestigial remains: organs in the human body with little or no present biological function, which were valuable at an earlier time in our history. Some of these vestigial remains, such as gill arches and gill grooves, appear only in the human embryo and then vanish. Our vestigial tail, the coccyx, while outside the body during the second month of embryonic life, usually folds under and disappears by birth. Occasionally, however, persons are born with short tails. But tails, like gills, no longer have any value for man other than to remind him of his ancient evolutionary journey. The appendix is one of the best-known vestigial remains. While its function in modern man seems to be restricted to providing bread and butter for the medical profession, it actually abets digestion in apes, monkeys, and other plant-eating animals. Wisdom teeth are also useful to a contented, cud-chewing herbivore, as is an extremely lengthy intestinal tract, but

Striking and independent proofs establish the theory of evolution. Within th human body are relics of the ancient animals from which man arose. Vestige of gills and tails, clearly visible in human fetuses, usually disappear befor birth; now useless wisdom teeth and appendixes remain throughout life. In th ground at sharply separated layers are fossils that trace the slow developmen of many forms of life. The drawings at left above show the development of th camel skull over millions of years.

EVIDENCES OF EVOLUTION

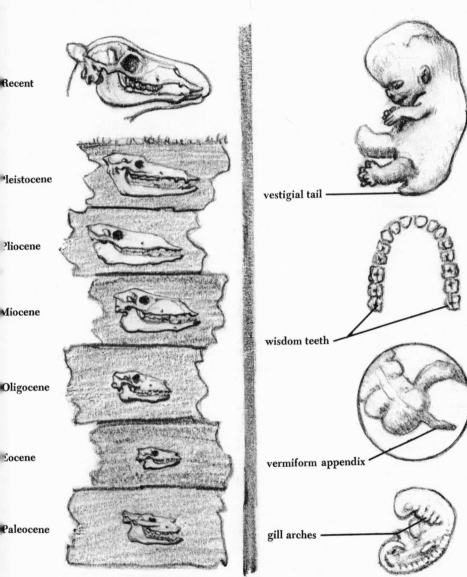

PALEONTOLOGICAL

Recent

Pleistocene

Pliocene

Miocene

Oligocene

Eocene

Paleocene

BIOLOGICAL

vestigial tail

wisdom teeth

vermiform appendix

gill arches

neither is needed by modern man. In fact, the frequency of impacted wisdom teeth and infected appendixes shows that ancient assets have become modern liabilities. Ear wiggling must still be considered an asset, since it amuses small children, but it functions as an automatic sound funnel only in the family cat and other animals. These and other vestigial remains clearly point to the emergence of new species from earlier forms through biological modification.

Man's evolution from lower forms is the success story of a strain of life struggling through almost impossible difficulties to a position of total dominance on earth. Told as it actually happened, it is a far more moving and dramatic story than any of the old myths could ever be. Man need not apologize for his lowly beginnings. His climb has been all the higher because of them. Nor need he forsake his faith that behind it all lies a larger plan or a divine intelligence. Scientists should not and, as a rule, do not argue this point. They can tell us *how* the miracle of evolution occurred in terms of the mechanics and biochemistry of the process. The *why* of it is something else again. No scientist speaking as a scientist presumes to know the meaning of creation or of evolution, although some may speculate about it. And theologians would do well to reflect upon their own history of bad guesses before pressing upon us too strongly their explanatory concepts.

HOW EVOLUTION OCCURS

Evolution is the product of several basic conditions and processes: (1) conception and individual variation, (2) mutation and species differentiation, (3) isolation and inbreeding, and (4) genetic drift.

Conception and Individual Variation / All major forms of animal life conceive their young through sexual activity. Specifically, conception involves the union of male and female sex cells, with the fusion of inherited potentials carried by each. Both the male cell (sperm) and the female cell (egg) are called gametes. Their fusion produces a fertilized egg, or zygote, which through rapid cell division becomes first an embryo, then a fetus, and finally a newborn animal. Each sperm or egg cell contains chemical units, called genes, that control the development of the animal—make it grow into a mouse or a man. There are an estimated 30,000 such genes in the human sex cell.

Geneticists no longer think of a gene as a fixed quality or carrier of a unit character, but as an inherited "push" toward development in a certain direction. A given gene at any point from conception onward contains the potential for the next step in the individual's development rather than determining absolutely individual traits like hair color. Accordingly, the basic genetic potential of a newly fertilized egg is better thought of as the capacity for cell division and growth. Understood in this fashion, genes are seen to be dynamic in nature, capable of modification through interaction with the environment. Far from operating in a fixed, changeless manner, fertilized eggs and their genes take nourishment from and are modified by the environment of the mother's womb. From fertilization onward any number of minute changes in the prenatal environment may influence the development of the organism. As anthropologist Ashley Montagu points out in his *Anthropology and Human Nature,* "A gene on the verge of expressing itself may be affected by random variations in the constitution of the cell substance." The fact that genes are chemical compounds further suggests that they, like other chemicals, may be altered through changes in pressure, temperature, atomic radiation, or the like. The possibility of controlling genetic modification is fascinating, but, we are reminded by geneticist Theodosius Dobzhansky, "it is much easier to destroy a gene than to have it changed and remain a gene."

The interaction between physiology and environment is more easily illustrated after the birth of an individual. Bone size, for example, is limited by the genes, but improper diet may result in bones smaller than the original possibility. Again, while genes are initially responsible for the development of our central nervous systems, lack of cultural opportunity may dwarf what could have been a giant intellect.

When you consider the foregoing facts concerning genes and their environments with reference to developing individuals, you appreciate the enormous opportunities for human variation. Inheriting as we do from each parent some 30,000 genes, each of which has varying tendencies toward development and operates in somewhat different prenatal surroundings, it is little wonder that we vary substantially at birth.

The remarkable thing is that in spite of infinite individual variaations, most of the basic gene-directed patterns for all human beings are the same. In most fundamental aspects the human body is standardized, as is the leopard, the cow, or the gibbon body. A medical student can learn anatomy from some general charts and a single well-dissected body. He need not hack his way through a hundred corpses in order to comprehend basic human anatomy. Noses vary in

19

a great many ways, but humans still have human rather than dog noses. Once you learn most of the facts about one human nose, you can be assured that, regardless of size and shape differences, the structure and functioning of other human noses that you encounter will be basically the same. In spite of countless physiological variations between individuals, due to genetic and environmental differences, genes themselves are remarkably stable and resist environmental modification of their basic structure.

Mutation and Species Differentiation / Yet genes do change from time to time, fundamentally and dramatically. What is more, these basically altered genes occasionally survive and reproduce themselves, perhaps producing for the first time a sort of lung instead of gills, or an eye sensitive to color and not just to shades of gray. Basic genetic changes of this magnitude are called mutations, and, as far as we know, occur naturally among animals on a random basis, probably as a consequence of cosmic radiation.

Mutations lie behind the stupendous climb of man in the animal world. Spread over millions of years, successful mutations have produced a world full of very different creatures, a world with lions and lizards, lice and men. Knowing what we now do about the nature of mutations, we may assume that there have always been far more undesirable than desirable ones. Even before mutations gave woman a large pelvis, other mutations probably caused an occasional large-headed child and thereby claimed the mother's life. Mutations assuredly gave us warm blood with the miraculous capacity to stem its own flow from most cuts. But mutations also produced hemophilia, a condition that delays or prevents the clotting of blood. Mutations grace us with ample-breasted, beardless women, but occasionally burden us with web feet, six fingers, human horns, or lack of a cerebrum. In spite of the frequently undesirable or even lethal nature of mutations, we must emphasize that every creature on earth owes its form, its functions, and its present existence to beneficial mutations. Although prehistory is a graveyard of unsuccessful mutations, any creature that lives today has inherited a great number of different physical qualities that enable it to adjust to the environment in which it lives.

Isolation and Inbreeding / Before mutations can produce new forms of life, or major variations among old forms, the animals concerned must be relatively isolated for a substantial period of time, and there must be intensive inbreeding among them. It can be seen that a mutation producing long fangs will have a much better chance of enduring if the long-fanged individual mates within a closed group.

Some of its offspring will possess the mutant; they in turn will mate within the same group, bearing more offspring with the mutant. We assume that most major divisions of the biological world (phyla, families, species, etc.) were produced in this way. The endurance of a mutation is also encouraged if, as in the instance of long fangs, the mutation contributes to survival. A mutation for heavy fur has little survival value to a tropical monkey, but may be of basic importance to an arctic fox. The hump of a camel is full of fatty tissue which serves as a water storage sponge. In desert conditions a hump has survival potential, but in temperate climes it only gets its owner behind bars as a zoological oddity. Traits with survival potential generally enable the animal to adjust better to his circumstances, perhaps live just a little longer, mate a few more times and, in consequence, produce more and more creatures with the desirable trait. Thus, while Darwin knew nothing of mutation, his theory of natural selection was quite accurate in describing the mechanics through which many mutations tend to perpetuate themselves. He made the following statement more than a hundred years ago:

. . . any being, if it vary however slightly in any manner profitable to itself, under the complex and sometimes varying conditions of life, will have a better chance of surviving, and thus be *naturally selected*. From the strong principle of inheritance, any selected variety will tend to propagate its new and modified form.

Genetic Drift / The formation of new and varied physical types has probably been further abetted by a process known as genetic drift. It is believed that when small groups of animals become isolated from others of their kind, occasionally there may not be a complete representation of the genetic potential of their species among them. As long as they remain isolated, they cannot reproduce all the original genetic possibilities of their kind. Of course, in a species having relatively few genes, genetic drift probably does not operate, since a few creatures can carry the entire range of genetic possibilities. In more complex species, a large group of animals is needed if the full gamut of genetic variation is to be represented. Consequently, lost, strayed, or ostracized members probably will begin traveling down a somewhat narrower-gauged evolutionary track than before. Even if the separated group possesses all the original genetic potentials, it is unlikely to have them in exactly the same ratios as exist in the parent stock. In this case, the mathematics of breeding will increase the most common genes, deplete or eliminate the least common ones, and gradually make the group different.

In human beings, genetic drift is considered responsible for variations in blood type among members of the same race who now inhabit different geographical regions. This can be illustrated by contrasting Chinese and American-Indian Mongoloids. North and South America were first settled by small, nomadic bands of Mongoloids who pushed across the Bering Strait into genetic isolation. Over the years blood group frequencies have changed remarkably between these migrants and their forebears. Thus it has been shown that whereas approximately 31 percent of the Huang-Ho Chinese tested had type A blood, only 7 percent of the North American Sioux and 2 percent of the South American Toba have this type. Even more impressive

Although the Chinese, Sioux, and Tobas are all Mongoloids, their blood types differ markedly. Type B is found in 28 percent of the Chinese, but in only 2 percent of the Sioux and in none of the Tobas. Apparently the small groups of migrants from Asia who populated the Americas did not bring the full blood group potential of their race with them. Isolation and inbreeding through the years further modified the original distribution of types to its present American distribution and introduced a secondary difference between North and South America.

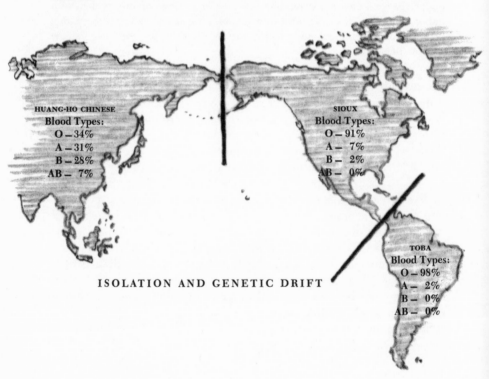

HUANG-HO CHINESE
Blood Types:
O – 34%
A – 31%
B – 28%
AB – 7%

SIOUX
Blood Types:
O – 91%
A – 7%
B – 2%
AB – 0%

TOBA
Blood Types:
O – 98%
A – 2%
B – 0%
AB – 0%

ISOLATION AND GENETIC DRIFT

differences exist in the incidence of B and AB blood. Twenty-eight percent of the Chinese have type B, but only 2 percent of the Sioux and none of the Toba have it. And while AB blood is present among 7 percent of the Chinese, neither American Indian group has this variety. In comparing these figures, the selective genetic screening effect of both the Bering Strait and the Isthmus of Panama may be appreciated.

Through mutation, natural selection, and genetic drift our line has not only survived but has risen to biological greatness among animals. It can be seen that this spectacular climb is the direct consequence of countless biological variations through time. Far from being liabilities therefore, physical differences in our ancestors have brought us to where we are today. Consequently, only the most shortsighted or prejudiced can view the current biological variations among men in any but a favorable light.

CHAPTER 3

Animals, Apes, and Men

For man is an animal
with peculiar biological traits
as a species which make him human.

WESTON LA BARRE

OF ADAM AND EVE

Contemporary men of science tend to take evolution so much for granted that they forget that few people really grasp the grandeur of the concept and are able to use it in their thinking about other animals, apes, and men. I recall vividly my first lecture on evolution to mid-twentieth-century college sophomores. It was one of those occasional days known to all professors when the words flowed well, the illustrations came easily, and the feeling of creative teaching took hold. The class was awake and participating with a high level of attention. Then came the questions, gratifying, thoughtful ones. And finally the one I have since learned to accept as inevitable from time to time: "It's a very nice story but where does this leave Adam and Eve?"

"Back in the Garden of Eden" is no answer, because the question is always asked seriously. It raises the old issue of sacred myth versus secular fact. Of course there is nothing wrong with believing a myth if you are willing to live and let live, to let someone else decide which facts or myths he wants to believe. People have held and cherished myths for thousands of years, and life has been better and more secure because of many of them. But myths vary so much from society to society that you are almost forced to disbelieve and perhaps to belittle the myths or even the facts of your neighbors if you believe your own. This is especially true if your own story of creation states that in the beginning the first man was of your race or ancestral to it, or that your people have evolved further than all others physically and mentally. If man holds such myths too strongly, it is plain that he will always have difficulty in putting himself and his fellow man in realistic perspective.

Then there are the apes. When one teaches the evolution of man, sooner or later one has to talk about apes. While people seem to like apes in the flesh—behind bars—an ape in the family tree is something entirely different. Maybe the flat-nosed, thick-lipped Negroids are related to them, but certainly not we long-nosed, thin-lipped Caucasoids.

What then are the facts about biological relationships between men and animals? How much animal and how much ape in a man? And where indeed does this leave Adam and Eve?

MAN'S PREHUMAN ANCESTORS

In thinking of man's evolutionary development, we must rid ourselves of any notion of a small manlike fish living 350 million years ago, who then became a manlike amphibian and so on. Whether we like it or not we have to think of our remote ancestors as being actual fish. Subsequently, with the aid of mutation, isolation, inbreeding, and perhaps genetic drift, these fish became amphibians, then reptiles, then mammals, then primates, then men.

Fish, Amphibians, and Reptiles / Actually the fish state is a good place to look in upon man's development; in the fish many basic aspects of human anatomy first took form. Internal skeletons, for example, as opposed to the hard external shells of clams or shrimp, first developed in fish. At that point, however, no creature could have been less promising than one whose protection lay in swift motion rather than in tough armor. If you have experienced an exoskeletal lobster pinch on an endoskeletal toe, you still may not be sure who has evolved best. Yet be assured, it is always the lobster who ends up in the pot.

In addition to internal skeletons, fish were the first creatures to have segmented backbones. This gave them great suppleness of body, suppleness that in modern times can often throw them free of a hook.

Correlated with these developments were two supremely important ones in terms of their significance to man: a central nervous system and a heart which circulated blood through the body. All these marvelous things were first developed by fish. They are now ours because we evolved from fish. Note, however, that this progression was a fantastically long one: the miraculous lung which liberated a few fortunate fish from the water required some 100 million years of evolutionary process. Another 100 million years were needed for the cold-blooded reptilian descendants of these amphibians to evolve into warm-blooded mammals.

Mammals / The emergence of mammals was another great event in our family history. Mammals not only retained the most useful traits of their forebears, but developed some highly important features of their own. Basic among these was internal sexual fertilization, and the economy of reproduction that this afforded. Fish have to lay thousands of eggs in order to ensure the survival of their kind; reptiles lay a dozen or so. But mammals can incubate their fertilized eggs safely within their bodies, usually in batches of not more than a half dozen at a time. The placenta, a superb and exclusively mammalian device, made possible internal growth of the young. Instead of being at the mercy of predatory creatures, the elements, and occasional shortages of food and water, the placenta-tended young rode in safety. As long as the mother lived, fetal chances of survival were excellent. Once born, the young mammals found in another unique development—the mother's breast—a constant food supply, independent of most external circumstances. The placenta and the breast then virtually guaranteed mammals their ability to perpetuate themselves indefinitely upon earth.

Primates / Mammals developed in more than one direction and dimension. Through the years different forms such as primates, carnivores, insectivores, and rodents came to exist. Man's line, the primates, emerged about 70 million years ago as relatively small, nimble, tree dwellers. Their arboreal existence indicates that mammalian mutations for movable limbs and grasping hands had taken place and that they had definite survival value. They got the creatures off the ground and into the trees away from danger. Had there been no trees or if the primates had not had the sense to climb them, it is doubtful if man would now have his free-moving limbs or his unspecialized hands with their amazing versatility. This does not mean that the primates gained this hand-manipulative ability through practice in climbing and through moving from tree to tree and then passed the trait down biologically (although some scientists have mistakenly thought so). What probably did happen was that those creatures who possessed a certain mutation-derived hand and arm formation found these features to their advantage in the trees. As a result they survived longer and so reproduced more times than primates without the mutation, thereby increasing the probability of passing these traits to subsequent generations.

Anthropologist Carleton Coon observes that primates living in trees feared snakes and falling. Grasping hands and mobile limbs were great assets in dealing with both of these problems. Hands could swing one along from branch to branch with relative safety; they could reach for a branch in a fall. Hands could also flail away at snakes and even hurl them out of a tree. Equally valuable in preventing falls were good eyes, and, through mutation and natural selection, primates acquired them. The surest grip in the world would amount to little if the distance to a limb were misjudged by weak eyes. And snakes gave few second chances to primates who failed to see the differences in coloring between reptiles and the surrounding vegetation. Good eyes meant a good chance of survival. For the first time in animal history, eyes evolved which could perceive depth as well as color. That this was a product of prolonged tree dwelling seems certain; of all creatures, only primates have both three-dimensional and color vision. It is interesting that birds, which fly rather than climb trees, have color but not three-dimensional vision. On the other hand, many animals (including the bull) have depth perception but do not see colors—not even red. If you find yourself upset about your ancestors having lived in trees, try to imagine a world without color.

While living in the trees, early primates probably lived principally upon fruit, nuts, seeds, and birds' eggs. For several million years this diet and a tree existence seemed ideal for our sharp-eyed, nimble ancestors. Fortunately for us, either the food gave out or their bodies grew too heavy for arboreal life, and they came down out of the trees. If, as seems most likely, sweeping climatic changes reduced the food supply and forced them down, they must have experimented a great deal with new kinds of food. Survival depended upon the ability to eat almost anything. The omnivorous primate digestive system was the result. Apparently our ancestors considered almost anything that grew or wiggled a candidate for caloric honors. A world-wide analysis of contemporary dietary habits will convince even the most skeptical that this invaluable capacity has been handed down to us almost intact.

MAN'S EVOLUTIONARY DEVELOPMENT

APPROXIMATE TIME IN MILLIONS OF YEARS BEFORE PRESENT	EMERGING GROUP	EMERGING BIOLOGICAL TRAITS STILL RETAINED BY MAN
1,500	Kingdom: Animal	Man is an animal, able to move around.
1,000	Subkingdom: Metazoa	He is constituted of many cells.
420	Phylum: Chordata	As an embryo man reveals a notochord, antecedent of the spinal column.
350	Subphylum: Vertebrata	Man possesses an internal skeleton, his brain is contained in a bony case, and his central nervous system is housed in a jointed backbone.
200	Class: Mammalia	In his hairy, warm-blooded body man possesses lungs and a 4-chambered heart; his body is separated by a diaphragm into lung and abdominal cavities; the female suckles her young, which are born alive.
140	Subclass: Eutheria	The human female carries her unborn young in a placenta, a membrane through which food, oxygen, and wastes can pass.
70	Order: Primates	Man has a flexible skeleton, nails instead of claws, a grasping hand, a thumb opposite to the other fingers, omnivorous diet, and a strong sense of sight along with a reduced sense of smell. The brain is large and the snout shortened.
45	Suborder: Anthropoidea	Man has large eyes, a *foramen magnum* that tends to be under rather than in back of the skull.
5	Family: Hominidae	Shorter arms, longer legs, larger brain, smaller canine teeth evolved at this stage.
1 ½	Genus: Homo Species: Sapiens	Man stands fully erect. His brain has increased in size to 1/7th his body weight at birth.

By about 35 million years ago, our line of primates was out of the trees and relatively well established upon the ground. Their well-developed upper bodies were of great use to them. Hands could be used for obtaining food, for eating, and for defense. In addition they could help to balance bodies that were striving to become erect. The anatomical possibility of erect posture was, in fact, the next great mutational development made by our ancestors. Once again, biological variation gave us the key to survival. On the ground, well-developed legs became almost as important as arms and hands had been in the trees. With natural selection at work, a near-human group emerged with long, strong legs, an arched foot, a large pelvis, and the ability to do a wide range of two-footed tricks while maintaining an erect posture. From a biological point of view they were almost the kissing kin of modern man.

Apes and Monkeys / At this point, the question of the relationship among monkeys, apes, and men comes into focus. Certainly there is kinship among them, since all are primates. Yet we are at least 35 million years away from whatever ancestral line we share with modern apes and monkeys. In other words, at about this ancient time mutational shifts, genetic drift, and natural selection began to move the then-existing primates into various directions. The ultimate human line diverged from all other primate lines, never to converge biologically again. If Uncle Joe resembles an orangutan, it is not because he is somehow more closely related to apes than you or I. All human beings have an equally ape-free lineage back to a certain point.

Most anthropologists accept the Huxley hypothesis that both men and apes evolved from a common ancestor. This view has recently been challenged by the Boule-Straus hypothesis which sees us more closely related to monkeys than to apes. Whatever our position, however, we should be cautious in attempting to describe this common relation. There is a strong tendency to think of other primates as not having changed at all during this immense time span and to visualize a modern ape or monkey as our ancient ancestor. But apes, like humans, have evolved through a number of intermediate forms, so that until the archaeological evidence is more complete, any description of a common ancestor can be little more than an educated hunch.

Australopithecus / By a million years ago, man's line had taken great evolutionary strides away from all other primates. Fossils and artifacts found in South Africa by Raymond Dart and other archaeologists indicate that at this time (beginning of the Pleistocene, or the

30

"Age of Ice") our relations were comparatively small in size, had brains of approximately 600 to 700 cubic centimeters, walked erect, made crude pebble tools, and hunted baboons for food. Collectively known as the *Australopithecinae* (Southern Apes), these manlike primates very likely lived in other climatically congenial areas of the world as well as in Africa. Their brains were still not developed enough for these primates to be called true men, and they probably did not use symbolic speech. But as anthropologist W. E. Le Gros Clark points out, "apart from the question of brain size, the evidence of skull structure, dental anatomy and the details of the pelvis and limb bones, establishes fairly clearly that the *Australopithecinae* are to be regarded as exceedingly primitive representatives of the family which includes modern and extinct types of Man."

THEORIES ABOUT THE EMERGENCE OF EARLY MEN

While there is increasing scientific accord that an australopithecine of some sort is in the mainstream of human evolution, there are several theories about the specific way in which our species, Homo sapiens, emerged. One school of thought conceives of the development of a number of human and near-human types in mid-Ice Age times, followed by the gradual extinction of all but one main line. This surviving species is Homo sapiens, who is thought to have evolved as recently as 35,000 to 50,000 years ago. According to this theory, races developed even later, perhaps only 20,000 to 25,000 years ago.

A variation of this theory postulates an ancient Homo sapiens who existed concurrently with various "ape-men" and "man-apes" perhaps as much as 500,000 years ago. According to this conception all other human or near-human types died out before modern times, but races may have begun to develop soon after the rise of Homo sapiens.

A third theory, one that I lean toward, hypothesizes that modern man has evolved from the small-brained australopithecines through the medium-brained species, Homo erectus, into the large-brained species, Homo sapiens. It assumes that the development took place at uneven rates around the world, reflecting differences in mutation, isolation, and genetic drift. The theory also assumes that the first Homo sapiens had emerged by 250,000 years ago, and that all the erectus species had completed the transition by about 20,000 years ago. As Carleton Coon puts it, "Homo erectus became extinct, not by ex-

31

The hands, arms, shoulders, and rib cage are part of our legacy as former tree dwellers.

The legs and pelvis acquired their present form when our line descended to the ground, and a premium was put on upright posture and two-legged agility.

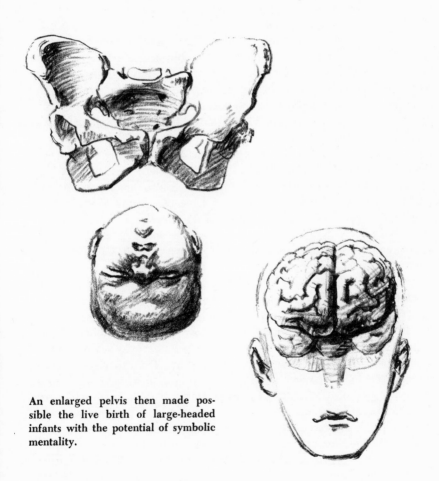

An enlarged pelvis then made possible the live birth of large-headed
infants with the potential of symbolic
mentality.

termination, but by evolving into someone else—in this case, modern man." According to this theory, certain basic racial differences were already developed in Homo erectus, and in many cases were simply inherited by emerging Homo sapiens forms.

From the overall standpoint of evolutionary theory, it makes very little difference which of the three conceptions is correct. Still another theory may be necessary to encompass new materials as they become known. We may be sure, however, that the general picture of man's development from a tree-dwelling to an erect, ground-dwelling primate, and from a small-brained to a large-brained man is correct. An occasional critic of physical anthropology may suggest that the current divergence of professional opinion indicates that the entire theory of evolution is set upon a rickety and haphazard base. If applied elsewhere such thinking would have us question thousands of facts known through research in atomic physics, since there are at present several contradictory theories about the internal structure of the atom. Actually, disagreement among scientists is a sure way to stimulate the thought and research necessary to settle disputed issues.

Although our theoretical views may differ about ancient man's specific line of development, his fossil remains make the basic aspects of his physiological evolution quite plain. All his forms continued to inherit the grasping hands and mobile arms which were the fruit of his tree-dwelling past. All human types also developed upright posture. The most ancient remains we have of a Homo erectus type (*Pithecanthropus erectus* or "Java man") clearly indicate that he stood erect. Even Neanderthal man (*Homo Neanderthalensis*) is now known to have had upright posture: The remains from Chapelle-aux-Saints, France, that once were interpreted to indicate a stooped, slouched-forward carriage for all Neanderthals have recently been shown to be those of a man forty to fifty years of age who was bowed over from a severe arthritic condition in his jaw, neck, and spine.

In addition to their unique hands and posture, all human types appear to have continued to inherit keen primate eyes as well. That man kept them after his ancestors came down from the trees seems largely due to his having assumed an upright posture. Four-footed creatures rely on their noses far more than on their eyes; had man returned to all fours, his nose probably would have become his dominant sense. For survival, it is far better to have good eyes than a good nose. Eyes allow us to penetrate reality much further than any other sense; danger can be seen at a much greater distance than it can be smelled. And how do you get downwind from a pair of sharp eyes?

IT TAKES BRAINS

The foregoing qualities were probably possessed by all ancient men and near-men in comparable amounts. Clearly then, the big leap from australopithecine to Homo erectus, and from erectus to Homo sapiens was not in these areas. It lay in the growth of the brain. This is considered to be the third and probably the greatest basic development in man's body. As is true with so many of our most valuable physical assets, the brain did not develop in isolation, but coordinately with variations in other bodily areas. Man's erect posture and need for swift movement on two legs made a large human pelvis highly desirable. As a consequence of the increased size of the pelvis, mutations for a large-headed baby no longer meant certain death for both mother and child. Upright posture is therefore directly related to our large human brain and, for that matter, to our human tendency toward ample bottoms as well.

In the lower animals the brain acts primarily as a relay center. It receives nerve impulses and shunts them along fixed routes to activate certain glands and muscles. We call the resulting behavior instinctive. A fair amount of learning is still possible in some animals, such as dogs, seals, and chimpanzees; in others, such as giraffes and hippopotamuses, so much of the brain is committed to inborn or physiologically derived patterns that little learning is possible. In addition, the brains of lower animals are for the most part smaller than man's both in absolute size and in the ratio of brain weight to body weight. This does not imply that we can directly connect brain size to learning ability or intelligence; a very small dog may have a very small brain and yet learn many tricks. But if we know both the brain size and the body size of a particular creature, we can predict learning ability and intelligence pretty well. It appears that there must be a certain minimum size for various levels of intelligence to exist, but if a good-sized brain is related to too large a body, then most of the brain becomes committed to the normal maintenance and operation of the body. This is true of the elephant, who has a larger-than-human brain but so much body to be regulated that his main intellectual feat has been to persuade human beings that he is far more intelligent than he is.

If we look at the figures for the ringed seal and the domestic dog in the drawings on pages 36 and 37, we see that the ability to learn tricks obviously has more to do with the brain to body ratio than with the absolute weight of the brain. This is further illustrated with

35

RATIO OF BRAIN WEIGHT TO BODY WEIGHT

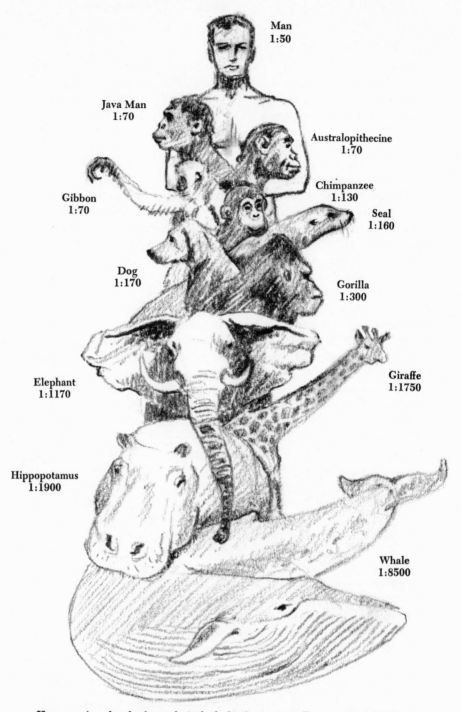

Man
1:50

Java Man
1:70

Australopithecine
1:70

Gibbon
1:70

Chimpanzee
1:130

Seal
1:160

Dog
1:170

Gorilla
1:300

Elephant
1:1170

Giraffe
1:1750

Hippopotamus
1:1900

Whale
1:8500

Homo sapiens has both a relatively hefty brain as well as a very high brain to body weight ratio. Even the smallest human brain has a higher ratio (more brain per unit of body) than the chimpanzee, who is considered to be the smartest of the apes, and almost twice as much brain bulk. It can also be seen

Whale
14.77 lbs.

Elephant
12.57 lbs.

Man
3.31 lbs.

Java Man
2.20 lbs.

Hippopotamus
1.59 lbs.

Giraffe
1.54 lbs.

Australopithecine
1.32 lbs.

Gorilla
1.10 lbs.

Chimpanzee
.97 lb.

Seal
.55 lb.

Gibbon
.20 lb.

Dog
.18 lb.

that the gorilla, who comes closest to man in brain size (500 cc.), has the least advantageous primate brain/body ratio (1:300). The gibbon, on the other hand, has a very promising ratio of 1 to 70, but its brain is less than one tenth the absolute size of a modern human brain.

the figures for the giraffe and the hippopotamus, both of whom are as lacking in brain as they are overloaded in body. In contrast to the hippo, the elephant is a genius—but only in contrast to the hippo. Compared with man, he has four times as much brain controlling one hundred times as much body. The results are inevitable. A final inspection of the illustration makes it obvious that it was the neurosis of Ahab, not the brilliance of Moby Dick, that gave the victory to Melville's whale. For with only sixteen pounds of brain maneuvering 136,000 pounds of body, grand battle strategy is out of the question. One may even suppose that, while sounding, many a whale has forgotten why he went down in the first place.

With dexterous hands, upright posture, superior eyesight, omnivorous appetite, and a large, complex brain, man rose to dominate the animal world before the close of the Old Stone Age. Although each of these qualities was important in his climb, it is believed that it was his transition past about a 900–1,000 cc. brain that brought the potential for symbolic thought and speech. The ability to manipulate symbols internally has been termed "algebraic mentality," and is the pivotal factor in man's superior intellectual accomplishments, his capacity to learn rapidly, to reason, and to create. Early men either made this critical step or died out, for by 20,000 years ago only one human species remained on earth—Homo sapiens, with an average brain size of 1,400 cc.

Of course human variation did not suddenly stop at this point. Mutations, isolation, inbreeding, and genetic drift were ceaselessly producing new physical trends. Most of these differences were less radical than those that had divided erectus from sapiens, but by this time in history man had begun to perceive these differences and to worry about them. Not understanding the biological significance of racial variation, man created myths to explain it, myths which were almost always highly unflattering to those outside his own group. Even now, technologically sophisticated though he is, he has not yet comprehended that the processes that created race are the same ones that placed him at the pinnacle of the animal world and that could guarantee his safe conduct into the future.

CHAPTER 4

Race: Myth and Fact

Genetic diversity is mankind's
most precious resource. . . .
THEODOSIUS DOBZHANSKY

RACIAL MYTHS

Myths about group differences in personal appearance constitute an extensive and fascinating part of man's cultural history. In many of them, as in his myths of creation, we see man's imagination and intellect grappling with the unknown in a prescientific world. In the more recent myths, however, we find an easy justification of the *status quo* coupled with an emotional refusal to face the uncomfortable facts of science.

From paintings in the royal tombs of Biban al-Muluk (Valley of the Kings) we know that the ancient Egyptians differentiated four racial groups on the basis of skin color: red, black, yellow, and white. Since these men are depicted at various distances from the god Horus, it is assumed that their relative positions indicate the regard in which they were held by the Egyptians. That an Egyptian with deep red skin is at the head of the group lends weight to this assumption. Following the Egyptian is the figure of a black-skinned Negro. After the Negro, a pale-yellow-skinned Asiatic appears, and bringing up the rear is a white-skinned, blue-eyed, tattooed European.

The Egyptians are not the only peoples who have ranked the white man last on their list of peoples. According to the Eskimos, for example, the Great Being tried his hand at man-making two times.

His first attempt was a failure and resulted in an inferior creature called *kob-lu-na* or "white man." Profiting from this unsuccessful trial run, he then created a perfect man called *in-nu*, who of course was ancestor to the Eskimos.

Other early Americans also had stories to account for the different races with which they were familiar. Here is a myth told by an old Iroquois chief to a British officer in 1766.

After the Great Spirit formed the world, he made the various birds and beasts which now inhabit it. He also made man, but having formed him white and very imperfect and ill-tempered he placed him on one side of it where he now inhabits and from whence he has lately found a passage across the water to be a plague to us. As the Great Spirit was not pleased with his work, he took of black clay and made what you call a Negro with a wooly head. This black man was made better than the white man, but still he did not answer the wish of the Great Spirit; that is, he was imperfect. At last, the Great Spirit, having procured a piece of pure red clay, formed from it the Red Man, perfectly to his mind, and he was so well pleased with him that he placed him on this great island, separate from the white and black men; and gave him rules for his conduct, promising happiness in proportion as they should be observed.

In their reaction to white men the ancient Chinese were even less flattering. Historians of the third century B.C. Han dynasty commented on the yellow hair, green eyes, and prominent noses of the Caucasians and described them as looking "just like the apes from whom they are descended." More recently the Chinese have reported that white men —especially their women—have a vile body odor which most resembles that of a dead person.

The Chippewa Indians were apparently less concerned about the white man's anemic look, bad temper, and ape-like appearance than about his deficiency of brains. One of their standard expressions for describing foolish behavior was "as stupid as a white man." A Moorish scholar in eleventh century Toledo made a similar observation. Said he, "Races north of the Pyrenees are of cold temperament and never reach maturity; they are of great stature and of a white color. But they lack all sharpness of wit and penetration of intellect."

If members of other races have believed some rather unflattering things about the white man, he has had no hesitation in returning the insults a thousandfold. One of the most ancient examples comes from the white-skinned, Indo-European–speaking people (usually termed Aryans) who conquered the dark-skinned people of the Indus Valley in India about 1500 B.C. Although the residents of this area had a much more highly developed culture than their conquerors, the Aryans described them as looking like apes and barking like dogs. Since the conquered people were not accepted as equals, it was inevitable that they should be placed at the very bottom of the then existing social hierarchy. Even before the Aryans arrived in India, they had begun to develop a stratified society. Among them rank was based upon comparative wealth and power as measured by the number of cattle a person owned and could successfully keep in his possession. While social position was by no means fixed and unchanging at this early date, historians see this early emphasis upon rank as the first phase in the lengthy development of the Indian caste system.

By about 1000 B.C. four distinct divisions existed in Indian society: the Brahman, the Kshatriya, the Vaisya, and the Sudra. There is reason to believe that originally only dark-skinned people were relegated to the Sudra level of society. As time went by, these social divisions became increasingly rigid; individuals remained all their lives within the caste into which they were born. Myths appeared, sanctioning this arrangement. It was believed that certain innate "qualities" existed which were supposed to equip an individual for life in one specific caste and no other. Since these qualities were inherited, they could not possibly be acquired or changed after birth. Here is the way in which the ancient Hindu epic, the Mahabharata describes one's caste-fated nature.

> The work of Brahmans, Kshatriyas, Vaisyas, and Sudras, . . .
> Is fixed by reason of the Qualities
> Plated in each:
> A Brahman's virtues, . . .
> Born of his nature, are serenity,
> Self-mastery, religion, purity,
> Patience, uprightness, learning, and to know
> The truth of things which be. A
> Kshatriya's pride, born of his nature, lives in valor, fire,
> Constancy, skillfulness, spirit in fight,
> And open-handedness and noble mien,
> As a lord of men. A Vaisya's task,
> Born with his nature, is to till the ground,
> Tend cattle, venture trade. A Sudra's
> State, suiting his nature, is to minister.

At about the same time that the myth of inborn qualities was taking hold in India, another myth appeared in the Levant which was destined to justify Negro slavery some 2,000 years later in the Western

41

world. This was the story in the Old Testament about a rather excessive punishment meted out to a son who happened to discover his father drunken and naked. The father was Noah, the son was Ham, and the account appears in the ninth chapter of Genesis.

And the sons of Noah, that went forth of the ark, were Shem, and Ham, and Japheth: and Ham is the father of Canaan.

These are the three sons of Noah: and of them was the whole earth overspread.

And Noah began to be an husbandman, and he planted a vineyard:

And he drank of the wine, and was drunken; and he was uncovered within his tent.

And Ham, the father of Canaan, saw the nakedness of his father, and told his two brethren without.

And Shem and Japheth took a garment, and laid it upon both their shoulders, and went backward, and covered the nakedness of their father; and their faces were backward, and they saw not their father's nakedness.

And Noah awoke from his wine, and knew what his younger son had done unto him.

And he said, Cursed be Canaan; a servant of servants shall he be unto his brethren.

. . . . .

God shall enlarge Japheth, and he shall dwell in the tents of Shem; and Canaan shall be his servant.

According to this judgment, even if one does not construe the relationship "servant" to mean "slave," a specific group is fated to be socially inferior to another. This particular biblical passage is one that I have heard quoted as a modern justification for racial discrimination. It is surprising how many of one's acquaintances seem to remember that "somewhere in the Bible" one may find racial inequality prescribed or explained.

Anthropologist Ruth Benedict has pointed out that the white man needed no elaborate racial theories to justify his exploitation of darker-skinned peoples during the great age of discovery and exploration. It seemed entirely evident to him that he was dealing with inferior beings. Records of early Spanish reactions to the Indians of the West Indies are replete with statements such as these: "They eat human flesh and they've no notion of justice; they go about naked and eat spiders and worms and lice, all raw. . . ." "When we cut the ears off one of them they all stick by him just the same." "The Indian is better off as a slave, among men, than as an animal on his own."

Many men actually felt a sense of religious duty to make captives of the native peoples they encountered. It was believed that only through bodily bondage to the white man could the "heathen" souls be saved. Convinced of his own cultural superiority, the white man traveled throughout the world with a gun in one hand and a Bible in the other. That this belief was popular and long-lived is indicated by its recurrence in the pro-slavery writing of mid-nineteenth-century America. The writer William Simms had this to say on the subject: "Slavery has elevated the Negro from savagery. The black man's finer traits of fidelity and docility were encouraged in his servile position."

Of course, a theory of slavery based upon saving heathen souls was bound to require new justification as more and more slaves became converted to Christianity. It became increasingly difficult to rationalize the enslaving of another man's body if his soul was destined for the same place as one's own. And so the belief gradually began to take hold among white men that natives were not actually human at all, that they were in fact subhuman and had not fully evolved.

Some took the theories of Darwin to mean that all men had descended from the apes, but that primitive peoples had only recently broken off from the family tree and were therefore not entirely human.

In time, numerous other myths found their way into the white man's collection. Many of these confused a lack of technological progress with a lack of basic intellect. Some of them evaluated primitive fertility rites by a Victorian scale and found the native not only without morals and ethics but actually a savage animal in heart and mind. Others romanticized him as a simple child. All these ideas, this potpourri of guesswork, came to be associated with race, with the presence or absence of skin coloring in man. Because of these myths and others like them, great injustices were done to millions of human beings. Merciless beating, mutilation, rape, the slaughter of infants—all were commonplace for over four centuries in the exploitation of primitive peoples. This treatment—of Africans, Indians, Melanesians, and Orientals—is all the more reprehensible today because of the self-righteousness of those who meted it out.

Few societies in the contemporary world still condone the ruthless exploitation of other peoples. Yet many racial myths live on. In twentieth-century America it is not unusual to hear impressions such as these: "They are not as human as we are." "You can't trust them." "They are still savages underneath." Even the full weight of anthropological and biological research has not dislodged some of these

43

old racial inferiority myths. Unfortunately this has led certain anthropologists to produce a new kind of myth—the notion that race itself is a myth. The rationale of this view is not difficult to understand; it probably goes like this: "People exaggerate differences. They believe that those with different skins and faces are not human, are not like themselves, whereas actually the shared physical traits of all races are vastly more numerous than the variations. If only I can persuade them that races do not exist, that physical differences are insignificant when compared with similarities, I can teach them to love and not to hate." There is no dishonesty here, only the confusion of one's facts with one's wishes.

Other specialists accept race as a fact but emphasize that skin color is one of the least reliable criteria for its delineation. They know that most of the world's peoples can be classified correctly by color and external appearance alone into one of the three primary stocks: Negroid, Mongoloid, or Caucasoid. But they also know that, if visible clues were the sole racial criteria, several million people would be incorrectly classified. As a result they insist that external differences are unreliable guides to race. Although they are technically correct, this position creates much confusion by denying what is obvious to any man.

Both of these "hide-race" points of view are nonsensical to the average person—of whatever race. All his life he has seen Negroes, Indians, Orientals, and whites, if not in the flesh then in pictures. Although he has probably had little experience with composite races, he can easily see visible differences between pictures of a Hindu, a Polynesian, and a quadroon. To him group differences in human physiology and appearance are as real as breed differences in dogs, this being a much-used analogy. And he is right—not in most of the implications that he may draw from these differences, but in his perception of them. Races do exist and the basic stocks are easily identified by anyone.

I suspect that the attempt to minimize or deny racial differences is often rooted in the same unconscious feelings that may lead others to magnify the same differences. There is probably the same lurking uneasiness toward human variation, a vague feeling that if a particular man or group of men can be shown to be different, then this difference will be to their disadvantage. It seems more realistic to acknowledge and classify obvious racial differences and, wherever possible, to explain their significance by using the facts of science rather than the fantasies of myth. There is nothing to be gained by replacing the myths of two thousand years with still more myths.

44

RACIAL CLASSIFICATIONS

A race may be defined as a biologically inbred human group with distinctive physical traits that tend to breed true from generation to generation. For the most part, the traits that are used to differentiate races are the obvious, the visible, the physical qualities that characterize large groups of people. The anthropologist and biologist, therefore, simply take for granted the thousands of more subtle, not-so-obvious, anatomical and biological similarities that exist between races, while highlighting differences. Once we are sure that both horses and cats are mammals, the known similarities underpin a subsequent search for specific differences and the establishment of new categories. Once we know that both men and apes are primates, our attention may turn to the classifiable differences between the two. In cataloging dogs, we implicitly recognize their common caninity, but we explicitly point out breed differences. In like manner, we approach human variation with the realistic acknowledgment that all races have many thousands more biological traits in common than they have traits that distinguish them. Such an acknowledgment does not deny the fact of race; it indicates that the traits we share make us mammals, primates, and humans, whereas the others make us races. Some of the generally accepted biological criteria used in differentiating the three primary racial stocks of Caucasoid, Mongoloid, and Negroid appear below.

FEATURE	CAUCASOID	MONGOLOID	NEGROID
Skin	White	Yellow; brown	Dark brown; black
Eyes and hair	Varied colors	Dark brown; black (epicanthic fold of eyelids)	Dark brown
Hair	Straight; curly	Straight	Woolly
Body hair	Medium amount	None; slight	None; slight
Prognathism (protrusion of mouth and jaw)	None	Slight	Marked
Brows	Medium size	Small	Small
Forehead	Sloping	Upright	Upright
Chin	Marked projection	Medium projection	Slight projection

45

FEATURE	CAUCASOID	MONGOLOID	NEGROID
Nose	Narrow	Medium size	Broad
Lips	Thin	Medium size	Thick
Body fat	Moderate amount	Much	Little
Head	Varied shapes	Round	Long

Since lists always appear somewhat stiff and uncompromising, it is important to note that our chart of racial characteristics is both incomplete and general. It does little more than indicate that there are at least a dozen immediate physical ways to differentiate three great races of men. It does not indicate the numerous smaller biological clusters of men within these races or the many human clusters between these major racial divisions.

Yet the more intensive our analysis of racial variations becomes, the more certain it seems that there are smaller groupings, called subraces, within the major categories. Among Caucasoids, for example, there is a tall, fair-skinned, long-headed, aquiline-nosed group, but there is also a short, swarthy, round-headed, short-nosed one. Negroid types may be extremely tall, long-nosed, and smooth-skinned, or they may be dwarfish, flat-nosed, and wizened. Mongoloids may be short or tall, slant-eyed or not, and yellowish or red. A number of additional intraracial differentiations may also be made. Moreover, interracial mixing has complicated classification still further by producing a number of composite racial groups. Members of composite races generally show characteristics of all races involved; if left to breed among themselves, they will produce offspring of remarkable consistency in overall appearance, that is, a new racial category.

While the primary and composite races of man seem well enough established, a number of highly respected anthropologists, including Clyde Kluckhohn, have questioned the validity of subracial designations. Their position is that a classification such as Nordic or Alpine is primarily a statistical exercise, since few, if any, pure subraces exist. Other anthropologists share the view of Mischa Titiev, who points out in his *The Science of Man* that "each stock does comprise so many different-looking groups that it seems justifiable to make an effort to fit them into the most logical arrangement possible." Whether or not one believes that subraces are valid biological classifications is probably not overly important, so long as one has an appreciation of the tremendously variable and adaptable nature of man. As Coon has said, "In an atom-age world in which men of all races are coming into increasing contact with one another on a basis of equality and cooperation, a knowledge of what a wonderfully adaptive thing the human body is, is a much healthier commodity than the recently traditional hide-race point of view."

Like phyla, species, families, and the other biological categories, races were probably produced by the complementary processes of mutation, intensive inbreeding in isolation, and genetic drift. Additional racial characteristics appear to be the result of aesthetic selection—a process to be discussed later. Yet, as is obvious from the above list of traits, the differences between races are not remotely as great as the differences between species.

This is further shown in the matter of inbreeding. All of us know that members of different orders (monkeys and wildcats, for example) cannot mate. All of us except certain late Nazi racists and a few Deep South diehards know that apes and men cannot reproduce. Most of us know that all fertile human beings are capable of interbreeding regardless of their race—or our approval. Paradoxically, it is the very knowledge of this proof of the biological kinship of races that often frightens man into inventing fictitious family trees for himself and for those whom he dislikes. An acquaintance of mine apparently never saw the logical contradiction involved in not wanting his daughter to marry a member of the race he designated as "black apes." To make his point, he and others like him list certain real or imagined similarities in appearance between Negroes and apes, usually quite unaware that the list may be expanded to show that the white man has his apelike features as well. Consider the following chart:

FEATURE	MOST APELIKE	LEAST APELIKE
Nose	Negroid	Caucasoid
Jaw	Negroid	Mongoloid
Body hair	Caucasoid	Mongoloid
Lips	Caucasoid	Negroid
Hair form	Mongoloid	Negroid
Eye color	Mongoloid	Caucasoid

From this we can see that the Caucasoid racist may well describe the Negro's broad nose and forward projection of the mouth as apelike. But he will certainly need convincing that his own abundant body hair and thin lips are in the same category, although they most assuredly are. When we tell him that the Negro's large lips and woolly hair are the *least* apelike of all races, he will probably be persuaded

47

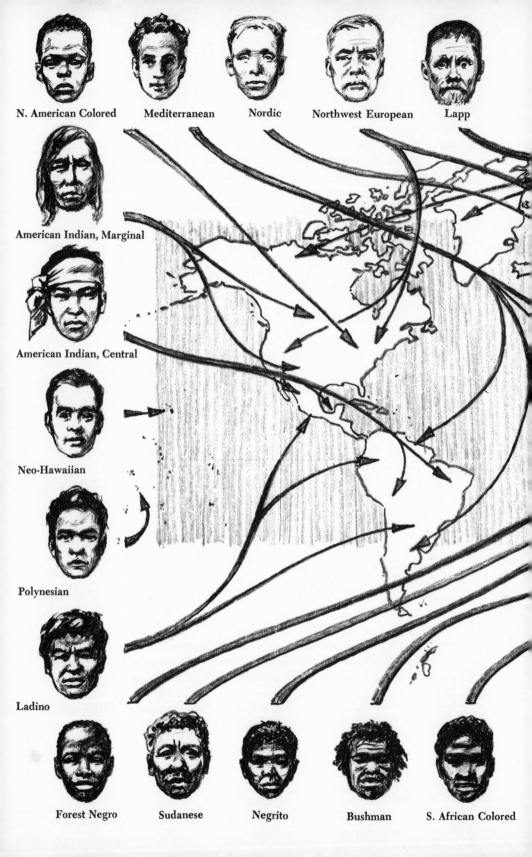

N. American Colored   Mediterranean   Nordic   Northwest European   Lapp

American Indian, Marginal

American Indian, Central

Neo-Hawaiian

Polynesian

Ladino

Forest Negro   Sudanese   Negrito   Bushman   S. African Colored

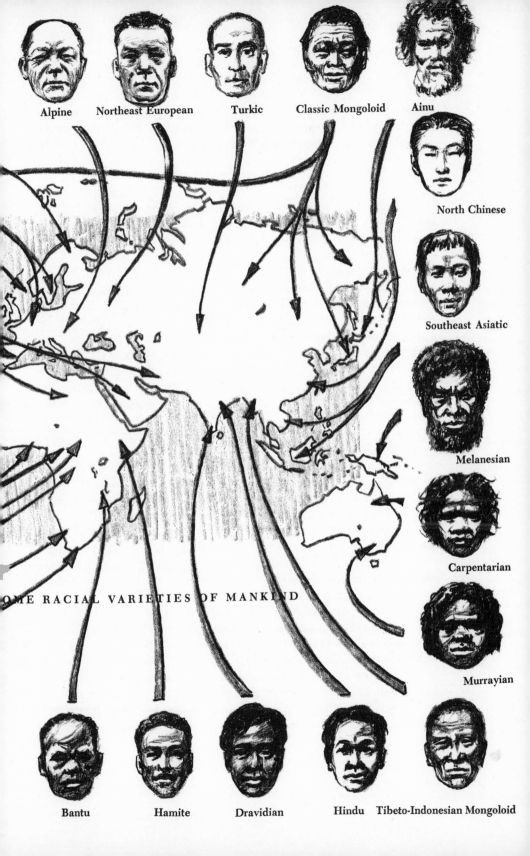

Alpine Northeast European Turkic Classic Mongoloid Ainu

North Chinese

Southeast Asiatic

Melanesian

Carpentarian

Murrayian

OME RACIAL VARIETIES OF MANKIND

Bantu Hamite Dravidian Hindu Tibeto-Indonesian Mongoloid

that we have taken leave of our senses. Yet, all races have features that resemble apes. These common features simply restate what we already know: that all human beings share a common though remote relationship with the apes. The man who points to the apelike aspects of the Negro points to the primate in us all.

THE ORIGIN OF RACES

Exactly when in prehistoric times races began to differentiate is not easy to determine. As we saw earlier, one theory holds that human varieties were late in developing, perhaps having appeared within the past 20,000 years or so. This concept is usually joined with the idea that Homo sapiens did not completely evolve until somewhat less than 50,000 years ago. If, however, as now seems likely, Homo sapiens is much more ancient than was previously suspected, and evolved from Homo erectus at different times and places, then it is probable that at least some of the races are also quite ancient. This theory sees Swanscombe man and Steinheim man (250,000 years ago) as early or evolving Caucasoids, Peking man (350,000 years ago) as proto-Mongoloid, and Rhodesian man (20,000 years ago) as Negroid. Be this as it may, man, while still erectus, apparently migrated over much of Europe, Asia, and Africa, and long before the end of the Old Stone Age was situated so that the forces of nature and society began to produce the various races.

Professional opinion varies about the value of race differences, once they appeared, for man's adaptation to his environment. Writing in the affirmative, Carleton Coon builds his case upon several ecological rules already formulated by zoologists and which he believes apply equally well to man. In discussing coloration for example, he cites Gloger's rule, which says that "animals living in wet forests tend to have black or red coats; those in arid regions buff or gray ones." Coon relates this to the darker-skinned races, and to their ability to withstand the high ultraviolet radiation and the infections that characterize equatorial Africa. On the other hand, fair skin is considered to be highly adaptive to areas such as Scandinavia. This is because it is able to utilize the relatively weak ultraviolet rays of these regions in the production of essential vitamin D. Coon applies another ecological rule to racial differences in hair amount. This is Rensch's hair-length rule, which states that animals living in colder regions have longer hair than members of the same species whose homes are hot. More hair tends to preserve an animal's body heat, less hair allows heat to escape the body. Other ecological principles are utilized by Coon to explain body size and amount of body fat.

Taking the opposite position, anthropologist Weston La Barre is convinced that very few, if indeed any of man's racial variations came about because of their adaptive or survival value. Here, from *The Human Animal*, is his devastating critique of skin color and hair form as racial adaptations.

In the first place, it is not immediately apparent to the heating engineer just why either a dark skin or kinky hair is adaptive. If insulation from a hot tropical sun is required, then longer and looser hair which trapped many air spaces would be more efficient thermodynamically. (But no, that will not do, because Caucasoids have that, to insulate them from the cold! —and also why do Mongoloids, who live in the same high latitudes and even colder continental climates, have long hair that is merely straight?) Actually, the Negro in Africa has short, tight, kinky hair—which in some of its extreme forms actually leaves the bare skin exposed to the sun's rays between knobby "peppercorns" of hair. Likewise, a dark skin absorbs heat rays more readily than a light skin does—and it is not very clear just why Negroes need skins adapted to keeping them warm in the tropics. Indeed, many such alleged racial "adaptations" may actually be maladaptations. As a matter of fact, we could cling to the belief better if our logic did a flipflop: a better case could be made for supposing that a dark bare skin (and nearly bare pate) can better radiate body heat than a light-colored hairy skin can. But this at best leaves our Negro "adapted" only so long as he stays in the shade; he is severely maladapted as soon as he steps out into the sun. Also, one is a little puzzled as to why the Negroid Melanesians, in the same hot moist climate as the Negroid Africans, should by contrast have immense mops of kinky hair, sometimes a yard in diameter, on their black heads.

To comprehend this critique of racial adaptation somewhat better, let us briefly review La Barre's general position. In a closely reasoned and profound analysis of race, he indicates that for the most part human biological evolution ceased when man learned to control his environment to a reasonable extent. This would be at least 100,000 years ago, probably more. His point is that once man learned to coordinate his brain and his hands and began to shape his environment, he stopped being shaped by it. La Barre designates this as a monumental shift by Homo sapiens from an "autoplastic," environment-created, anatomically adaptive type of evolution to an "alloplastic," create-one's-own-environment, nonanatomically adaptive type. Specifically, once man learned to control and to make fire, and to use the skins of animals for clothing, his survival no longer depended upon mutations for thick hair and fatty skin. When he learned to make a club and a spear, he was freed once and for all from any dependence on adaptive mutations in his fight against his strong-pawed, but uninventive animal rivals. La Barre's position, then, is that whatever biologically adaptive traits man possesses were acquired when they had survival value, before he became skilled in the use of tools, weapons, and fire. Therefore, he is convinced, racial differences do not represent biological adaptations to the environment at all. They are primarily the result of variations which appeared in isolated groups through mutation or genetic drift, and which probably came to have an aesthetic or perhaps ethnocentric appeal to the group concerned. According to this position, man himself more or less created races because different people had different ideas of beauty. The appearance of dark skin in one society may have offended its members, and the dark-skinned man or woman may not have mated or may have mated late, thus diminishing the opportunity to produce dark-skinned offspring. On the other hand, some societies may have looked upon dark skin as highly attractive and condemned the light-skinned person to a barren life. In either case, group skin differences would have resulted from man's aesthetic preferences rather than from the process of natural selection.

I am convinced that La Barre's position represents a brilliant advance in our thinking about race. Yet we need not totally discard adaptation as a concept useful in explaining early racial development. Certainly there must have been a long period in human history when man was learning to use his brain, when his evolution was neither wholly autoplastic nor completely alloplastic. Man was not shivering, naked, and fireless one night, and skin-clad and hearth-warmed the next. Thinking, reasoning, and inventing required much time, time in which adaptive mutations could have occurred. It seems reasonable, therefore, that a number of adaptive racial traits may have appeared during this autoplastic-alloplastic transitional period. In this connection, Coon's argument that dark skin is adaptive to ultraviolet radiation, infection, and cancer is more compelling than La Barre's that it is nonadaptive to infrared heat. Yet it is probably naive to insist that all racial traits are adaptive just because a few clearly are. There is every reason to believe that La Barre's basic concept is correct, that once man began to control his environment there was a gradual decrease in the appearance of naturally selected traits and a gradual increase in aesthetically selected ones. Genetic drift bolstered by divergent aesthetic concepts may well be, as La Barre assures us, all that was required to produce Negroid hair that is short and tight in Africa but long and loose in Oceania.

THE COMPARISON OF RACES

Probably most conversations about race between average Americans deal with comparisons. We are concerned about the relative physiology, the relative intelligence, the relative morality, and the relative potential of the races. We want to know if the average Negro is innately more indolent and stupid than other races, if Orientals are naturally furtive and emotionless. In discussions of this type we often confuse nationality with race; we frequently speak of socially produced characteristics as inborn traits. Comparisons are further confused by the use of popular notions about various peoples, some of which have a basis in fact, but none of which apply to all members of the groups concerned. These ideas depict Jews as cunning and greedy, Indians as thieves, Frenchmen as effeminate, Germans as efficiently cruel, and Dutchmen as dully honest.

Unfortunately, clear-cut yes and no answers are not yet possible for some of these questions, or the explanations are so complex that few wish to take the time to understand them. In many cases no objective research has been done. Scientists who reject racial discrimination, who respect Negro or Oriental colleagues, and who know how avidly the bigot distorts racial differences, have not been enthusiastic about exploring racial variation. Other investigators, as we have seen, have been so outraged by the prejudice against minority groups that their own research has been colored by a desire to prove that people are not different—that all so-called differences are superficial. Whatever the reasons, research in this area has been so unpopular, or biased in one direction or the other, that even the simplest questions remain scientifically unanswered.

For example, instead of a controlled chemical analysis of racial sweat, we allow well-meaning but completely biased opinion to prevail. We are assured that the only reason Negroes smell different from whites is because of their poverty, which makes bathing difficult. Thus, all unwashed human bodies have an unpleasant smell and there are more unwashed Negroids than Caucasoids. I have smelled enough races to have a strong opinion that this explanation is hogwash. When definitive studies are finally made I expect them to show a qualitative chemical difference in sweats, with each race having an odor that may offend nonmembers.

Another illustration concerns the possibility of race differences in special aptitudes. As things now stand, many educated Negroes reject the suggestion that their race has extraordinary inborn rhythmical capacities, because they interpret this as an effort to set them apart. They have learned to resent any implication that they are not exactly like the white man except for a few visible features. This attitude, while perhaps understandable, makes much racial research both unpopular and difficult.

Perhaps the major intellectual hurdle that one must overcome in making racial comparisons is to accept the fact that physical differences do not automatically indicate racial superiority or inferiority. On the other hand, it is naive to assert that racial differences are totally meaningless. From a biological and climatic point of view certain racial features are definitely desirable and others undesirable. Subsequent research may also uncover race differences in such areas as creative potentials; artistic, musical, linguistic, and mathematical aptitudes; ability to endure stress; and basic temperament. At this point no one can say. What is needed is racial research founded on the philosophy that men do not have to be the same to have equal opportunities. This research should examine every aspect of human variation. The search should be for truth, not for materials that support a pet theory about race, be it liberal or conservative. Some research of this type has already been done; more is in progress. Much more needs to be undertaken. Already two things are quite clear. First, it is highly difficult to isolate true racial predispositions and tendencies from the social situation of the race being studied. Second, each race has its share of assets and liabilities. Both of these facts are evident in the material below.

Biological Comparisons / Since many racial differences represent biological adaptations to climatic conditions, it follows that no one race can possibly have a body superior for all environments. The dark, tough skin of the Negro is demonstrably an asset in Africa and Melanesia since it provides protection from ultraviolet penetration and insect bites. Negroes in Scandinavia, however, require vitamin D supplements. Light-skinned Caucasoids have little difficulty in the geographical north, but must continually use sun creams and insect repellents in the tropics. The long Negroid forearm allows efficient cooling in intense African heat and provides an all-important edge

PERUVIAN ADAPTATION TO THIN ATMOSPHERE
ATOP HIGH MOUNTAINS

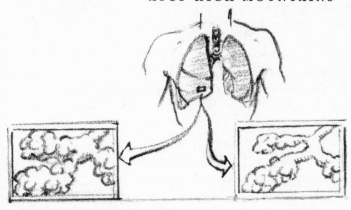

Lung air sacs permanently dilated

More hemoglobin

More blood

Bigger heart

Bigger red cells

Compact body build

in American boxing. But these same long fat-free extremities afford very little protection from the cold. Such comparisons could be greatly extended.

If we consider racial vitality or resistance to disease an index to racial superiority, we are confronted with a similar situation. Certain illnesses appear to be linked to race, but a race can hardly be termed superior or inferior on this basis. The following chart will make this clear.

RACIAL PATHOLOGY IN THE UNITED STATES
Almost Certain Racial Basis

HIGHER INCIDENCE FOR WHITE

Diphtheria	Psoriasis
Yellow fever	Lupus
Hemophilia	Trachoma
Peptic ulcer	Surgical suppuration

HIGHER INCIDENCE FOR NEGRO

Sickle-cell anemia	Keloid tumors
Whooping cough	Nephritis
Fibroids in womb	

Some Probability of a Racial Basis

HIGHER INCIDENCE FOR WHITE

Scarlet fever	Coronary occlusion
Measles	Gallstones
Infantile paralysis	Urinary stones
Angina pectoris	Most cancers
Arteriosclerosis	

HIGHER INCIDENCE FOR NEGRO

Lobar pneumonia	Syphilitic heart disease
Hypertension	Cancer of female
Cerebral hemorrhage	genitalia

It can be seen that there are both physical strengths and weaknesses inherent in racial membership. The races are obviously not the same, but who can measure the relative superiority of angina pectoris to hypertension?

Intelligence Comparisons / Probably the most controversial of all race comparisons deal with brains, learning, and intelligence. Many people have once and for all decided that the white race is vastly ahead of all others in intelligence and that is that. On the other hand, racial-equality enthusiasts are just as certain, but with no more real evidence to go on, that there could not possibly be race differences in intelligence potentials. Neither position is scientifically defensible. The plain fact is that at present we are able neither to confirm nor to deny the existence of an intellectually superior race.

Racists make much of the fact that the brain size of the Negro seems to run about 100 cc. smaller than that of the white man. This is, of course, believed to indicate automatically less intelligence in the Negro. The fact is, however, that once man has about 1,000 cc. of brain tissue, there is no evidence that a person with an additional 300 cc. is less intelligent than one with an additional 400 cc. When I first began to teach anthropology, I generally used the fact that the brain of the average Caucasoid female is from 100 to 150 cc. smaller than that of the male to indicate that brain size is not of critical importance in intelligence after the 1,000 cc. level is reached. I soon discovered that, far from clinching my point, I was actually confirming what many male members of the class had always suspected—the inadequacy of female brain power. Nowadays to make my point I refer to the average Eskimo brain, which is about 100 cc. larger than that of the average white man. We can argue that brain volume equals intelligence only if we are willing to admit that we are mentally inferior to the Arctic Mongoloid.

Even within a given racial group there is a fair amount of variation in brain size. But while we speak of intellectuals as "eggheads," no one feels intellectually inferior just because he has to settle for a size $7\frac{1}{8}$ hat rather than a size $7\frac{3}{8}$. There is no evidence that the genius has a consistently larger or smaller brain than the idiot. Once the capacity for algebraic mentality exists, the richness and complexity of the neuron network within the brain appears to be vastly more important than sheer bulk in determining intelligence.

Unfortunately, there is no existing test which can determine the basic intelligence of persons reared under different cultural conditions. This is to say that, at present, innate intelligence cannot be measured without at the same time testing to some extent the opportunities and background of the person concerned. There are a host of factors that have thus far prevented the development of such a test. In the first place, every society responds to certain aspects of its environment, but either rejects or fails to sense other features. This blindness to various aspects of reality is not found within any specific race. It is a matter of learning and often simply indicates that these

57

aspects of the world are of no real importance to the way of life of the group concerned. In the second place, every society rates by its own scale of values the relative importance of the many things to which it does respond. Thus the Cheyenne brave, unlike the Hopi, is taught everything about hunting with a horse and a bow, but knows nothing about farming. The ancient Greeks learned to see beauty in whatever had balance and harmony, but were apparently blind to any wild, asymmetrical, or unstructured beauty. The modern American learns that steak and ice cream are good to eat but scorns even the idea of snails and grasshoppers.

When it comes to constructing and standardizing an intelligence test for use in a society we are almost forced to test the familiar and accepted areas of that specific society. If we take our test out of the society for which it was made and use it in a society with a different set of values, sensitivities to things, and word-meanings, it seems obvious that any results we get will be worthless. We cannot realistically ask the Cheyenne about farming or the Zuñi about buffalo hunting. Nor can we expect all people to share the Greek ideal of beauty or American dietary tastes. Yet during the past fifty years we have been just this unrealistic in our cross-cultural intelligence testing; in every case our subjects have obliged us with thoroughly miserable performances. While we can excuse most of the early investigators in this area for honest mistakes in the intellectual down-grading of exotic peoples, we can be eternally grateful that the psychologist Stanley Porteous got to the Australians with his tests before they got to us. How would you like to make a *woomera*, train a dingo, find water in a desert, and answer questions about an eight-dimensional exogamous kinship system or be handed the racial dunce cap by an Australian native?

One standardized test of intelligence for an American child involves the ability to match all the similar colors within a group. Ruth Benedict notes that this test was worthless among the Balinese because "the Balinese children spent all their time putting harmonious colors together 'for a pretty belt.' The Balinese are very sophisticated about color and they could not accept the idea of wasting time putting the same colors together when they might be showing their taste in color arrangement."

Difficulties of this nature exist in almost every aspect of contemporary intelligence testing. If colors are to be grouped, we learn that different societies group them in various ways, all equally good but not amenable to intercultural testing. If objects are to be arranged or related, the same problem arises. As an American you would classify a yam as an edible vegetable and that would be that. A Melanesian Trobriander, on the other hand, would see it as an object loaded with powerful magic and symbolism. Food would be its secondary, not its primary function. Tests of synonyms or vocabulary richness are likewise of limited value, since each society builds its words around those areas of reality that are most important to *it*, not to others. Thus there is little testable common ground between our automobile-rich vocabulary, the camel-rich vocabulary of the North African, and the caribou-rich vocabulary of the Chuckchee of Siberia. Test items that deal with mathematics or aspects of time encounter another variety of difficulties, since there are no universal ways of conceiving of space, quantities in space, or of events in space, that is, time. Thus, while there may well be fundamental pan-human laws of perceptual organization or gestalten, it has yet to be demonstrated that they are more powerful than the cultural forces in which they operate.

Finally there is the all-important matter of the testing situation itself. How can you adequately test a youngster who has been taught all his life never to answer any question unless he is absolutely sure of the answer? In American society we encourage the "educated hunch"; our use of the multiple-choice examination question illustrates this. Our children are taught that it is commendable at least to make an effort, even if they are incorrect. Consequently, on test items which require a child to recall as much of a story as possible, American children do well. But among many American Indian tribes children have been taught all their lives to say nothing unless they are correct in every detail. Either total recall or no recall is their choice. Moreover, among the Pueblos, it is in very bad taste to try to win in competitive activities, and American teachers have discovered that good Indian students often refuse to admit having finished an exercise ahead of everyone else in the class. Even if one day we have a culture-free intelligence test, the problem of how to make competitors of subjects outside of our own competition-oriented society may still remain unsolved.

Testing the intelligence of two races within the same society might appear easier than cross-cultural measurement, but here too are formidable difficulties. In America, for example, some fifty years of I.Q. investigation has settled nothing about the comparative native intelligence of the races. Although scores of studies have been made, none has yet tested adequate numbers of persons matched for region, sub-culture, and educational background—varying only in race. You may have heard of the Army tests where northern Negroes outperformed southern whites, or of southern studies where Negroes are shown to be at least two years intellectually inferior for each age level. Unhappily, there are enough studies to support any position one wishes to take so long as one does not insist on adequate numbers of comparable subjects and rigorous testing standards.

We should, of course, recognize the possibility that racial differences may be found in intelligence if and when we are able to test adequately for them. Even if overall racial intelligences prove to be about equal, we may discover specific aptitudes or tendencies that are racially linked. The important thing to remember, however, is that the average member of any race is intellectually competent to live in modern society; he can be taught any profession, learn to enjoy art, literature, and music, speak other languages, and keep his behavior on a high ethical plane.

Character Comparisons / Like other areas of racial comparison, this is a highly complex one to analyze. In America, many champions of equality refuse to believe that any differentials exist between racial rates of crime, illegitimacy, venereal disease, and the like. Others are willing to accept objective government reports on these matters, but lay the entire blame on the inferior socio-economic situation of the Negro. The first approach is the by-now-familiar one of seeking to deny all differences between the races. The second is quite extreme in holding the white race responsible for all Negro shortcomings. The white bigot, of course, reverses the blame and sees all Negroes as born savages at heart, lusting for his women, and coveting his possessions.

Much research is in progress in this area, and we may expect an increasing stockpile of sound information in the years ahead. Already, scientists have agreed that inborn predispositions toward vices and virtues do not exist. Traits such as greediness, industry, laziness, sadism, and so on are clearly learned, not racially inherited. Indeed, perhaps the major intellectual triumph of twentieth-century sociology and psychology has been a thoroughgoing revision of the older instinctivist theories concerning the natural tendencies of man. As a matter of fact, it is not necessary to bring race into such a discussion at all. All men, regardless of their race, develop their basic personalities through social situations, not through the inexorable unfolding of inborn traits. Character is learned rather than inherited; otherwise there would be no errant sons of model ministers. Aggressiveness, sociability, moral laxity, and all the rest are products of society, not of race (see Chapter 8). When we cite the high incidence of cer-

60

tain types of crime among Negroes, we are referring to a complex social condition, not a racial characteristic. When we demonstrate the sadistic tendencies of the Germans and Japanese, we are dealing with the end result of specific social systems on personality formation, not with a biological quirk of race. And we may be quite sure that it is Russian society rather than Russian genes that has given the world a taste of Russian impassivity and hypocrisy as well as Russian vodka.

It is probable that much of the lawless behavior that is associated in our society with the Negro will disappear as he achieves increasing equality. For years kept out of much of the mainstream of our culture, the Negro has developed his own subculture with differing values, ethical prescriptions, and controls. As he now begins to participate fully in the ways of the larger group, he will discover, whether or not he enjoys the prospect, that his own subculture will gradually disintegrate.

RACIAL FUSION

Before commenting on the highly explosive question of racial fusion, it may be well to summarize some of the points made thus far in the chapter.

1. All men are Homo sapiens, and have been for at least 20,000 years.
2. No race is any more animal-like or closely related to the apes than any other.
3. It cannot be established that races were produced as a divine punishment for a particular group or that a given race is predestined to be inferior to any other race.
4. It has not been established that racial differences in overall intelligence exist. Regardless of future findings, it is obvious that average members of all races have the necessary intelligence to live valuable and useful lives in modern society.
5. There are no inborn racial tendencies toward immorality, greed, laziness, sadism, and the like.
6. Racial differences in physiology do exist, and represent the adaptation of man to his various physical and social environments.
7. Some differences, such as color, demonstrate man's ancient ability to "roll with the punches" of his environment, by becoming physically adapted to the outside world of light, humidity, and temperature.
8. Differences such as high and low resistance to various diseases also show that men have lived in different environments and have

adapted themselves in varying degrees to unfriendly insects and microbes.

9. Other differences, such as hair form and length, may represent social choices based on concepts of beauty rather than environmental adaptation.

10. A number of other physical differences are only now coming to light. For example, various blood factors appear to be race related, as well as differentials in body chemistry. The significance of most of these differences is not yet known.

11. As racial research continues, it is likely that variations in creative potentials, certain aptitudes, and psychological processes will come to light. To judge from present findings, it is also likely that each race will be found to inherit its share of both assets and liabilities in these areas.

With the foregoing facts in mind, we may be sure that inbreeding between races will not produce apes or physical "throwbacks." We may likewise be confident that interbreeding is not against some divinely ordained plan for racial "purity" as heard in the racists' line, "If God had intended for the races to mix, he would have mixed them." Of course, the undesirable consequences of mating a black Angus beef cow with a white-faced Hereford bull have been sketched for us by numerous racists, as has the danger of "mongrelization" among both dogs and men. The basic weakness of these analogies lies in the fact that with cows and dogs we know what we are breeding for and we admit it: more flesh, more milk, longer hair, or perhaps a longer muzzle. With human beings it is different. White racists proclaim their biological fitness, but they ignore the cancer and infection proneness of white skin in favor of its symbolic superiority. Thus, while "mongrelized" skin may better equip us biologically for sunbathing, socially it may prevent us from using the beach in the first place. Should the day ever come when man truly wishes to breed himself for the strongest and most disease-resistant bodies, together with the best minds, the geneticists will probably be able to tell him how to do it. But even now it is quite obvious that man would have to do two highly controversial things in order to accomplish it. First, he would have to breed selectively within each racial group for those biological qualities he values most highly. Then, he would have to take some of the best representatives of each race who had been produced in this way and interbreed them.

Since man may never wish to conduct such a large-scale program of controlled development, it is more realistic to inquire into the present situation and probable future consequences of modern racial separatism and fusion. The answer to these questions is truly surprising, if not confusing. It suggests that at present both the racial purist and the racial fusionist are probably unwittingly contributing to man's continued differentiation and hence to his chances of ultimate survival. The racial purist may actually be instrumental in the creation of new human traits, since he is a modern force which makes for restricted human inbreeding, insisting as he does on marriage within his own race, his region, and perhaps even his particular community. And while he may not be motivated by humanitarian reasons in putting up his marriage restrictions, we cannot ignore the fact that inbreeding for whatever causes has been one of the basic factors in man's evolutionary development. The fusionist, on the other hand, helps to spread to all humans new traits that may develop and reshuffles existing genetic traits into new and potentially adaptive combinations. Each response in effect appears to be inadvertently contributing to human biological diversity, and indirectly to man's chance of survival on earth. That man is doing less and less of the intensive inbreeding necessary for the development of adaptive traits is highly obvious. But it is, nonetheless, possible that with the recent increase in radiation to human genes, due to atomic fallout, we may already have produced men whose skins and organs are more than usually resistant to radiation. If we have, then man may yet outlive his racial and political intolerance. If we have not, then the bigot had better learn to put up with his neighbors regardless of their race, at least until he can successfully inbreed a mutant gene to save himself.

CHAPTER 5

Human Society and Culture

No single culture can be accepted
as the final and best for all peoples. . . .

LAWRENCE K. FRANK

GROUP LIFE

To a large extent it was physical variation—changes in hands and hips and heads—that made our line the most successful of animals. Other differences in color and construction allowed man to adapt to almost any environment on earth. In more recent times, however, physical change has become much less important in human survival. This is because man no longer needs to wait for the painfully slow process of biological evolution to solve his problems. He invents the solutions himself. This remarkable transition appears to be related not only to the fact that man developed a large brain but that he was living in groups when he did.

We do not know when in history the human line adopted group life or the way in which instinctive herding gave way to learned association. We do know that man was not the first creature to live in groups and is not the only one doing so today. Bees, ants, and termites live in colonies; cows, sheep, and elephants in herds. A fairly common mistake even today, however, is to assume that all social behavior, be it in the apiary, on the trail drive, or in suburbia, is the product of what is sometimes called a "gregarious" instinct.

If you happened to be a creature with a very small brain, or perhaps even a good-sized brain in a hulking body, you would be fortunate that your gray matter functioned on a predetermined plan. Luckily for you, there would be neural patterns that organized and limited your external behavior about as neatly as they did your digestion and metabolism. But if your brain were then suddenly stripped of its tight little system of patterning, you would be out of the evolutionary contest immediately. An ant trying to learn its way through life would be as fatally frustrated as a man trying to adjust to modern society on instinct alone. Thus, while both ant and man are social creatures, the nature of their sociability is vastly different. The ant has no choice whatever—he must follow the built-in "grayprint," and one of its specifications is for group life. Fortunately, man has no such irrevocable orders. He obviously prefers and sustains a group rather than a solitary existence, but there is little doubt that this preference is now based on the learned pleasures and satisfactions of a social setting. Most social scientists agree with Aristotle that man is "by nature" a political or social animal, but there is also accord that this aspect of his nature is primarily a social, not a biological creation. Where man's "natural" sociability is concerned, we are born with the capacity to be sociable or antisocial; the content and quality of our experiences will establish both the degree and direction of the capacity.

Since most men, ancient and modern, have elected to live with others of their kind, we may be sure that there were advantages involved, and that these outweighed the attractions of isolation. As a matter of fact, it seems certain that part of the general primate tendency to prefer group life began long before man's early relations left the trees. In the comparative safety of the heights, life was casual and serene. Food came easily and long hours must have been spent in pleasurable social exchanges. Mating, nursing, grooming, and playing—all of great primate interest—involve give and take among individuals. Cooperation, mutual concern, and at least the rudiments of affection may consequently be additional assets that tree dwelling gave our ancestors, assets as desirable and as human as our good vision, our versatile hands, and our readiness to vocalize.

When our line left the trees, it was fortunate that group life had already been established, since existence on the ground was far more precarious. With large meat-eating rivals all about, the problems of food getting and protection could no longer be solved through aerial acrobatics. In all likelihood, group living was the key to the survival of our ancestors during this time. Remember that this was several million years prior to the first deliberately made weapons. Other than their numbers, these prehumans had nothing but their physical and mental agility to aid them. The screams of one set of vocal cords and the rocks hurled by two hands could at best only briefly delay the progress of a tiger toward a meal. But two or three or four cooperating creatures would change the situation. They not only could help protect each other but might actually kill the tiger for a good meal themselves. Groups, especially those with brainy cooperating members (that is, near-human or human), may immediately turn the hunter into the hunted.

Group living, then, gave the human line increased protection in a hostile world and greatly multiplied its chances of survival. Moreover, several hunters could kill game that one would not dare attack alone and could thereby substantially increase the food supply. The advantages of greater protection and more food, and the knowledge that they came through group cooperation, must be considered fundamental ties that bound early man into groups. Moreover, man was still primate enough to enjoy many of the old tree-society patterns as well. There is every reason to believe that our ancestors from arboreal times onward have enjoyed games, grooming, and lovemaking.

PROBLEMS OF HUMAN SOCIETY

Obviously, group life assisted man in coping with problems related to the physical environment. But one of the most notable facts about group living is that, while it bestows benefits upon its members, it also engenders problems that they must solve. You will have noticed this somewhere along the line. In fact you could find many supporters if you wished to argue that society has created more problems than it has solved. While some anthropologists may be willing to concede this, the general opinion is that most contemporary societies must have solved about as many problems as they have produced, or they would not exist. Some problems are tied up with the relation of the group to the outside world of nature and other groups; some with the interaction between group members. Still others concern the individual as a member of society. As a whole the problems tend to fall into large clusters, which appear to characterize all human societies, ancient or modern, of which we have any record. These are the general areas:

1. The problems connected with communication between group members: the world of symbols, language, gestures, and writing.

EVIDENCES OF MAN'S INCREASING CREATIVITY

10,000 YEARS AGO
Rock drawings of dancing women from South Africa

40,000 YEARS AGO
Jewelry used in Aurignacian times. Each unit is made up of two sets of four fish vertebrae, three gastropod shells, and one canine tooth.

70,000 YEARS AGO
Skin scrapers of flint made by Neanderthal man.

1,000,000 YEARS AGO
Crude bone tools used by Australopithecus.

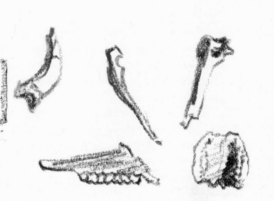

2. The problems concerned with the production, distribution, and consumption of goods: the world of technology, weights and measures, means and media of exchange, property, and wealth.
3. The problems involved in mating and child rearing: the world of courtship, sex, personality formation, and education.
4. The problems concerned with law and order: the world of status, rights, privileges, obligations, social controls, government, war, and peace.
5. The problems related to the unknown: the world of religion, magic, myth, ritual, divination, and science.
6. The problems of self-expression: the world of art, music, literature, dance, and play.

While other animals face and solve a limited number of these problems from day to day, man is the only creature who copes with them almost completely without an inborn, prearranged plan of action. Instead he carries into battle a large brain, sharp eyes, versatile hands, upright posture, and vocal ability. Together these traits enabled early man to test his environment, to experiment with his world in a way totally unknown among other animals. Singly, none of these traits would have mattered—man would have been just another animal. Elephants had larger brains, moles had better ratios of brain to body weight, and monkeys had grasping hands. Birds had good eyes, walked upright, and vocalized beautifully. But in man alone did all these qualities exist in combination, and in combination the effect was miraculous. With these, man became able to think creatively and in so doing rose to true greatness among animals. Anthropologists call the fruit of this creative wrestling with the environment "culture"; man alone both produces and stockpiles it.

CULTURE

We know nothing about the first culture of man—his ideas and how he translated them into actions and things. But archaeological evidence shows us some of the slow steps that he made along the way into the present. African caches of stream-worn pebbles miles from their source show us that a creature (Australopithecus) was learning to see cause and effect and to plan future action. Pierced skull bases and split bones show us a hungry Peking man, but, more importantly, a highly perceptive and manually dexterous one. Bones of an arthritic old Neanderthal tell us that men had come to love and care for helpless members in their midst. Drawings of animals in the depths of

Man's first stone tools were probably sharp fragments from smashed pebbles. Later he learned to flake and chip in a more precise way with pointed bones and stones. By half a million years ago he had developed enough skill and feeling to make flint hand axes such as this one from the banks of the Thames, England.

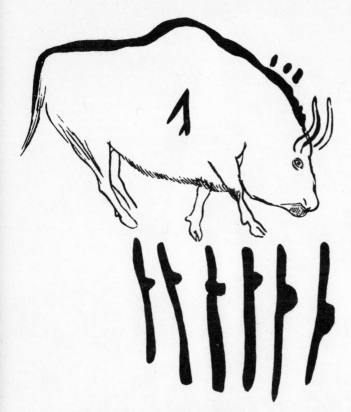

FROM MAX RAPHAEL,
Prehistoric Cave Paintings
(PANTHEON BOOKS, NEW YORK,
1945).
COURTESY OF THE
BOLLINGEN FOUNDATION

Before the end of the Old Stone Age, man had created a wide range of culture in addition to the basic necessities of life. Beginning about 50,000 years ago, he etched and painted the forms of many game animals on cavern walls. This drawing of a hunter-wounded bull from a cave at Pindal, Spain, shows the magical, wish-fulfilling nature of much of this early art. (See Chapter 10)

French caverns indicate that man had discovered the anxiety-calming practice of magic. And shells and teeth with holes drilled in them show us that man was conscious of beauty.

These cultural developments and other hundreds like them were the products of man's creative responses to the world about him, a world of nature but also a world of other men. More specifically we may say that most of man's culture represents a uniquely human response to problems in one or more of the basic areas of human social life. In fact it is likely that group life among men was probably one of the preconditions for the emergence of culture in the first place and was of as much ultimate importance in its development as the biological prerequisite of a large brain. Far from inhibiting creativity, as may be true in many social situations today, the conditions and problems of group living have for hundreds of thousands of years been its spur.

The early thought-directed activities of men were probably quite drab as compared with the elaborate affairs of beavers and termites. At first glance a creature who collects a rock rather than a nut or apple seems rather absurd. But precisely because man can foresee a future need and act through will rather than instinct, he can break away spectacularly from all other animals. In this leap, culture emerges. Now, while it is true that various animals learn a great deal, animal innovations are rare and haphazard. Moreover, we have no evidence that animals other than man ever deliberately teach their young actions or ideas that they themselves have learned or discovered. Their relatively small, simple, instinct-committed brains probably preclude symbolic mentality. Man alone creates and enriches his posterity with the fruit of his creation.

How significant is man's leap to culture believed to be? Probably as significant to what man has and will become as mutations were in transforming a fish into a man in the first place. Just as mutations provide for endless biological variation, culture gives man the capacity for endless behavioral variation. For millions of years mutations have allowed creatures to vary enough to adapt successfully to different and changing environments. The fact that man emerged in precisely this way is testament enough to the ultimate value of physical variation. But with culture, man seems now to have the means to do as he pleases, to cope with his environment even without mutations, to evolve, as La Barre points out, "alloplastically" rather than "autoplastically." Culture is the new nonbiological way to have fur in the Arctic and water-storage in the desert. Man can now inhabit these and other environments with or without adaptive mutations, so long as he produces appropriate culture devices. The use of thermal suiting, bottled oxygen, heat shields, "toothpaste" foods, and the like testify eloquently to man's cultural rather than biological adaptation to the new environment of outer space.

The thesis of the remainder of this book is that, whereas biological variation through mutation was the key to man's development in the past, cultural variation is the key to our future. Before testing this idea in the great problems of man's experience, however, we

71

should examine the basic causes of cultural variation. We understand much about why men are biologically different; now we need to know why they are culturally different. Why do men speak different tongues, eat different things in different ways, dress differently, and have different social organizations, religions, and arts? What is the difference between a primitive tribe and a civilized society, and what is responsible for these differences?

CAUSES OF CULTURAL DIFFERENCES

A search for the causes of cultural differences, whether among nations, regions, races, or individuals, must at the outset recognize the danger of the one-dimensional, deterministic viewpoint. A simple, pat explanation is often attractive, especially so if it bolsters an emotionally held position, but it is hopelessly inadequate. Man in all his marvelous variety is a product of both biological potential and environmental limitation. What is true of his body is also true of his culture. A given level of cultural development is no more due solely to his biology than to his habitat or to his specific social organization. In any human society these factors interact. It is no simple matter to tell you why Joe Arunta wears his nosebone rather than a bow tie, or has thrown his lot with tribal rather than Melbourne society. Generally speaking, however, we may think of four broad groups of interrelated factors which are responsible for cultural variation in human groups: (1) biological and psychological factors, (2) geographical factors, (3) intragroup factors, (4) intergroup factors.

Biological and Psychological Factors / These include a great range of internal possibilities and limitations which influence the creative capacities of a given individual. It can be seen that whatever forces within a person abet or limit his ability to innovate ultimately make for cultural differences among individuals and among groups. While much is known about this dimension of human creativity, much more remains to be learned. Current research has isolated several interesting variables relating to some highly creative Americans. As a group they are reasonably intelligent though not brilliant, not very interested in small details, strong in aesthetic and theoretical values, relatively open in emotional expression, at home in complex situations, wide-ranging in their interests, more interested in possibilities than in facts, and in general intellectually nonconformist. Detailed knowledge of this nature is invaluable in furthering our understanding of cultural innovation within a society; when

BIOLOGICAL. The Negro's black skin, which seems to be an advantage in the tropics, lends itself to decoration better with scars than with tattoos or cosmetics.

GEOGRAPHICAL. He wears little clothing to accommodate to tropic heat and uses local materials to construct his dwellings.

INTRAGROUP. He believes in several gods, each related to forces and experiences he does not understand in a physical sense. He also believes in polygamy, both as a convenience and as a sign of status.

PSYCHOLOGICAL. He may have racially based talents for rhythm that encourage music and the dance.

INTERGROUP. Until very recently he did not develop alphabetized writing, a cornerstone of our civilization. On the other hand, he independently produced some of the world's great wood carving and developed a tonal language which may be transmitted by drumming.

THE SHAPING OF THE ESKIMO

BIOLOGICAL. The Eskimo's thick layer of subcutaneous fat helps make possible an arctic existence. Even so, he wears clothes most of the time and therefore restricts all skin decoration to his face.

INTRAGROUP. Following tradition, he settles most of his arguments by wrestling or by an insult-singing contest. When old he will insist that his children allow him to freeze on the ice rather than jeopardize the precarious welfare of the group.

GEOGRAPHICAL. Although severely limited by his environment, he has learned to exploit every aspect of it, *e.g.*, using frozen snow blocks for housing, old sea ice for salt-free drinking water, and fresh frozen urine to repair cracked sled runners.

PSYCHOLOGICAL. He appears to have mechanical aptitude, and has developed many ingenious devices which aid in his survival.

INTERGROUP. Isolated in the Arctic, he has only recently learned of metals and writing, but has adopted both with ease and confidence. Possessing the world's best reservoir of information on arctic survival, his wisdom is now a part of all U.S. armed forces survival manuals, and his clothing designs are standard issue.

tested in other societies, it will certainly throw much light upon the entire area of cultural differences.

Other biological and psychological factors which probably play a role in levels and directions of creativity are sex and race. We have very little objective information in these areas. Yet even a casual review of cultural history shows clearly that women have occupied themselves for the most part with the creation of children and homes rather than empires, and Negroes, until recently, with the arts rather than the sciences and technology. Whatever the explanation, this is the way it has been. Of course, the equalitarian is not happy with the thought that the sexes and the races are different, whereas the racist sees every difference as a sign of inferiority. From my point of view, it is a fine thing that women lavish their creativity upon children, and I think it is unfortunate that we have convinced the Negro that our science is better than his art. I am convinced that creative expressions are partly, but by no means purely, biological in nature. The social and geographical factors are of far more importance than a person's sex or race in limiting and directing his creative thrust. But insofar as creativity is concerned, sex and race are still scientifically untested areas. To dismiss them as unimportant in understanding cultural differences is as irresponsible as it is unrealistic.

Geographical Factors / Man's physical environment is of such importance in shaping culture that some scholars, such as Ellsworth Huntington, have seen it as the basic determinant of civilization. As a group, anthropologists do not take such an extreme position, although few persons have had a better opportunity both to see and to feel the impact of various environments first hand. Elman Service was alluding to this experience when he dedicated his fine book *A Profile of Primitive Culture* to anthropological field workers, "Who have been defined as 'otherwise intelligent and literate persons who do not accept the germ theory of disease.'" Yet even with their personal familiarity with the forces of nature, most anthropologists see man's geographical setting as a broadly limiting factor rather than a specifically directing one in the cultural development of a group. Thus, for example, while the Eskimos orient their innovations toward existence in the extreme cold, it is impossible to predict what they will do simply on the basis of a knowledge of climate and resources. Men plus cold do not equal the same thing every time. Some men may freeze to death; some may immediately migrate to a warmer land. Others, like the Eskimo, may eat the fat and wear the skins and feathers of available animals, while utilizing rocks and frozen snow for

VARIETIES OF RESTING POSITIONS:
HOW CULTURE MODIFIES PHYSICAL POSSIBILITIES

While all men are endowed with essentially the same physiology, they rest—
sitting, kneeling, leaning, squatting—in many different ways, each in a pattern
specified by his own society.

protective housing. Still others, such as the Ona of Tierra del Fuego, may depend on biological mutations for fat "stovepipe" ankles and high rates of metabolism for basic protection from the cold, and instead of fur clothing may decide on a good fire in the open and animal fat smeared on their naked bodies for further protection.

Many additional illustrations suggest themselves. Consider, for example, the Pueblo Indians of the American Southwest. Look at their surroundings—arid semidesert lands, scanty and unpredictable rain-

77

fall. Look at their lack of rivers and of domesticated animals other than the dog. On the basis of these facts how could you know or even guess that these people are fine agriculturists and in fact have geared their entire way of life to soil and water? And if man's geography determines his way of life, how do we account for the use made of Miami beach or the Pennsylvania hills in the fifteenth century as compared with the twentieth? The climate and resources are virtually the same, but the ways of life have almost nothing in common. In all such cases it is plain that the geographical environment limits but does not direct the line of cultural innovation.

Yet climate and resources do play an important role in cultural variation, and I do not intend to minimize it but to place it in proper perspective. Eskimos have no choice but to orient their entire way of life toward survival in the cold, just as African Bushmen must toward the heat. No Eskimo wastes time on designs for keeping himself cool or attempts at growing palm trees. No Bushman's wife wants a fur coat either for warmth or status, or, if pregnant, develops a sudden nocturnal craving for whale blubber. Geography saw to it that Micronesians could not discover metallurgy since there are no metals in the area. Within any geographical region, however, we usually find substantial cultural variation and in some cases behavior completely the reverse of that expected. Thus, although the Ona live near water abounding in fish, they are not fishermen since they greatly fear the water. Some hunting groups surround game animals with so many totemic restrictions that they either do not hunt them at all or must do so in a rigidly prescribed manner.

Intragroup Factors / Here we see culture influenced by a complex constellation of forces. They include the goals and values of a society, its relative rigidity, the gaps or needs it recognizes, and the presence or absence of writing. Each factor affects the stance that a society takes toward new ideas and new inventions whatever their origin may be.

The overall values of a society seem to be of enormous importance in spelling out for its members the areas of life where creative effort is most acceptable. This is to say that the pressures, rewards, and punishments of a society both direct and shape the creative expressions of the individuals in its midst. For example, consider the comparative rewards for the creative scientist and the creative artist in modern America—the remarkable thing is that we have any artists left at all. Yet in Bali the creative composers of music or the creative dancers are the most honored persons in the land. Society not only delineates the basic areas of acceptable creativity but also the degree to which an individual realizes his creative potential. In this connection it seems that creative Americans function far better in a social environment encouraging individual activity and decision as opposed to group participation and goals. As a matter of fact there is much evidence that in our society at any rate, the group process actually inhibits creativity.

At least part of a society's treatment of its innovators is a function of its internal rigidity. This rigidity may exist for many reasons. A dominant group may perceive all change as a threat to its established position. It may reject cultural innovation from all sources, both from within and without the society. History provides countless examples. The great Oriental resistance toward westernization demonstrates much of this rigidity, as does the classic struggle between science and the Christian church. Resistance to cultural change is often more than a matter of institutional rigidity, however. The habits of an individual usually continue throughout a lifetime, not because change would result in a loss of control or dominance, but because it is far easier to continue to do things the way we learned them first, than it is to acquire a new set of habits. This tendency to continue old behavior patterns because they are easier than new and perhaps even superior patterns is sometimes termed "psychological inertia." In varying degrees it appears to characterize all people everywhere. Who in our society is interested in newly designed eating devices to replace the knife, fork, and spoon? How even less inclined we would be to adopt chopsticks. And who doubts that a Chinese farmer would be as resistant to the adoption of our culinary tools as we are to his?

For a society to welcome innovations, either created by its members or borrowed from other cultures, there must generally be a sense of need somewhere within the group. Someone will have felt some dissatisfaction with old techniques and ideas or will have encountered problems which left him remarking frustratedly, "If there were only some way . . ." These cultural gaps or needs afford the creative person an opportunity to rise to the occasion and may also open the door for the diffusion of ideas or objects from other societies. Indeed, the rapidity with which a group borrows from another may often be less a matter of the excellence of the material borrowed than the felt need of the borrower. Conversely, many fine new ideas are ignored by societies who feel no need to change, more out of apathy than of rejection. We may value our religion as one of our best items for export, but before pressing it too strongly on the rest of the

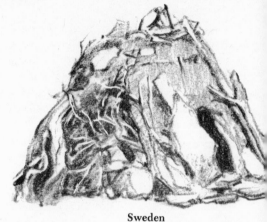

Sweden

VARIETIES OF HOUSING:
DIFFERENT SOLUTIONS TO IDENTICAL GEOGRAPHICAL

DESERTS

Lebanon

TROPICS

Each of these three climates, with its own set of requirements for comfortable housing, can be found in many places the world over. Men have invented a number of quite different solutions to meet the same requirements.

Philippine Islands

Switzerland

Japan

India

Syria

West Africa

Samoa

world we need to reflect on Gandhi's observation that "To the millions who have to go without two meals a day the only acceptable form in which God dare appear is food."

The presence or absence of writing must also be considered to be a major factor in cultural variation among societies. Where writing exists, culture may accumulate for generations. There is no urgent necessity to teach everything orally to the next generation or have it lost forever. With a written record we have far more freedom to question old techniques and ideas, to test and discard, add and modify. After all, if the new procedure does not work out, we can always go back to the old recorded methods. If the new does work, then we have alternative procedures, both of which may be written down and passed along to subsequent generations. When there is only an oral tradition, however, teaching must generally say, "This is the way it is. This is the way we have done it. Learn it well and you will survive. Ignore it or question it at your peril." Cultural alternatives are consequently far fewer in nonliterate societies than in literate ones. Where man's culture is only as rich as his memory, there is little advantage to a new technique if it duplicates the function of an old one. Better to leave the old one alone and use one's inventiveness in less disruptive ways.

Intergroup Factors / These include all conditions which contribute either to the isolation or the interaction of two or more societies. In the development of civilized as opposed to primitive groups these are the most crucial forces. In isolation each group must be totally self-sufficient or perish. It cannot borrow techniques and ideas, or trade its surpluses to supply another's shortages. In the remote island jungles of Melanesia and the deserts of Australia and Africa, no one was able to borrow the rare and precious inventions of alphabetic writing, metallurgy, and agriculture until recently because there were no trade caravans, no merchant fleets, or even conquering armies. Consequently, for the most part, the story of civilization is a story of cultural diffusion, while the story of primitive tribes is one of isolation. Yet it is commonplace to hear these differences naively ascribed to superior and inferior brainpower, superior and inferior races. The remarkable fact is not how far civilization has come through wholesale culture borrowing and literacy, but how ingeniously primitive man has survived virtually on his own.

For thousands of years an isolated location in the world has been a potent force making for cultural difference. Conversely, an accessible location has historically promoted borrowing and therefore cultural similarity. There are, however, many exceptions to these generalizations. Isolation is much more than mere geographic remoteness, and interaction more than the proximity or even the contacts between two societies. Isolation depends not so much upon geography as upon means of communication and transportation. For centuries Athens was relatively remote from the cultural centers of the Near East and could not support herself through her own agriculture and stock breeding. Yet these conditions were overcome because of a fine harbor and extensive trade. Ships removed Athens from her isolation, and cultural diffusion made her great. On the other hand the ancient Hebrews lived in the direct center of a cultural highway that led from Mesopotamia to Egypt and yet were remarkably successful in preserving much of their own tradition. You will recall that, in spite of repeated conquests and even a Babylonian Diaspora, a central core of Hebrew belief and practice remained intact, and indeed has survived to this day.

Thus, while contact between peoples is a necessary first step in cultural borrowing, diffusion is by no means an automatic consequence of such contact. As I have previously suggested, people must have a willingness to respond, a sense of cultural need, perhaps a problem to be solved, or a new pleasure to be enjoyed. With the stage so set, cultural borrowing becomes possible, though certainly not inevitable. Moreover, people may alter what they borrow. They may do this deliberately in order to make the new addition fit more perfectly into an existing cultural framework. A black Christ on an African crucifix is not in the least unusual. On the other hand cultural alteration often results simply from an imperfect understanding of the new material. Word pronunciations and meanings often reflect this possibility. The word "taboo," for example, was our imperfect rendering of a Polynesian word actually sounding more like "tapoo" or "tapu." With the word, we borrowed the generalized idea of the forbidden or disallowed, but we left behind the complementary concept of "mana," which in Polynesia gives tapu its powerful and compelling significance. In terms of lost meaning, it is something like borrowing the concept of Christ without the correlated concept of God. While diffusion may promote cultural similarity, under many circumstances it may result in further cultural variation.

These then are some of the known reasons for the existence of cultural differences among human groups. Human beings everywhere are faced with a number of similar problems—problems dealing with communication, the production and distribution of the necessities of life, social organization, the unknown forces about them, and self-expression. Every society extant has found successful, workable answers to these problems or else it would not now exist. But while the problems of man are similar, his answers vary enormously. This is due to at least four sets of influences that are at work in any society —the biological-psychological, the geographical, the intragroup, and the intergroup factors. There is no simple way to explain a preference for a nosebone instead of for a bow tie, just as there is no easy explanation for physical variation in man. This is why the purely racial or geographical theories fail. They oversimplify man by exaggerating the importance of only one set of factors in his life.

Most anthropologists are thoroughly skeptical about the possibility of ranking the cultural solutions of society A with those of societies B and C. Since an entirely different constellation of factors led to the solutions made by each group, intergroup comparisons are probably both impossible and meaningless. The important, the exciting, the truly spine-tingling fact is that man has spread himself over the face of the earth and has dominated his world through the creative use of his mind. Once you really feel this fact, once you see what this has to mean in terms of man's capacity to prevail, you cannot feel disgust that some of our kind eat rats, others enjoy intercourse during female menstruation, and still others torture themselves to gain a religious experience. Our greatness as animals came from our capacity for physical variation; our greatness as men is and will continue to be due to our capacity for cultural variation.

CHAPTER 6

Symbol Systems

There are certain things that one language
can do supremely well which it would be
almost vain for another to attempt.

EDWARD SAPIR

VARIETIES OF COMMUNICATION

The range and variety of the symbol in contemporary culture
is enormous. It includes speech, gestures, writing, drawing, sculpture,
weights, measures, numbers, indicators of wealth, position, age, sex,
education, occupation, and so on and on. So marvelous is man's
power of association that almost any idea, action, or thing may in
some context come to stand for any other idea, action, or thing. A
fish may symbolize a religion, a simple motion of the hand may be
insulting, and some drawn lines may stand for spoken sounds.

Of all the creatures on earth, man alone has the fourfold capacity
to learn and create symbols, to manipulate them, and to teach them.
He may learn that certain situations and animals are dangerous,
think about these facts at length, and then invent a sound to symbolize distress and the need for assistance. This sound symbol can
then be taught to all the members of the group. While many animals
have cries that they emit in distress situations, for the most part these
are quite automatic and evoke equally automatic responses in others
of their kind. Even so this does not indicate that learning is totally
absent in animals or that they do not communicate. Rather it shows

85

that in species other than man the neural patterns seem to be pretty well laid out, so that both of these activities, learning and communication, operate within relatively tight limits. In this connection let us consider a classic study of gibbons in which anthropologist Clarence R. Carpenter observed nine types of sounds with their probable functions:

VOCAL PATTERN	PROBABLE FUNCTION	GROUP RESPONSES
1. A series of hoots with rising inflection, rising pitch, increasing tempo with climax followed by two or three notes of lower pitch. Duration 12–22 seconds.	Exploration. Defensive actions. Protection of territory.	Same group: same vocalizations, orientation, rapid swings on high-pitched climax. Other groups: same vocalizations, at times withdrawal.
2. Single discrete calls, a series but may be repeated over and over. Similar to beginning note of Type 1 calls.	Localizes group in its territory. Avoids conflicts.	Other groups: similar calls, simultaneously or alternately.
3. A loud, high-pitched note. A shout. Repeated but not in original series.	Alarm, warning defensive when group is surprised by a hunter, observer, or possible enemy	All groups: similar calls with avoidance behavior.
4. Single note with rising inflection. Seems questioning at times.	Employed when a member of a group gets lost. Keeps group together and directs attention.	Same group: assembly, searching.
5. High-pitched, distinctive. Several seconds duration. Given in series of three to twelve.	Not known.	Most groups: similar calls.

6. Deep-throated growl.	Defensive sound when a group is closely pressed by observer or hunter and greatly annoyed.	Same group: aggressive behavior typical of rage response.
. . .	. . .	. . .
7. Little chirp or squeal.	Facilitates play, encourages or stimulates approach.	Play associates and mother: more play, embracing and greeting behavior.
. . .	. . .	. . .
8. Fretting cry.	Begging in a disturbed situation or when confined in captivity.	All animals present.
. . .	. . .	. . .
9. Chatter or series of clucks.	Means of directing group progression.	Same group: following.
. . .	. . .	. . .

In interpreting the significance of the gibbons' "language," you should keep several things in mind. First, of all animals, primates and birds are the most vocal. Undoubtedly this is directly related to tree existence, present or past. When you live in the trees you can make all the noise you please, because nothing can surprise you easily except a few large snakes. And once you've become a rather noisy species, if you are not bird-brained, you may descend to the ground in relative safety and actually use your vocal capacity to help you survive. This seems to be the way our line did it. Among primates making almost as much noise as man are the gibbons and the howler monkeys, but both groups are tree dwellers. A noisy ground creature cannot survive unless he has the brains of a man or the brawn of a lion. Another fact to remember about the versatile vocalization of the gibbon is that, although his brain is small, his ratio of brain to body weight is high: 1:70 (close to man's 1:50). This gives him a fair amount of uncommitted brain tissue. Moreover gibbons appear to be monogamous, and as a result of close family association have opportunities for the intensive interaction and repetitive behavior which underlie successful communication in man. Three facts, in sum, contribute to gibbon vocal proficiency: tree life, a good brain to body weight ratio, and a fairly permanent family situation. Even so, there is no reason to believe that the gibbon can make many sounds beyond those observed, that he can switch his sounds around to confuse his enemies, or that he can deliberately teach his young the significance of these sounds. In short, as Carpenter tells us, "gibbons have capacities for making complex perceptual social responses and certain responses to symbolic cues such as gestures or meaningful facial expressions, but they do not have capacities for employing more complex, generalized, 'higher level' symbols." In addition, he comments that, among gibbons, "gestures and vocal signals must be instrumented; a warning growl will eventually lose its social function as a warning signal unless reinforced occasionally by a cuff or a bite." Apparently man alone can create a complex world of symbols and regard it as being as real as the physical world about him. This great power frees him from the conditioned reflex, but it has its own perils because it allows him to build a word-world without roots in reality. Still, most of us would agree that the ultimate possibilities of culture are easily worth the risks of schizophrenia.

THE ANTIQUITY OF LANGUAGE

Symbolic speech in early man probably developed as a natural consequence of his tree-born vocalizing, his ground-born large brain, his sex- and security-based society, and the pressures of his environment. In all likelihood, he began to create and respond to symbolic sounds and gestures at about the same time that he started working out elementary social relationships and producing his first tools. Anthropologist Harry Hoijer, in *Man, Culture, and Society*, edited by Harry L. Shapiro, cites three groups of evidence that establish the great antiquity of language.

First, cultural continuity depends upon some type of symbol system. An isolated invention means very little unless it can be taught to others. That early man did teach his offspring is clear. "As we study the several chronological phases of culture in any given area of the world," Hoijer points out, "there is revealed a slow but steady advance both in the number of tools made and in the complexity of their manufacture. The men of successive generations did not begin anew each generation to fashion their cultures but built upon the techniques which had been discovered in the past and transmitted to them by their ancestors." This transmission must have been largely effected by the use of symbolic speech and gestures.

Second, there are today several thousand mutually unintelligible languages. That many of these tongues may be shown to be related argues for their antiquity, since linguistic change is a fairly slow process. The common roots of English, Russian, Greek, and Sanskrit lie well back of recorded history. Moreover, at a certain point, linguists are unable to relate some forty to fifty linguistic stocks or families. This suggests that if any of these stocks ever had a common origin, it was so long ago that all traces have disappeared. Of course, the existence of some of these nonrelated language stocks may indicate that several groups of ancient men independently invented symbol systems at about the same time. There is no good reason to believe that all men ever spoke a common tongue.

Third, there are no primitive languages as opposed to highly developed ones. All known languages, ancient or modern, have well-developed systems of sounds, adequate and flexible vocabularies, and well-delineated grammars. As Hoijer points out, "Language has so long been a human possession as to have developed to about the same level among peoples the world over. There remain today no traces of an earlier and cruder stage of linguistic development." You can see that this puts the Indian grunt language right back where it came from—in the great white father's somewhat biased brain.

Language then is probably man's most ancient and valuable symbol system. Through it he has been able to transmit and increase his culture from generation to generation. In this process each language has come to reflect to a remarkable extent the culture, the society, and the conditions of life that have nurtured it. Consequently, while all languages are equally developed, they vary enormously from group to group. These variations occur along three basic dimensions —sound, vocabulary, and grammar—and it is to these that we now turn our attention.

CHARACTERISTICS OF LANGUAGE

Sound / Most human spoken language is produced by a stream of air forced out of the lungs through the larynx, over the tongue, and through the teeth and lips. Each of these phases may affect the final sound, as may the nasal passages, tonsils, and cheeks. In the so-called "click" languages, "stream-of-air" sounds are supplemented by kiss, cluck, and pop sounds from the mouth area. The resulting language is so unusual to European ears that the Boers contemptuously designated those who spoke it "Hottentots" or "stutterers." Today we know that, although there may be stutterers among the Hottentots, the language itself is as developed as our own. Indeed it should be emphasized that from a linguistic point of view there can be no superior or inferior sounds. Any sound that a human being can make

Eskimoan	Chibchan
Na-déné	Arawakan
Algonkian	Cariban
Penutian	Tupi-Guaranian
Hokan-Siouan	Quechumaran
Uto-Aztecan	Gê
Mayan	Araucanian

The existence of so many separate families of languages, together with the several thousand

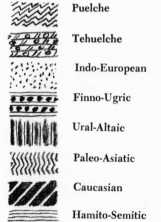	Puelche	
	Tehuelche	
	Indo-European	
	Finno-Ugric	
	Ural-Altaic	
	Paleo-Asiatic	
	Caucasian	
	Hamito-Semitic	

Central Saharan	
Niger-Congo	
Macro-Sudanic	
Click (Khoisan)	
Dravidian	
Sino-Tibetan	
Malayo-Polynesian	
Austro-Asiatic	

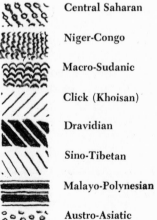

utually unintelligible tongues they encompass, argues for the **antiquity of all languages.**

can be given a meaning and become part of a symbolic speech system. Theoretically this would have to include burps, body slaps, and throat clearings, as well as Hottentot clicks and Oxford vowels. Our symbol system includes hand clapping for applause, tongue and lip vibration for jeering, and whistling to show male approval of female appearance. Man can produce thousands of different and repeatable sounds, any one of which is as legitimate as another for symbolic purposes. However, most languages incorporate remarkably few of the total range of human sound possibilities. In fact few languages utilize more than twenty to forty basic sound units, and these are generally stream-of-air sounds known as phonemes.

While phonemes are the basic sound units of most languages, great variations in these sounds may occur without loss of meaning. For example, if you ask ten American men of the same race, class, and region to read the sentence "Go get the girl with the green gloves, George" and record the sound on an oscillograph or a smoked cylinder, each reading will be measurably different and yet each will be perfectly understood by everyone. If we introduce a few men of other races, classes, and regions, the sound differences will become more noticeable, but the sentence will continue to be understood. Add some women, some young boys, some young girls, and some octogenarians; even more sounds appear, but there is still comprehension. The sentence continues to be understood in spite of the fact that, although the same phoneme "g" is used seven times in the sentence, only in the word "George" do two phonemes have approximately the same sound. The obvious but surprising fact is that a phoneme may be sounded with dozens of variations and still be understood. This is because listening is a dynamic process; we are able mentally to gloss over a great many specific sound variations and still get the general meaning of what is said.

On the other hand, phoneme differences may reveal important information about the speaker, and in some tongues even the meaning of the words he uses. As a rule we can establish a person's sex and age by hearing his voice. Race, subculture, and nationality may also frequently be discerned by sound differences alone. Further, variation in phoneme duration makes it simple to differentiate a Southerner from a New Yorker. Almost any Memphis belle can easily turn an efficient "Yes, Bill" into a thoroughly wasteful but attractive "Yea-us, Be-yul" with her phoneme drag. In Chinese an increase in volume usually indicates anger, whereas in English it may connote the exhilaration of "Oh boy!" the anger of "The devil you will!" or simply an attempt to monopolize the conversation in a committee

HOW LANGUAGE VARIES

It is largely through phoneme differences that we distinguish the native from the outsider.

> Ni-yo ah can heah you, Jaw-wige.

> Now aie heer you tew, Georgette.

VOCABULARY

The content and richness of a vocabulary depend on the importance of things or activities to a society. The Chuckchee, for example, have twenty-six words for reindeer, three of which are shown in the drawing.

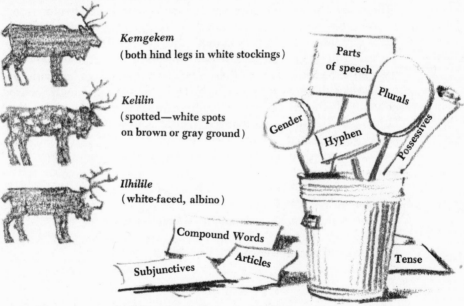

Kemgekem
(both hind legs in white stockings)

Kelilin
(spotted—white spots on brown or gray ground)

Ilhilile
(white-faced, albino)

GRAMMAR

The meaning of a language resides in its agreed-upon combination of symbols, not in universal rules of structure. Some tongues do without such elements of grammar as gender, tense, plurals, parts of speech.

meeting. In many languages of the world, such as Chinese or Burmese or Yoruba, differences in pitch actually are meaningful in themselves. This is to say that a word may contain identical phonemes, but its meaning will depend upon the pitch with which the word is sounded. Thus, in the Chinese Mandarin dialect, *ma* has four different meanings, each a function of pitch variation.

> *ma* (high pitch) = mother
> *ma* (rising pitch) = hemp
> *ma* (low-rising) = horse
> *ma* (low-falling) = scold

I may as well confess that one of my ethnographic ambitions is some day to hear someone in Peiping say something like "Tie that horse with hemp or mother will scold."

Once we accept the fact that phonemic variation is quite natural among languages, and that there is no objective way to rate or rank a tongue, there are exceptionally absorbing things to be learned about man's symbolic use of sounds. Unfortunately, few people ever discover this. In effect, all of us are told from the cradle to the grave, "These are the sounds that we fashion words from in our group. Learn these sounds. Repeat them often. No, that's baby talk! No, that's a nonsense sound! No, that's vulgar! No, that's the way the X class or the Y race or the Z region would say it!" Little wonder that we tend to be intolerant of others who use our language but with pronunciations different from our own. Thus we may be smugly amused or annoyed when the Chinese laundry man says "It's belly cold today." Or we may be convinced that the British "accent" is strictly an affectation. Certainly if we are from Brooklyn we think a Southerner ridiculous when he drops his "er's" and "ir's" and substitutes "ah's" and "uh's."

BOY TO GIRL. "Come ovah heah, sugah."

GIRL TO BOY. "Yes, suh."

But the man from Dixie is equally offended when he hears Brooklynese which changes "ir," "ur," "or," and "ear" into "oi," "the" or "th" into "da" and perhaps even a "them" into a "dem."

> Out at thoid?
> Dat's absoid!
> Dem bums never loined to play!
> Out at foist?
> Dat's da woist!
> Da umpire went blind t'day!

94

Thus reared in our provincial linguistic settings we quite naturally find German too guttural, French too nasal, Spanish too staccato, Chinese too sing-song, and African and American Indian tongues full of grunts and sounds that we cannot duplicate. Our language has its preferred sounds; unless we are encouraged to try other languages with their sounds, particularly in childhood, these languages will probably always sound rather strange to us. The unfortunate thing about this is that unfamiliar sounds, like unfamiliar sights, tend to throw most of us on the defensive. We are threatened by words we do not understand, perhaps offended by sounds acceptable in an exotic tongue, but vulgar or ridiculous in our own. For the most part, the societies of the world do not prepare their peoples for the linguistic realities of the world. And should you think that the answer is a universal language—English of course—you might reflect on the fact that our language has been widely described as the "hissing" tongue.

Vocabulary / A second characteristic of every language is its vocabulary or the total stock of words that it contains. Words encompass and represent the meaningful experiences of a society, since they generally stand for or symbolize some object, action, or idea of importance to the people involved. Just as there are no superior or inferior sound units among languages, there are no superior or inferior meaning units. The French or Japanese or Hottentot words for "wife" or "music" or "rain" are as useful and meaningful as our words. Further, comparative linguistic research has clearly demonstrated that no language has a "primitive" or inadequate vocabulary. No human groups have crude languages with only a few hundred words, no human groups must use elaborate gestures because they lack adequate speech symbols, and no human groups lack vocabularies flexible enough to express shades of meaning or theoretical concepts. The truth is that all vocabularies allow their speakers to express themselves adequately, to communicate effectively with one another, and to handle any new ideas and experiences that may occur.

There are of course marked differences in the size and complexity of word systems. The tendency is to interpret these differences as signs of language inferiority or superiority, but there is overwhelming evidence that this is not true. Actually, the more important a particular thing or activity is to a given group, the more words the group will have to describe and delineate it. In Eskimo society, for example, where culture is existence-oriented, there is no elaborate technical vocabulary. On the other hand, in matters concerning snow, which is extremely important to them, we find an extensive vocabulary. Snow is of slight importance to us, so we have one basic word for it and a number of qualifying adjectives. To the Eskimo, however, the form of snow is often of crucial significance to life itself, so the Eskimos have a word for wind-driven snow, another for snow on the ground, and still another for snow packed hard like ice. There are other words for slushy snow, soft-falling snow, drifting snow, and the like. Among the Chuckchee, who are Siberian Eskimos, we find a similarly elaborate vocabulary describing reindeer, on which their way of life depends. In addition to many words which convey the size, sex, and antler development of reindeer, there are twenty-six different words whose only use is to describe the colors of reindeer skin. Separate words indicate "whitish, with brown stripe along the back," "one hind-leg in white stocking, body gray or brown," "underleg grayish, light-gray spots under the legs and on the groins, body brown," and so on. Many other examples demonstrate how closely vocabulary expansion follows cultural interest. In fact, once we know the vocabulary of a people, we may often surmise the major emphases of their way of life with little difficulty. Knowledge that the Aymara Indians of Bolivia and Peru have more than two hundred words for potatoes is as deeply revealing as the fact that Arabs of North Africa have a thousand words for sword, and that the Maori of New Zealand have nine words for the shape of the clitoris and twelve for the penis. In each case an area of dominant cultural interest determines the extent and richness of the vocabulary. You may have already reflected on our own heavy linguistic involvement with science and government, and if you own a television set, you will also sense our national concern for sex, sadism, painkilling, keeping clean, smoking, and drinking.

Vocabularies are dynamic. They grow and shrink and change. A vocabulary, like all culture, is constantly modified through the processes of innovation and diffusion. Because of this flexible quality, any language can adjust rapidly to the new things and experiences that may confront a given society. Where innovation is involved, it is possible though not very frequent that entirely new words may be coined by combining phonemes in a novel way. A newly discovered microbe could simply be called a "mog" or a "rog" since we have not yet given these phonemic possibilities meaning. Drug companies have their lawyers copyright dozens of important sounding nonsense combinations in order to have adequate names available for yet-to-be-invented preparations. More common is the practice of giving an existing word a new meaning in place of or in addition to the old one. By now most of us know that the word "cat" may mean a jazz addict or a prostitute as well as a feline pet. Not as well known, however, are some of the more recent colorful additions to American teen-age "jive-talk."

ANCHORED. Pinned or engaged

BRAIN CHECK; *sometimes* SWEAT SLIP. Report card

BOP. Go (Let's bop to my pad.)

ESCAPE PIT. The movies

FANGSVILLE. A hen party

FACTORY. School

FEATHERS. Beard

GAS UP. Eat

HAM AND EGGS. A couple going steady

HAWKS. Overly aggressive females

IG. Ignore (The opposite of "she digs me" is "she igs me.")

JUDGE. Anyone over twenty

JUICE SHOOTER; *also* CARBURETOR. Soda jerk

NAILS. Cigarettes

ONE-EYE. Motorcycle

OARS. Ears

RAINMAKER. Someone who tells everyone his troubles

THE SNAKE. The subway

THREADS; *sometimes* SKINS. Clothes

UMBRELLA. An alibi

VAULT. Wallet

Of course, few if any of these terms will endure, but they illustrate a basic type of linguistic innovation quite well. To appreciate the tremendous use standard English makes of this technique, you might look up in a good dictionary the definitions of a few words, such as "horn," "pitch," "court," and "pan."

Vocabulary innovation occurs in a third way through combining existing words to produce a new composite word or phrase. For example, the Dakota Indians named the horse a "big dog," and the Shoshone Indians called it a kind of deer. When introduced to cattle, the Crow Indians called them a type of buffalo and then redesignated buffalo as "genuine buffalo." The Crows aptly named the gun an "iron bow" and scissors "two knives." On the other hand, native Australians saw scissors as "two teeth." The fact that some of these word coinages are amusing may tend to obscure the fact that each represents a language innovation in response to a new object in the environment. Each is based upon structural or functional similarities between familiar objects and the new object. Still, to call a horse a big dog seems slightly absurd to us, and we may feel that "primitive" languages are incapable of the fine distinctions that we make in English. Yet many new English words are amusing, but descriptive. We call a tall building a "skyscraper" and protective metal bars either "bumpers" or "cowcatchers." And though the expert knows better, the layman generally sees a gibbon as a "big monkey." In short, peoples the world over use words with which they are familiar to describe the new and the unfamiliar. Furthermore, every language has many words and expressions which make little or no sense if they are taken literally. Consider "Indians" meaning native Americans, "hot dogs" meaning links of beef, and "baby" meaning a grown woman. What is significant is that all languages are flexible enough to adjust to new things and experiences either through innovation, as we have seen, or through the process of diffusion.

In vocabulary diffusion, one language simply borrows a word and its meaning, or an approximation of them, from another language. The extent to which languages expand their vocabularies in this manner is truly phenomenal. The terms "O.K." and "Yank" were virtually internationalized during World War II, as were various American swear words. A good five years after the end of the war, prostitutes in Casablanca's Bousbir were smilingly coaxing American visitors with such invitations as "O.K., how about it, you chicken ───── Yankee S.O.B.?" Our own language is rich with borrowed words. To mention only a handful, "plaza," "sarong," "potato," "pizza," "roulette," "patio," "tobacco," "liqueur," "tattoo," and "tomato." It should be added that in many cases the spelling and pronunciation of a word are considerably altered in the borrowing process. This can be illustrated in the fact that our word "coffee" is an alteration of the Arabic "qahweh," which in turn is derived from the Ethiopian province of "Kaffa." Loss of meaning occurs most frequently with more abstract and theoretical words, as was the case when we borrowed the Polynesian word "taboo."

Grammar / Structure or grammar is a third characteristic of all language systems. As with sound and vocabulary, grammatically superior or inferior languages do not exist. Further, there are no universal grammatical principles. Any rule of grammar in a given language will be ignored or reversed by some other language. Take gender for instance. All of us know that gender is unnecessary in a language. This is to say that all speakers of English know it. When we learn a tongue with gender, we find it tedious, since there is obviously nothing logical about the genders. The moment you decide that the French may be romantically correct in making the moon and the sea feminine, you learn that they have done the same for the Four Horsemen of the Apocalypse—war, famine, pestilence, and death. And you may find yourself muttering that Frenchmen especially should know that not all dogs and cats are male!

That grammar is arbitrary and often quite unreasonable is further shown if we look at the formation of plurals in our own language. To express the concept of multiplicity, English generally appends an "s" to the noun involved. In Hottentot one designates femininity in exactly the same way. There is certainly nothing wrong with either system, although both are arbitrary. English, however, is wildly inconsistent with plurals, as foreigners will tell you. The poor fellows cannot get it through their heads that even though the plural of "goose" is "geese," the plural of "moose" is not "meese." In fact, they think it should be "gooses" in the first place. When they finally learn the correct plural for "mouse," "die," and "man," it is outrageous what they do with "house," "lie," and "pan." Even some Americans have difficulty deciding whether "My feet hurts," "My feets hurt," or "My feet hurt." A few brave voices have occasionally suggested that we should drop all plural forms as the Chinese have done. Their point is the same one we make about genders—they are unnecessary. "I wish to check out five book." "Twenty man are on our track team." "Their house are full of mouse." These statements seem odd, but they communicate clearly without the use of plurals.

As a matter of fact, languages now exist without tenses, without parts of speech as we know them, and with almost every conceivable type of sentence structure. Yet in spite of the arbitrariness of all grammars, people in every society put words together into meaningful combinations which they prescribe as grammatically correct. To an extent this is necessary so that communication within the group may proceed in an orderly and fluid fashion. Even so, it is common knowledge that some of the "rules" are broken every day in a given society, and people still manage to communicate. To be accepted into certain subcultures within a society you must often break a number of grammatical rules. Your disclosure that "He come over and eat with me yesterday" may get you thrown out of the "Great Thoughts League," but it might well be your passport to acceptance down at the shop.

ONE TONGUE OR MANY?

These considerations of sounds, vocabularies, and grammars show clearly that, in spite of language differences, there are no superior and inferior symbol systems. Each language is effective for the society that uses it and must be considered adequate for its needs. But language differences, like other human variations, cause much misunderstanding and ill will. For this reason it is often said that if all the world spoke the same tongue what a happy place this would be. Toward this end, a succession of international languages—Volapük, Esperanto, Ido, Interlingua, Occidental, Novial, Nov-Esperanto, and Basic English—have been offered and for the most part rejected. Detractors point out that some of the most bitter wars in history have been fought by those who spoke the same tongue, wars like the American Revolution and the American and Spanish civil wars. Advocates correctly tell us that a man in danger cannot even shout for help and be certain of being understood on a trip across Europe unless he knows half a dozen tongues. "Help!" may produce results in England and America but the best sounds to make in other countries are:

> *Voethia!* (in Greece)
> *No pomoshtch!* (in Russia)
> *Imdat!* (in Turkey)
> *Socorro!* (in Portugal)
> *Aiuto!* (in Italy)

If new words are not your dish and you like to travel, you should arrange to get in trouble only in Germany (*Hilfe!*), Sweden (*Hjalp!*), Denmark (*Hjaelp!*), or best of all the Netherlands (*Help!*). While some sort of basic universal vocabulary would probably solve a number of problems by facilitating travel and aiding simple communication, it certainly would not prevent war or reduce ethnic or racial hostility. In fact there have come to be strong arguments for the preservation of different tongues throughout the world even if a common language should one day succeed. We shall look closely at some of these arguments and at the evidence that supports them.

LANGUAGE AND REALITY

We have described language as a part of the total culture of a particular group as well as the means through which most of the group's culture is handed down from one generation to another. Language, then, is both culture and the vehicle of culture. Since this is true, language is more than just a way to communicate within a group. It is a symbolic reflection of the basic values and points of view of a particular society. We have discussed, above, the intimate

HOW LANGUAGE AFFECTS OUR VIEW OF THE WORLD: NAVAHO VERSUS ENGLISH

The language of any people dissects the real world in a particular way, and those who speak it never doubt that this is the way things really are. Yet even simple descriptions of objects reveal how differently reality is perceived. In this drawing the English word "rough" is seen to cover all four depicted rough-surfaced objects—a road, a file, a rock, and a pimply face. In Navaho, on the other hand, much finer distinctions are made; three different words describe the four types of roughness. Only the pimply face and the nodule-covered rock are seen as similar enough to merit the same designation. Thus while Navaho and English both see roughness, each classifies what it sees in entirely different ways. Each dissects the world along different lines.

connection between a way of life and a vocabulary. Even when standing on the outside of a society looking in, we can know much about the group if we know its language. There is another side to this coin. Consider for a moment the children who are born on the inside of a particular social system. Far from having the world of nature and man spread out before them in the raw, so to speak, for their direct experience and interpretation, children learn to see the world around them through the language of their elders. This thing is pointed to, this event is commented upon, this idea expressed, and these things, events, and ideas are related. Other things, actions, and relationships are minimized or ignored. Thus the language of any society acts as a filter or a screen through which a child learns to perceive the reality around him. Since the words in any language represent attempts to capture things and experiences by symbols, they will be subject to all the errors and distortions, as well as the insights, of human perception, logic, and emotion. This means that a person reared in a specific language system will view the world in terms of the denotations and connotations of his particular tongue and no other. By virtue of his culture, he will inevitably be blind to or dismiss as unimportant many specific aspects of his environment that are as real as those he is taught to accept.

To illustrate this, let us consider several well-known cases from outside our Indo-European linguistic tradition. We can begin with a question. Do things change? Of course they do—in English, Russian, Greek, Hindustani, and almost any other language you care to suggest. Not so, says the Trobriand Islander. Things are, they exist, they have being, that is all. To Americans, a plant grows day by day, finally reaching maturity and ultimately dying. To us it is a process, a sequence in time, change. The Trobriander, on the other hand, accepts his world as he sees it. Today it is one thing, tomorrow it may be different; it has concrete being only at the instant of its perception. To this fact the Trobriander responds. Because he structures the world in this manner, anthropologist Dorothy Lee tells us, he has no terms such as "because," "so as to," "so that," and "why." The Trobriander point of view is much more complicated, but this should be enough to illustrate the remarkable way in which a language may structure the world for those who speak it. From our linguistic perch the Trobriander is all wrong. That things change and may be caused to change seems an almost automatic observation that even a child can make. But more objectively the Trobriander is probably at least half correct in his position. Perceptually speaking we are less sophisticated than he when we see our geranium as "the same plant only changed" from week to week. To him any visibly perceived difference in this "same" plant indicates something new. From any scientific, descriptively accurate point of view, he is correct. As a matter of fact, we are occasionally closer to Trobriander than we know: we do not seek to describe grandpa as "a baby with various changes"; we have specific words "infant," "child," "adolescent," and "adult." After all, an adult is not just a grown-up baby, but something qualitatively different. English, on the other hand, is probably more accurate in its perception that certain things may act upon others and "cause" their alteration. However, Lee advises us not to infer "that the Trobrianders are incapable of explaining a sequence of cause and effect, but rather that this relationship is of no significance" to them.

Let us take the concept of time. This is something all Americans are hyperconscious of. *"Tempus fugit,"* "My, how the time goes," and "Time and tide wait for no man," are expressions that reveal this concern. The past, the present, and the future are as real to us as the trees, the water, and the sky. We think of time as a flow or sequence of events that man observes and in which he participates. We want to know when an event occurred; some of the first questions we ask concern the year something happened or the year it is expected to happen. We want to know whether a television program is "canned" (a past event) or "live" (a present event). To the Hopi Indians, on the other hand, this concern over the sequence of events is meaningless. The important things to establish, from their point of view, are: (1) Can the event be established as an actuality by perception or recall? (2) Is the event only anticipated, not yet going on or completed? (3) Does the event occur with regularity? Instead of verb forms for the past, present, and future, the Hopi language has verb forms for statement of fact, expectation, and regularity. A language which blurs the past and present in this manner obviously was produced by a society with cultural values which ignore an area of reality that is of great importance to us. This blind spot in the Hopi, however, is matched by our own linguistically unrealistic method of expressing characteristic behavior. To describe regularity we use the present tense and state that "He plays golf," even though his present observed activity may be beer drinking. In Hopi this dimension of reality is neatly handled with a separate verb form.

Other examples that illustrate how languages dissect nature in different and fragmentary ways are not difficult to find. Anthropological linguist Benjamin Whorf has pointed out that, in Hopi, occurrences like "lightning," "meteor," "puff of smoke," and "pulsation" are verbs, because they are events of short duration. English is more arbitrary here, classifying all of the above events as nouns. The Nootka Indians of Vancouver Island, on the other hand, do not perceive the world as a dichotomy of things and actions, of nouns and verbs. Instead, Whorf tells us that they have "a monistic view of nature that gives us only one class of word for all kinds of events. 'A house occurs' or 'it houses' is the way of saying 'house,' exactly like 'a flame occurs' or 'it burns.' " You may wonder how such a language would handle several different actions performed by the same subject. It is not difficult at all. The Nootka have a large variety of prefixes and suffixes to inform them whether "it dogs," "it running dogs," or "it black and white dogs" and so on. If you will think about this a moment, you will see there is an internal consistency and beauty to this conception of the world. It is in effect a gestalt or holistic point of view that expresses with words about what Einstein did with a formula, that is, mass and energy (noun and verb) are actually two sides of the same coin.

In *Mirror for Man*, Clyde Kluckhohn provides us with an excellent summary of the relation between language and reality:

Every language is also a special way of looking at the world and interpreting experience. Concealed in the structure of each different language are a whole set of unconscious assumptions about the world and life in it. The anthropological linguist has come to realize that the general ideas one has about what happens in the world outside oneself are not altogether "given" by external events. Rather, up to a point, one sees and hears what the grammatical system of one's language has made one sensitive to, has trained one to look for in experience. This bias is the more insidious because everyone is so unconscious of his native language as a system. To one brought up to speak a certain language it is part of the very nature of things, remaining always in the class of background phenomena. It is as natural that experience should be organized and interpreted in these language-defined classes as it is that the seasons change. In fact the naive view is that anyone who thinks in any other way is unnatural or stupid, or even vicious—and most certainly illogical.

. . . From the anthropological point of view there are as many different worlds upon the earth as there are languages. Each language is an instrument which guides people in observing, in reacting, in expressing themselves in a special way. The pie of experience can be sliced in many different ways, and language is the principal directive force in the background.

We should not consider diversity of language as something to regret or to rectify, but as one of the most valuable aspects of man's culture. Each language represents a human attempt to deal symbolically with experience. Each language gives us a unique view of the world; each expresses reality in a different way. Sometimes the differences are superficial, sometimes fundamental. It is by now obvious that no one symbolic view can apprehend or describe the nature of all external things and events and their interrelationships. It is equally obvious that languages vary greatly in how they deal with the richness and depth of human emotion and thought. Consequently, the more languages we study, the more interpretations of reality we have, the more varied our linguistic screens are—the more we will ultimately learn, and the fewer blind spots there will be in our ambitious quest to understand ourselves and our universe. It is here that we find the inestimable value of linguistic variation in man.

CHAPTER 7

Man at Work

There is probably no culture extant today
which owes more than ten percent
of its total elements to inventions
made by members of its own society.

RALPH LINTON

EARLY TECHNOLOGY

All creatures, except for some captive or domesticated animals
and a handful of men, "work" for a living. In their native habitat
gibbons often spend about eight hours a day finding food and eating
it, eight hours commuting to and from feeding areas, and eight hours
sleeping. Like gibbons, most herbivores occupy themselves almost
completely during the daylight hours with getting food. Carnivores
generally work shorter hours than the herbivores, but their efforts are
far more strenuous and frequently go unrewarded. Only pets, race
horses, zoo occupants, and estate beneficiaries are able to secure a
steady supply of food without laboring for it. The rest of the animal
world toils mightily for its sustenance.

Over the centuries man has improved his food-getting techniques
to such an extent that he now works to obtain other things as well. He,
in total contrast to all other animals, works for clothes, shelter, transportation, jewelry, and life insurance, as well as for less tangible
things like self-esteem and social status. Underneath this expanding
structure of wants, however, lies his basic animal need for adequate

food. Take away man's food long enough and the rest of his elaborate material goals collapse in a heap.

Our line's urgent concern for food after it left the trees was one of the factors crucial in producing a noninstinctive social life and the first culture. Of central importance in this successful struggle for food was the development of a digestive system that could handle meat as well as most other organic materials. Being omnivorous is a far greater asset than one might immediately suppose. In addition to broadening the supply of food, meat offers energy in a concentrated form. As a result, man could spend much less time eating. A cat whose time is thus released sleeps and plays a good deal. Man, not having fangs and claws to fall back on, wisely began to exchange the work of almost continuous feeding for the work of thinking and creating. It was an epochal change, for, as we have seen, culture was the result.

At first, man probably scavenged much of his meat, entering the scene after carnivores had made the kill and sated themselves. Perhaps at about the same time he was using his bare hands to choke or pull apart small game. Later he probably threw rocks and picked up sticks and bones for clubs. Thus, man may well have developed his taste for meat while he was a tool-user but before he was a tool-maker. Kenneth Oakley comments on this possibility in *Social Life of Early Man*, edited by Sherwood Washburn:

By the time that the Hominidae had evolved into tool-makers, they were evidently largely carnivores—quantities of meat bones were associated with the remains of *Pithecanthropus pekinensis*. It is easy to see how the one habit led to the other. Although the killing of game may have been accomplished easily enough in some such way as that suggested above, the early hominids must often have encountered difficulty in removing skin and fur and in dividing the flesh. In the absence of strong canine teeth, the solution would have been overcome most readily by using sharp pieces of stone. Here, surely, was the origin of the tradition of tool-making. Where no naturally sharp pieces of stone lay readily to hand, some of the more intelligent individuals saw that pebbles, which broke on the ground when thrown, provided the solution. By breaking pebbles, fresh sharp edges were produced. Once the tradition of tool-making had begun, the manifold uses of chipped stones became obvious. They were useful for sharpening sticks for digging out burrowing mammals; for making spears sharp enough to be effective weapons in hunting larger game; for scraping meat from bones, splitting them to get at the marrow; and for chopping the meat into convenient mouthfuls. All the main uses of stone tools were, I suggest, connected in the first place with adoption of semicarnivorous habits.

An additional consequence of man's increasing ability to make tools and weapons was his discovery of fire. There is evidence that man used fire for warmth, protection, and possibly for cooking in early Paleolithic times, but there is none that he could actually produce fire. His earliest fires were probably collected. That is, they were produced by natural causes such as lightning, volcanoes, and spontaneous combustion, and then taken as embers and brands to man's camps and caves. Such fires would have to be tended carefully, since no one knew how to rebuild them. Oakley believes that it was not until man had learned something about the manufacture and use of tools that he discovered how to make fire. He points out that an early man working in dim light would obviously have noticed sparks that occurred when he struck certain stones together. And while the sparks from flint striking flint would not be hot enough under normal conditions to produce a fire, sparks made by an iron pyrites hammerstone striking a flint node could easily do so. The fact that abraded nodules of pyrites have been found at late Paleolithic sites lends support to this position. Fire by friction rather than by percussion seems to have been an even later invention, not occurring until man discovered how much heat was produced in grinding, sawing, and boring various materials.

The control and production of fire were critical steps in man's technological progress. In addition to shielding him from the cold and protecting him against nocturnal carnivore prowlers, fire also served as a hunting weapon. Man could use burning sticks to drive animals over cliffs and into pits. Moreover, Carleton Coon notes that man can masticate cooked food in a fraction of the time required for raw, and so gain further time for more creative activities.

Three crucial Paleolithic cultural "breakthroughs"—symbolic speech, tool and weapon making, and fire control and production— allowed man to increase in numbers and to spread all over the world. With these creations he was able to challenge any animal and any environment. In doing so, he discovered that because conditions of life changed constantly, his survival was often directly related to his ability to adjust. What was a cultural asset in the moist tropics might actually be a liability if one were suddenly confronted with a desert situation. A hunting society in an area where game was scarce could save itself through cultural flexibility alone. With man situated in so many locations and conditions about the world it was both necessary and inevitable that his work and its fruit should vary prodigiously. He learned to like many foods, to create many types of clothing and

Weapons

Symbolic Speech

Fire

shelter, to enjoy varied luxuries, and to establish and accept different rules for the production, distribution, and accumulation of goods. Some preferences were determined by the environment. Others show clearly man's supple mind and imagination in action. Many early societies perished because they could not adapt rapidly or well enough to variation in environment. Nevertheless, mankind had the key to ultimate survival as our present-day cultural diversity proves. For wherever cultural differences exist, we see the evidence that man at work has successfully met his particular circumstances head on with his creative faculties.

In spite of the great diversity in economic arrangements among the peoples of the world, there are certain characteristics shared by work systems everywhere. All societies divide up the work among their members in some way; no one set of individuals does everything. Every society has certain products that it works for—things it considers to be either the necessities or the luxuries of life. Each society has a system for distributing these products among its members as well as for trading with outsiders. And, finally, each has a system and symbols of ownership.

THE DIVISION OF LABOR

Human beings living in societies have no choice but to divide the necessary work up along two basic lines—age and sex. Obviously babies cannot work at all, children can only do the lighter and easier tasks, and old people cannot perform heavy manual labor. The bulk of the productive physical work therefore falls on the shoulders of young and middle-aged adults. However, many societies exploit fully the energy of their children and the knowledge and dexterity of their old people. Sex also determines some of the work people do. In general, women are not as large and as strong as men. With rare exceptions, then, men do the necessary hunting and fighting and make tools and weapons for these activities. When pregnant, women become incapable of work requiring agility; later they are biologically equipped to feed infants, and infants must have much care and protection in the early months of life. These facts route women toward cooking, gathering edibles, and making clothing and household objects. The sexual division of labor, however, is not without variations. Among the Hopi Indians, for example, men spin the cotton, weave the cloth, and make the clothes for the family; they leave all but the heaviest of the

Societies differ in their notions of appropriate and stylish ways to protect, adorn, and display the body. This faience statuette from Knossos is of a priestess of the Cretan fertility religion. Modestly clad by the standards of the period, she holds aloft two snakes.

house-building work to the women. In areas where food is plentiful, such as Polynesia, men often do the cooking.

The work of a society may also be apportioned in terms of the knowledge and skill of particular individuals. As a rule, however, there are few specialists in a society that exists at a subsistence level, that is, with no product surplus over and above the needs of its members. A man may become highly skilled in a particular area only if he may exchange his products, whatever they may be, for necessities of life produced by others. Unless his society has a fairly high level of technology there will be no surplus available for such an exchange. This is why the discovery of the basic facts of horticulture and animal husbandry are such critical turning points in man's cultural history. Not only did this knowledge assure him of a stable source of food, it also meant that in many fertile areas he could produce a surplus and so afford the luxury of the work specialist. The eminent British historian Gordon Childe considers these discoveries of equal importance to any ever made by man and describes their appearance as heralding the "Neolithic Revolution." A revolution it was. Just as hunting had liberated man from the blind alley of continuous feeding, agriculture and stock breeding freed him from the hazardous maze of hunting. No longer did his fortunes depend upon the success or failure of the hunt. No longer was every able-bodied male forced to become a hunter or starve. Now a few men could feed many, and the many could learn to do other things. In time there could be specialists in any area that the creative mind of man chose to probe. Civilization became both possible and inevitable.

NECESSITIES OF LIFE

By the time of the Neolithic revolution, which began in the Near East, man had already settled extensively in Europe, Africa, Asia, both North and South America, and in many of the Pacific islands. People in some of these areas appear to have domesticated plants and animals independently. Other people, living in reasonably accessible locations, eventually borrowed this idea from traders and soldiers. Still others lived in areas too isolated to receive the good news and too barren to allow them to do anything about it if they had. It can be seen how great cultural differences between these societies—some still geared to hunting and gathering, some to herding, and some to planting—began to open up at this point. Many of these differences lay in the specific things that men valued and worked for, and a number of them have persisted into the present time. Because of their importance, we will consider the two basic product areas of food and clothing.

Food and Drink Variations / All men everywhere work for food, but as everyone knows there is fantastic variation in opinion as to what constitutes a good meal. Take a staple like flour or meal. We prefer wheat, rye, and corn, and we know that the Orient is largely committed to rice. But these are the preferences of food-growing economies. In societies still oriented toward food-gathering we find surprising variety. In West Africa dried bananas are pounded into meal as are breadfruits. Indians of Northern Mexico do the same with mesquite beans. A South Pacific favorite is a root called taro, while Indians of our Northwest coast make a fine meal from acorns. The Indians of the Amazon area have produced one of the most amazing staples. It is called cassava which, prior to an elaborate processing sequence, is a deadly poison. Thus far it is anybody's guess how they learned to turn a poison into a staple without exterminating themselves in the experimental phase.

While we may never answer the question "Which came first, bread or beer?" we do know that man now utilizes fully as many substances for alcoholic beverages as for flour. Our favorite hard liquors come from wheat, rye, and corn, our wines from grapes, and our beers from rice and barley. Familiar variations include potato whisky, or vodka; rice wine, or saki; and apple brandy, or Calvados. Not so well known is African palm tree sap wine; Central Asian kumiss, or fermented mare's milk; and the honey wine, or mead, of the Bolivian Indians and the ancient Greeks. Perhaps most extraordinary is the Chuckchee beer made from acorns and reindeer urine. This sampling should suffice to illustrate man's imaginative use of the flora and fauna native to his area. In view of the ingenuity with which man has concocted some of them, it is plain how determined he is to have his bread and wine.

Anthropologists enjoy stringing together lists of food from around the world to show how provincial and unquestioning our own dietary preferences are. Here is one such world-wide menu, compiled by Lister Sinclair for the record album *Ways of Mankind:*

SOUP. From China, made from the nest of a small bird that mixes little bits
    of fish with its saliva and lets it harden into a basin. Bird's nest soup.
ENTREE. From the Eskimos, seal blubber, the skin of the white whale (as
    full of vitamin C as orange juice), and the vegetable contents of diving
    birds' stomachs.

MAIN COURSE. Take a medium-sized sea creature, closely related to the spiders, boil it alive, and serve its muscles with the fermented milk of the cow. Lobster thermidor.

VEGETABLES. From North America, fiddleheads—the tips of growing ferns. And also the lumps on the roots of a plant of the deadly nightshade family that comes from the high Andes—potatoes.

SAVORY. Coagulated blood mixed with lumps of fat—the black pudding of northern England. Or fried witchetty grubs from the Australian desert.

DESSERT. A cake made from ground-up grass seeds (wheat flour) plus the secretion from the insides of small flying insects (honey).

FRUIT. Bananas, the staple food of much of Africa. The thickened and swollen stem of a relative of Spanish moss—the pineapple. And the dried flower cluster of a desert tree—the fig.

NUTS. All sizes, from poppy seed to the coconut.

BEVERAGE. Something fermented—grapes or tree sap. Something distilled —barley or potatoes. Something stewed out of a plant—tea or coffee.

While there are good reasons for the existence of all these foods, we are still shocked by the things that other people eat and mentally tend to downgrade them accordingly. None of these foods is inherently superior or inferior as a dietary object except in terms of nutrition. But no American waits for a vitamin-calorie-protein assay before rejecting grubs and worms, any more than he reflects on the origin of his honey. These are preferences that our society has made for us and taught us so thoroughly that we are actually emotionally committed to many of them. Cultural learning alone makes us reject juicy grubs in favor of insect juices, or relish shrimps rather than grasshoppers, to which they are related.

Man's food preferences are not all explained by what is naturally available in his geographic area. Many food choices have become thoroughly overlaid with religious and aesthetic and sentimental concepts. We do not reject worms, grubs, rats, snails, insects, monkeys, horses, dogs, cats, and liquid blood because these things are not available but for irrational aesthetic notions and sentiment. Although many Americans have eaten horsemeat, they have usually done so unknowingly; the general attitude was probably best expressed during World War II by the mayor of New York who indicated that it was morally wrong to do so. On the other hand, the Kirghiz of Central Asia, who are by no means a morally depraved group, find horsemeat superior to beef. Hindus, of course, reject our much-loved steaks on other grounds. To them, slaughtering a cow is one of the greatest sins a man may commit. One of their religious books, the Mahabharata, stresses this with the statement that "All that kill, eat, and permit the

113

slaughter of cows, rot in hell for as many years as there are hairs on the body of the cow so slain." Then there is pork. As a whole the Western world likes it, as do the Chinese, but to orthodox Jews and Mohammedans its use is sinful. Religious-sanctioned dietary differences relating to pork and beef, in fact, were important in the decision to create the separate nation of Pakistan out of India.

I have already commented upon some of our food aversions. Other societies have comparable dislikes for some of our culinary favorites. Take milk for example. Most Americans like milk or milk products. "Drink your milk" is perhaps our favorite advice to children, and "Milk, the perfect food," one of our national slogans. But the very idea of milk offends millions of Chinese, Japanese, Koreans, and Indochinese, who consider the milking of any female animal to be highly indiscreet, if not almost immoral. Or think of eggs, the favorite American breakfast food. To the French, eggs before lunch are as out of place as vegetables for breakfast would be for us. Still, the French do eat eggs, and their omelets are among the best. Many African peoples, on the other hand, view an egg with about the same composite religio-aesthetic horror that we reserve for their hot cattle-blood cocktails.

Finally, the act of eating, itself, is viewed in various ways around the world. To us, eating out in public is fun. Cafeterias, cafés, and restaurants thrive in our society. Although we do not enjoy crowds during mealtime, most of us feel vaguely uncomfortable dining alone in a restaurant. In total contrast, peoples like the Dobuans of Melanesia will turn their backs and walk away from the group to avoid being observed while eating. In many respects their modesty in eating is similar to ours concerning the equally natural functions of sex and elimination.

Clothing Variations / Throughout history man has labored for and valued coverings to protect his body from the elements. Like food, much clothing is closely related to the climate and geographical setting. We need only compare the fur parka of the Eskimo with the sarongs of the South Pacific. As we have seen, however, predictions are not easy to make on the basis of climate alone. You will recall the near-naked Ona of frozen Tierra del Fuego. You might also consider the skirt, sheer stockings, and fur-on-the-outside coat of a New York woman in January, or the coat, shirt, and tie of her husband in July. The native Australians, who endure a seasonal temperature range from 20° F to 115° F, wear nothing but a seashell or a tassel of fur on a string. Still, in spite of these contrary examples, most peoples

This fourteen-inch-tall cedarbark hat notifies other status-conscious Tlingit Indians that its wearer has had four successful potlatches, each disc standing for one. Using paint based in the oil from chewed fish eggs, these Northwest Coast people characteristically use eye designs in their representations of various animals.

In Tunis the author's blond wife in practical American costume observes veiled Moslem women. While their loose white robes provide protection from the North African sun, their veils, worn in the name of modesty, give anonymity and, with it, surprising freedom of expression to feminine eyes.

tend to regulate the type and amount of clothing they wear by the climate in which they live. A world full of climatic variations means a world full of different clothes.

There are additional reasons for differences in what people wear, reasons having to do with modesty, status, and beauty. Our cultural conception of modesty, for example, stands squarely in the way of getting cool in public on a hot day. Brazilian Indian women do not have this problem; they wear no clothes in the first place although modesty demands the wearing of nose ornaments, without which they are acutely embarrassed. North American Haida Indian women feel the same way about their lip ornaments. American women may accentuate their breasts by padding, lifting up, enhancing cleavage, and displaying their topsides. The women of ancient Crete, with a different notion of modesty, wore dresses designed to support and enhance the beauty of the breasts, but not to conceal them. Labrador Eskimos thoroughly bundle themselves against the elements while outside, but wear few if any clothes inside their dwellings. Their neighbors, the Naskapi Indians, to the contrary, go fully clothed at all times, since they consider it immodest to expose any part of the body except the hands and face. Some of these illustrations may convince you that there are people who lack a true sense of modesty. This is not the case. Anthropologists have found that all peoples have rules of modesty that relate to their bodies. Many, though not all, of these rules specifically concern the covering of the sexual areas. Almost every part of the body has been concealed in the name of modesty by one society or another. Modesty may in many cases not relate to dress at all, but to posture, a gesture, or facial expression. Certainly a fully clothed woman may be brazenly suggestive and a naked one demurely dignified. It was the ignorance and provincialism of Western missionaries, not their superior modesty or morals, that led them to put sacks on primitive peoples and to teach them shame for their organs of sex.

Clothing and ornamentation also vary because they may conveniently indicate status or position within a society. The Hopi, for example, use hairstyling to indicate a girl's marital status. If she wears her hair in large whorls on the sides of her head (symbolic of the squash blossom), she is unmarried; if she puts it into two long braids down her back (symbolic of the mature squash vine), she is married. The Kikuyu of East Africa have a whole series of items that are worn by women to indicate their progress through life. At puberty, girls receive a browband of beads and shells. When they become betrothed they are given a necklace, and this is exchanged for an iron collar at their wedding. Later, when one of their own daughters reaches puberty, they receive spiral copper earrings. With such a system, it becomes possible to see at a glance a woman's marital and family status. We do this to a limited extent with fraternity pins, engagement rings, and wedding bands. The Russians go further, awarding medals and titles for child production. The more children, the fancier both medal and title become. For five children a woman is awarded the "Motherhood Medal, second class," and for six the "Motherhood Medal, first class." There are three ranks of "The Order of Motherhood Glory" for seven, eight, and nine children. Finally, for ten children, she receives the highest honor of all—the award of "Heroine Mother," together, one would hope, with a much needed rest. Social rank and leadership is also often indicated by clothing and ornamentation. Among the Plains Indians, feathered bonnets are worn only by the best fighters, whereas among the ancient Incas, only the ruling class could wear large ear plugs. Royalty among the Shilluk is indicated by the possession of the lower incisors—all other persons must have these teeth taken out. Samoan and ancient Hawaiian chiefs submitted to a full body tattoo as a sign of their high office as well as their bravery in enduring the pain.

Man's quest for beauty and aesthetic satisfaction has also led him to great variety in his clothing and personal adornment. In this he has demonstrated an amazingly supple imagination. In the Western world he has painted his face, lips, nails, palms, and other body areas. In the South Pacific he has tattooed designs on virtually every part of his body, including in some cases the tongue, gums, and genitalia. In Africa and Melanesia he has cut marks and designs in his skin and deliberately made them heal slowly into raised, livid scars. Throughout the world he has pierced his ears, nose, and lips to receive rings, disks, and shafts. Congo Pygmies chisel their teeth down to points to beautify them and ridicule the white man for having teeth like the beasts. The Mangbetu of Africa and various Indians of the Americas bind the heads of infants in order to flatten them and thereby, in their estimation, improve on nature.

To speak of superior and inferior practices in clothing and ornamentation is impossible as far as beauty, modesty, and status are concerned. There is and can be no universal best way to be beautiful or modest or to show one's position in society. Each society has its own rules, and these are right for it. Cultural learning alone determines our preference for a plaid shirt rather than a chest tattoo, for pierced

In Alaska an Eskimo woman makes mukluks, chewing the sealskin sole to soften it. When her parka hood is up, the wolverine trim will prevent ice from forming around her face in sub-zero temperatures. While these clothes have no equal for outer wear, she has discarded much of her traditional dress in favor of factory-made cloth.

AMERICAN MUSEUM OF NATURAL HISTORY

ears rather than pierced lips. It alone made trousers seem so ridiculous to the Tupi Indians of South America that they called the Portuguese who wore them a derisive name usually applied to birds with feathers around their feet.

Objectively there is only one way to evaluate clothing from society to society and this is in terms of the protection it offers. We can measure the insulating efficiency of Eskimo furs, the water resistance of a Kazak felt raincoat, and the durability of several pairs of American boots. But, as we know, protection and comfort are often of secondary importance in social life. Almost any American woman will gradually deform her feet in order to wear what she considers beautiful shoes. And few American men will go to work barefoot or in sandals on a hot day even if they own the business or are in no danger of being fired.

DIFFUSION AND LEVELS OF TECHNOLOGY

Most societies produce more than food and clothing. They make shelters, tools, weapons, luxuries—and these also vary markedly from group to group. Just as the nutritive value of food and the protective value of clothes may be established, the other products of man's technology may usually be measured. Thus, tools, shelters, or machines may be compared in terms of cost of material and labor to produce as well as their functional efficiency. We can demonstrate conclusively the technical superiority of a steel axe over one of stone, a gun over a spear, a plow over an adze, a brick house over a lean-to, and so on. In this way we can clearly establish that some groups, like the Australian Arunta, have a very crude technology. The Arunta subsist on a meager hunting and gathering diet, wear no clothes, manufacture only a dozen or so useful objects, and possess virtually no luxuries. North Americans, on the other hand, have thousands of efficient technological products, related to practically every area of man's life. Differences of this nature are so profound and reflect such an enormous disparity in technology, that we tend to think of other peoples as lazy, perverse, and certainly not very bright. But, as we have seen, these differences stem from the various ways men have responded to natural resources, climate, isolation, diffusion, and cultural values and goals—for several thousand years. The differences do not in themselves indicate racial or cultural superiority or inferiority. The Arunta are one of the world's least technologically developed peoples, because they have been one of the world's most isolated peoples. Now that it is possible for them to reach into the human cultural stockpile, they also may rise to the technological heights if they choose. If you doubt this, consider a classic statement by anthropologist Ralph Linton, which appeared in *The American Mercury* in 1937, on the role of diffusion in creating the "American" way of life. It is a fine antidote to our tendency to think that we achieved our civilization unaided and that we alone are the great cultural innovators of all time.

There can be no question about the average American's Americanism or his desire to preserve this precious heritage at all costs. Nevertheless, some insidious foreign ideas have already wormed their way into his civilization without his realizing what was going on. Thus dawn finds the unsuspecting patriot garbed in pajamas, a garment of East Indian origin, and lying in a bed built on a pattern which originated in either Persia or Asia Minor. He is muffled to the ears in un-American materials: cotton, first domesticated in India; linen, domesticated in the Near East; wool from an animal native to Asia Minor; or silk whose uses were first discovered by the Chinese. All these substances have been transformed into cloth by methods invented in Southwestern Asia. If the weather is cold enough he may even be sleeping under an eiderdown quilt invented in Scandinavia.

On awakening he glances at the clock, a medieval European invention, uses one potent Latin word in abbreviated form, rises in haste, and goes to the bathroom. Here, if he stops to think about it, he must feel himself in the presence of a great American institution; he will have heard stories of both the quality and frequency of foreign plumbing and will know that in no other country does the average man perform his ablutions in the midst of such splendor. But the insidious foreign influence pursues him even here. Glass was invented by the ancient Egyptians, the use of glazed tiles for floors and walls in the Near East, porcelain in China, and the art of enameling on metal by Mediterranean artisans of the Bronze Age. Even his bathtub and toilet are but slightly modified copies of Roman originals. The only purely American contribution to the ensemble is the steam radiator, against which our patriot very briefly and unintentionally places his posterior.

In this bathroom the American washes with soap invented by the ancient Gauls. Next he cleans his teeth, a very subversive European practice which did not invade America until the latter part of the eighteenth century. He then shaves, a masochistic rite first developed by the heathen priests of ancient Egypt and Sumer. The process is made less of a penance by the fact that his razor is of steel, an iron-carbon alloy discovered in either India or Turkestan. Lastly, he dries himself on a Turkish towel.

Returning to the bedroom, the unconscious victim of un-American practices removes his clothes from a chair, invented in the Near East, and proceeds to dress. He puts on close-fitting tailored garments whose form

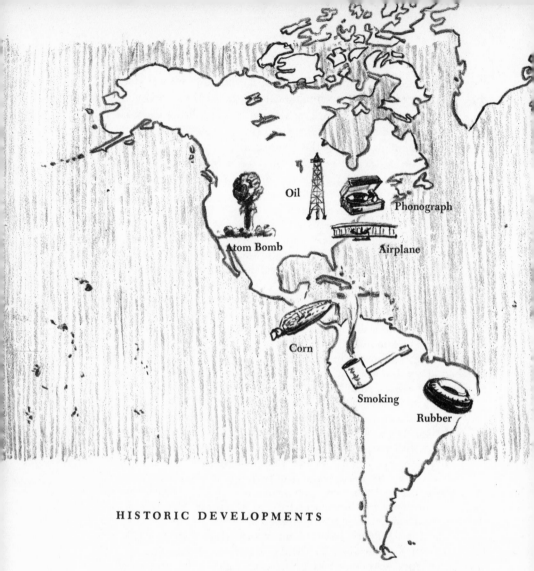

HISTORIC DEVELOPMENTS

derives from the skin clothing of the ancient nomads of the Asiatic steppes and fastens them with buttons whose prototypes appeared in Europe at the close of the Stone Age. This costume is appropriate enough for outdoor exercise in a cold climate, but is quite unsuited to American summers, steam-heated houses, and Pullmans. Nevertheless, foreign ideas and habits hold the uncomfortable man in thrall even when common sense tells him that the authentically American costume of gee string and moccasins would be far more comfortable. He puts on his feet stiff coverings made from hide prepared by the process invented in ancient Egypt and cut to a pattern which can be traced back to ancient Greece, and makes sure that they are properly polished, also a Greek idea. Lastly, he ties about his neck a

122

Man-made Satellite

Printing Type

Clock

Fork

Domestication of Horse

Spoon

Gunpowder

Soap

Bricks

Steel

Paper

ABC

Wheel

Silk

Alphabet

Tanning

Coffee

Mirror

strip of bright-colored cloth which is a vestigial survival of the shoulder shawls worn by seventeenth-century Croats. He gives himself a final appraisal in the mirror, an old Mediterranean invention, and goes downstairs to breakfast.

Here a whole new series of foreign things confronts him. His food and drink are placed before him in pottery vessels, the proper name of which—china—is sufficient evidence of their origin. His fork is a medieval Italian invention and his spoon a copy of a Roman original. He will usually begin the meal with coffee, an Abyssinian plant first discovered by the Arabs. The American is quite likely to need it to dispel the morning-after effects of overindulgence in fermented drinks, invented by the alchemists of medieval

123

Europe. Whereas the Arabs took their coffee straight, he will probably sweeten it with sugar, discovered in India; and dilute it with cream, both the domestication of cattle and the technique of milking them having originated in Asia Minor.

If our patriot is old-fashioned enough to adhere to the so-called American breakfast, his coffee will be accompanied by an orange, domesticated in the Mediterranean region, a cantaloupe domesticated in Persia, or grapes domesticated in Asia Minor. He will follow this with a bowl of cereal made from grain domesticated in the Near East and prepared by methods also invented there. From this he will go on to waffles, a Scandinavian invention, with plenty of butter, originally a Near-Eastern cosmetic. As a side dish he may have the egg of a bird domesticated in Southwestern Asia or strips of the flesh of an animal domesticated in the same region, which have been salted and smoked by a process invented in Northern Europe.

Breakfast over, he places upon his head a molded piece of felt, invented by the nomads of Eastern Asia, and, if it looks like rain, puts on outer shoes of rubber, discovered by the ancient Mexicans, and takes an umbrella, invented in India. He then sprints for his train—the train, not the sprinting, being an English invention. At the station he pauses for a moment to buy a newspaper, paying for it with coins invented in ancient Lydia. Once on board he settles back to inhale the fumes of a cigarette invented in Mexico or a cigar invented in Brazil. Meanwhile, he reads the news of the day, imprinted in characters invented by the ancient Semites by a process invented in Germany upon a material invented in China. As he scans the latest editorial pointing out the dire results to our institutions of accepting foreign ideas, he will not fail to thank a Hebrew God in an Indo-European language that he is a one hundred per cent (decimal system invented by the Greeks) American (from Americus Vespucci, Italian geographer).

DISTRIBUTION METHODS

Regardless of technological level, each society must work out methods for distributing its products among its members. Agreements or rules must exist to regulate who gets what and how much, as well as to dispose of group surpluses if they exist. In many societies these rules follow the basic divisions along which work is apportioned—age and sex. In societies where food is difficult to obtain, it is distributed with utter realism during periods of scarcity. Those who are responsible for obtaining food eat first and best, since their strength is needed to get more food; without them the group would perish. This normally means that vigorous young males will take precedence over women, children, and old people. In times of great famine among the Eskimos the oldest members voluntarily go out on the ice to

VARIETIES OF MONEY

Dentalium Shells
(Northwest American Coast)

Pearl Disc Money
(New Guinea)

Clam Shell Money
(West American Coast)

Fruit Bat Canine Teeth
(Solomon Islands)

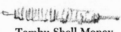

Tambu Shell Money
(New Britain)

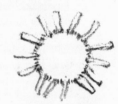

Cus-cus Teeth and Beads
(Solomon Islands)

Boar's Tusk
(New Guinea)

Money-Ring of the Tridacna Gigas Shell
(Melanesia)

Feather Money Necklace
(Banks Islands)

Copper Coin
(Congo)

Red Woodpecker's Head
(Hupa Indians)

Cowrie Shell
(Africa and elsewhere)

Stone Money (Fei)
(Yap Island)

freeze, in order not to jeopardize the existence of the group. On the other hand, the Arunta have an elaborate system of food taboos which ensures an equitable distribution of food to all members of the group. Even old people share in the available food, no matter how scarce, as long as it does not come from their totem animal.

Since most of the world's societies have an easier time of it than the Eskimos and the Arunta, distribution does not often become so intense a problem. Generally speaking, as anthropologist Daryll Forde points out, societies with little technical knowledge live and work together with a strong sense of group solidarity.

The economic unit is small and, save for occasionally bartered specialities, does not transcend the population of a small village. Social relations are of the personal, face-to-face kind. Everyone has known everyone else from childhood, everyone is related to everyone else. The sick and unfortunate are able to depend on the kindliness of immediate neighbors. The sharing of tools and of supplies to meet individual shortages are matters of moral obligation between kinsfolk and neighbors. Impersonal commercial relations hardly exist.

In view of the quality of the human relations within such societies, a low technical level of existence does not appear to be the curse we would imagine.

Once technology improves, surpluses become possible, intergroup communications tend to increase, and the probability of trade emerges. Trade, in addition to solving the periodic problems of economic scarcity and surplus, has been a great medium of diffusion through the years. In trading, one may swap something for something else, that is barter, or he may assign a fixed value to an object, which he then uses to evaluate, buy, and sell other things. Chance meetings between groups or individuals promote barter; regular or sustained contacts between peoples often result in fixed exchange standards and on occasion the development of a medium of exchange.

As a rule, the desire for profit is not a factor in primitive exchange, since each party has a surplus that he does not need and is pleased to obtain something that he needs but does not have. A reasonable amount of bargaining may take place before the relative worth of the items is agreed upon, but "shrewd deals" and "hooking the sucker" seem to belong to civilized rather than to primitive trade relationships. As a matter of fact, trading among many primitive societies is done with great finesse. For example, off the eastern coast of New Guinea, natives of the Trobriand Islands have an elaborate exchange relationship. No one island in this group is self-sufficient in raw ma-

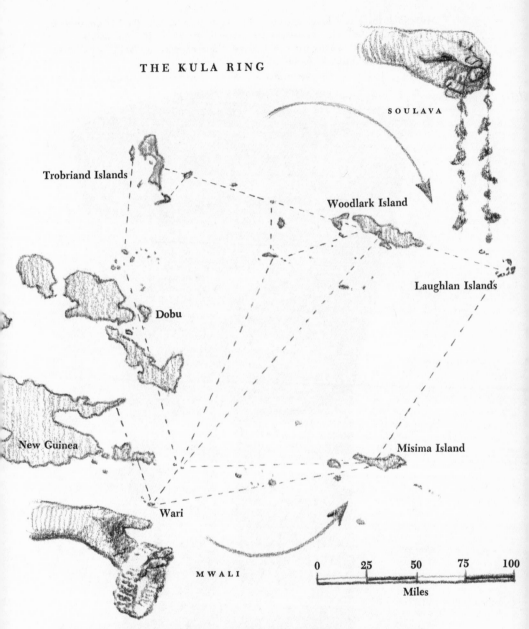

THE KULA RING

SOULAVA

Trobriand Islands

Woodlark Island

Laughlan Islands

Dobu

New Guinea

Misima Island

Wari

MWALI

| 0 | 25 | 50 | 75 | 100 |

Miles

Trade among the islands near eastern New Guinea follows these routes. As a prelude to commercial transactions there are elaborate ceremonial exchanges of *mwali*, white shell bracelets, and *soulava*, long necklaces of red shell. *Soulava* are always exchanged from island to island in a clockwise direction, *mwali* always in a counterclockwise direction.

More than three feet long, this copper symbolizes wealth to the Tlingit Indians. Beaten thin (this one measures one-sixteenth of an inch) and painted with family crests and designs from mythology, these coppers are used in potlatches to enhance the status of family and clan.

terials, technical skills, and products. Consequently, the people of each island regularly trade their surplus products for those of neighboring islanders. Preceding these trading activities, however, is a set of involved ceremonial gift exchanges collectively called *Kula*. Because the islands involved in successive trades form a rough geographical circle, the relationship is termed the "Kula ring." Two types of ritual trade objects are used in these activities: necklaces of red shell and bracelets of white shell. Since each participant must make a gift to the other, these objects move in opposite directions around the ring, the necklaces clockwise and the bracelets counterclockwise. The elaborate ceremonies accompanying these exchanges set the stage for the amicable trade relations that follow, and tie all the varied participants into a system of mutual understandings and relationships.

OWNERSHIP AND "THE GOOD LIFE"

Once trade becomes established among peoples, the concept of ownership tends to grow stronger. Symbols of ownership begin to be created, and social arrangements devised to indicate who may keep what and under what conditions. To identify personal property, man has produced hundreds of symbols ranging from the brands, monograms, deeds, and rings of the Western world to the teeth and smooth pieces of quartz of the Vedda of India. We also find remarkable variation in the conditions and circumstances of ownership. Primitive societies for the most part, such as the Kwakiutl and other Indians of the American Northwest Coast, stress family or local group ownership. Some societies, such as our own, have a strong heritage of and feeling for individual ownership, but are learning to accept increasing national ownership as well. Russia, on the other hand, and other collectivist societies favor national ownership, but accept some individual ownership as well. Much of the present friction in our world is directly related to a dispute about who has the best system of ownership and production. There is no scientific way to settle the argument. In fact, the evidence suggests that, given a high level of technology, almost any system of production and ownership will benefit the group concerned. This is not meant to disparage our own economic system; capitalism need not apologize for its great achievements. We should be realistic enough, however, to understand that other economic systems may be as good as our own and to recognize the possibility at least that someday something even better may come along.

A world full of different diets, clothing, technologies, methods of distribution, and symbols and systems of ownership seems to upset many people. At best these differences are considered to be quaint, and at worst downright anti-American. Yet our right to dislike certain foods, dress, or customs does not include the right to find the people who do like them perverse or inferior in taste and judgment. Moreover, even though millions of people are now being exposed to Western technology and values, if and what they wish to borrow remains to be seen. Just because our inventions are efficient and time-saving does not mean that they will be accepted. As we have seen, there are a great many other factors involved in cultural diffusion. Although all societies would probably predicate "the Good Life" upon having enough to eat, reasonable protection from the elements, and freedom from disease, little agreement would exist between them from this point on. It may please us to believe that all people everywhere would like to have our cars and houses and conveniences once they experienced them, but we have little justification for this assumption. These things must be worked for and paid for in one way or another, and their price is high in terms of the time, freedom, and often the loss of health that they require. There are hundreds of other worthwhile values and goals in life besides wanting "the highest standard of living in the world." Anthropologist Felix Keesing puts it this way in *Cultural Anthropology:*

The Westerner, on the one hand, tends to look at the local people as "lazy," "indolent," incapable of sustained effort, unreliable as workers, perhaps even biologically deficient in these respects, because they do not strain themselves in what by Western standards are counted worthwhile and profitable enterprises—and especially because they may not be willing to labor for wages in the white man's enterprises. The local people, on the other hand, far from seeing profit in such new lines of activity, may actually be secretly pitying the white man for having to work so hard for his living, regarding him as a kind of economic slave caught in the toils of time clocks, factory whistles, and the like, and being the more thankful that they themselves have a less hectic pace. True, the Western institutions and values are now being increasingly diffused. At the same time, in Western countries, the trend is toward shorter hours of work and the Westerner is having to learn what many so-called pre-industrial peoples have been adept at: how to relax and utilize leisure time.

An even more valuable insight will be ours when we finally learn that a preference for a nosebone, or hot animal blood, or collectivism, does not automatically compromise a man's intellectual power, his emotional maturity, or his ethical standards.

CHAPTER 8

Man and His Mate

> . . . the lesson is almost inescapable that a great
> variety of marriage and family practices seem to
> have worked. . . . More than this . . . the many
> workable arrangements all have loyal adherents who
> . . . would find it difficult to imagine themselves
> living under some radically different family type.
>
> WILLIAM F. KENKEL

BIOLOGY AND THE HUMAN FAMILY

One of the fundamental ties that binds human beings into social groups is the nonseasonal sexual availability of the female. This quality, developed only in some Old World primates, made it possible for a female to attract the same male for an indefinite period of time. With the world full of permanently sexed males, the social effects of this biological adaptation are far-reaching and difficult to overestimate. Certainly for the first time in animal history fathers began to have an ongoing social function in addition to their brief biological one. It has been suggested that once woman became aware of her capacity both to arouse and to satisfy man all year round, she made the most of it and demanded that he care for her and her offspring. While an early bargain of this nature may well have been made, this view may simply project our own experience into the prehistoric past. It also makes first-class philanderers out of the human males of ancient times. I believe it is more likely that man was intelligent enough to recognize the advantages of a continuing sexual alliance and also emotionally attracted to the variety of social relationships that repeated sexual intimacy makes possible. For "settling down" not only solves the problem of having to find and perhaps fight for an available female every few days, but it also encourages shared experience from which both affection and a sense of responsibility often emerge.

Correlated with this increase in the depth and permanency of male-female ties was the long dependence of human babies, who stayed longer in the womb and were more helpless than other animals after birth. These physiological facts wrote the guarantee to close relationships between mother and child. Carrying a child inside you for nine months does not necessarily make you feel affection for it, but you most certainly cannot ignore it. In fact, during the final weeks and days, you may be aware of little else. This new child is the world's most helpless creature and has absolutely no chance of survival unless it is cared for by its elders. Adequate food is of course essential and, as psychologist René Spitz has shown us, so in many cases is affection. Normal physical and psychological growth is a matter both of *being* cared for and *feeling* cared for. Actually the location of the female breasts, together with upright human posture which frees the hands, enables women to fulfill both infant needs at the same time. Since suckling is normally pleasurable for both mother and child, inevitably hands caress and fondle during feedings. That man now exists in such great numbers is a good indication that his women have adequately fed and cherished their offspring through history.

It can be seen that the fundamental biological ties of sex and infant dependence bind human beings together into family groups. It is also apparent that only between father and child is there no long-term biological relationship. Whatever bonds exist between a father and his offspring are socially learned. They are feelings that are made possible by his sustained attraction to the same woman and his inevitable close association with the children that result. And while this affords man the opportunity to develop an altruistic concern for others, it is, as we know, by no means an inevitable consequence of family life.

CHOOSING A MATE

Select a Beauty / The most powerful initial family bond is and always has been sex. In his early days in the trees man may not have been very selective in his choice of mates. But as sight gradually replaced smell as the key human sense, inevitably the female's appearance became increasingly important in the selection of sexual partners. To some extent this must have worked both ways, with females tending to respond more favorably to visually appealing males. Today the visual evaluation of a prospective mate is a widespread practice before—and even after—selection. To guide these choices properly most societies have well-defined standards of beauty. Even groups in which small children are betrothed exclude or place a low value upon ugly and deformed persons.

As in all other areas where man has thought creatively, his conceptions of beauty vary prodigiously from society to society. The prettiest girl by Hottentot standards would probably be the ugliest by our standards, and vice versa. In his *Race and Nationality* Henry Pratt Fairchild once visualized a truly international "Miss Universe" beauty contest in which the fairest girl from each of eight different societies was vying with Miss United States for the title. Here is the way he described the procession:

First in line is Miss Alor, a dusky maiden from an inconspicuous South Sea Island, displaying two rows of teeth carefully blackened and filed down to points. Next is Miss Botocudo from South America, with a huge disc of wood inserted in her lower lip. Behind her comes Miss Manganya who wears her plug in her upper lip. Following in line is Miss China, a slender slant-eyed miss who, being modern, is not kept from walking by having her feet reduced by binding to a mangled mass of bone and tissue as would have been the case with her mother. Then a couple of other Far Easterners, Miss Siam with her long fingernails protected by silver cases, and Miss Burma whose neck is so elongated by a series of brass rings that if she were to take them off she could not hold her head up. Then a group of dark-skinned girls hardly distinguishable except for the carefully worked out patterns of artificial scars on their cheeks, foreheads, and other parts of their bodies. Just behind them is Miss Bushman, a tiny maiden with an extraordinary development of the buttocks, recognized by the more scientific of the observers as *steatopygia*.

To this group I wish to add a number of beauties who, I believe, also deserve consideration. For example, here is Miss Mangbetu of the Belgian Congo with an artificially created, long, slanting head shape, further accentuated by a backswept hair style. Then we have Miss Samoa who, like Miss Bali, would feel more at home wearing a bathing suit without a top on it, especially since someone had mentioned that well-formed breasts were an important asset in a beauty contest.

*A "beautiful woman" reflects the aesthetic
standards of her own culture.*

The Burmese lady, a jeweled cloth between chin and traditional neck rings,
watches a dance festival.

The Butende girl's arms and legs were encircled with bangles when she was young. The developing flesh bulges above and below the bangles, but apparently this is not harmful or uncomfortable. The girl carries her basket on a wooden spacer.

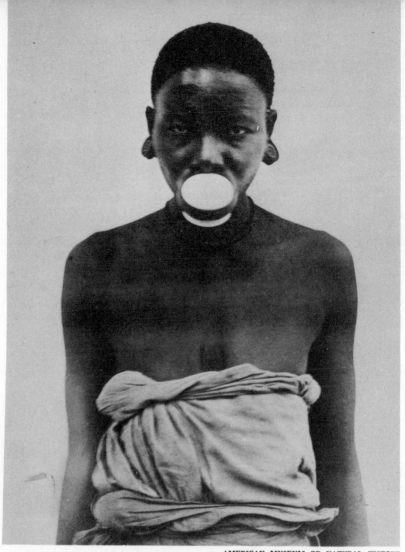

The Mohonde woman wears a handsome lip ornament.

A Bushman chief and his five wives in varied costumes.

The three young women of the Upper Congo are particularly proud of the richness of their scarified designs.

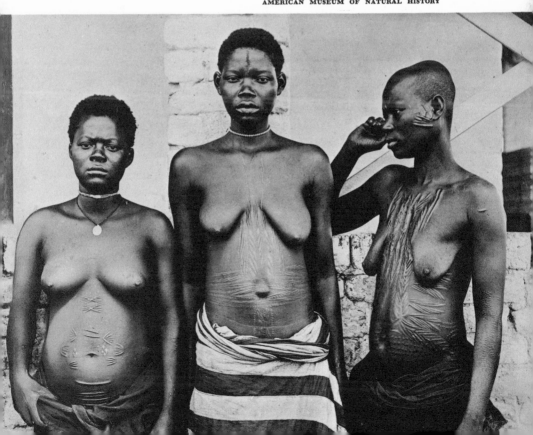

Miss Samoa is also rather proud of how yellow she has made her skin with coconut oil and turmeric. Next in line, Miss Witoto from Amazonian South America didn't want to wear a suit at all, but when forced to, insisted on cutting a triangular opening in the lower front portion. She further adhered to her cultural prescription for beauty by removing all her facial hair including eyebrows and eyelashes. By contrast Miss Ainu of Japan appears to be wearing a mustache, but closer inspection by the judges establishes that she has a fine blue-black lip tattoo around her mouth that extends almost to her ears. After her comes Miss Masai of East Africa, a six-foot six-inch tall, rather frail but proud-looking girl, followed by Miss African Pygmy, who is obviously just as proud of her compact four-foot six-inch size, her peppercorn hair and her fat, protruding abdomen. Behind them is Miss Azande from the Congo, who was selected to represent her group because her breasts were longer and more pendulous than her rivals'. Finally comes Miss United States, big breasted and long legged, the first effect being purposely exaggerated by her swimsuit, and the second by her high-heeled shoes. While she has shaved her legs and her armpits, she has, unlike the Witoto beauty, only plucked enough eyebrows to establish a thin line. To complete her culturally directed beauty treatment, she has had her hair cut and curled and has painted her mouth, fingernails, and toenails bright red.

There is, of course, little likelihood that such a contest will ever be held. Most non-Western societies feel that the deliberate public display of a scantily clad woman is disgraceful and morally reprehensible. More than this, a great many contestants would not be allowed on the stage, since their culturally approved costume or lack of it would be shocking to Western observers. Imagine the reaction if Miss Nama Hottentot entered the contest. Beauty in her society is partly determined by the extent to which the *labia majora* has been enlarged through deliberate stretching. Yet regardless of how unorthodox and startling any member of the beauty parade may have appeared to observers from other societies, within her own group she would be considered a very desirable woman. In a world full of different female types there can be no universally best face and figure. By the same token, in a world full of creative minds, there can be no universally best way to beautify or exhibit these faces and figures.

Select Outside This Group / While appearance is always important in the choice of a mate, societies usually specify many other conditions that must be met before courtship may begin. No matter how attractive you may consider your mother or father to be, and no matter which society you belong to, you will not be allowed to mate with either parent, even if widowed. The same rule, with a few exceptions, such as the ancient Incas of Peru and the Ptolemies of Egypt, prohibits your selection of your brother or sister. Requirements of this type are known generally as "rules of exogamy" and specifically as "incest taboos." In effect they say, "You must seek a mate *outside* of this particular group." All societies have additional rules of exogamy, but these vary greatly from group to group. The Chinese, for example, have historically disapproved of marriage between persons with the same surname. In the small villages of India marriage between members of the same community is not approved. Most rules of exogamy appear to serve at least two functions. Learned early and easily, they prevent constant fighting and bickering among males over females within given family groups. In addition, they help to extend economically beneficial social contacts beyond the narrow range of the family or the village. It seems unlikely that these rules were first created by an ancient group that grasped the connection between intensive inbreeding and genetic defect.

Select Within This Group / Often a society will not only require its members to seek a mate outside of a particular group, but also will designate certain other groups as the only correct place to look. Requirements and expectations of this nature are called "rules of endogamy." The caste system of India illustrates well such a rule. Caste members must seek mates from their own social stratum. To look elsewhere is to defy some of the basic concepts of the Hindu faith. Roman Catholics and Orthodox Jews also have strong endogamous beliefs. Everyone is familiar with the Catholic insistence that whoever does not conform to this expectation must nevertheless agree to rear all children in the Catholic church. A perhaps less-well-known practice is that of Orthodox Jews: A son who marries a non-Jew is considered to be dead, the burial service is read, the formal mourning period is observed, and his existence is no longer acknowledged. In the United States we are largely endogamous as regards members of other races, particularly marriages between Negro and white. In some states this is an expectation, in some a law. Restrictions which relate to a potential mate's comparative wealth and lineage are found throughout the world. In Polynesia, however, these factors are often less important than birth order. Here a person is supposed to marry someone with his own birth position: Ideally, a first-born son should marry a first-born daughter, and where possible even their ancestors should match in birth order comparisons.

139

While we are theoretically free to marry our first cousins, the practice is discouraged; when it occurs it is considered to be somewhat unfortunate. In contrast, many Melanesians, Africans, and American Indians consider this to be the ideal arrangement. They have set up certain restrictions, however, that must be observed. In the first place, once you think about it you will find that first cousins may be produced in three ways. Thus the offspring of two brothers and their wives would be first cousins. Two sisters and their husbands could also produce first cousins. And, of course, the children of a brother and his sister would be first cousins. The first two possibilities, that is, children of brothers or children of sisters, are called "parallel" cousins, and marriage between them is discouraged or forbidden by most of the societies that approve first-cousin marriage. The Bedouins of the Near East are an exception. The most preferred form of cousin marriage is between "cross-cousins," which is the third possibility described above. To complicate the matter further, cross-cousins come in two varieties. You may be the offspring either of a sister or of her brother, and your society may decide that this is important in selecting a mate. If you are a Haida boy, for example, you are encouraged to marry the daughter of your mother's brother, but not the daughter of your father's sister. On the other hand, if you are a Trobriander boy, the requirements are completely reversed, and you may only marry your father's sister's daughter. Some groups such as the Dravidians permit marriage of either type.

Perhaps the most extreme form of endogamy is found in those societies where young children are promised to one another by their parents and have no choice in the matter. In India, where this practice flourishes, the children go through one ceremony when the original arrangement is made, and another when they reach puberty and are ready to live together. Among the Arapesh of New Guinea also, children are often promised by their parents; to seal the bargain little girls go to live with the family of their prospective husbands, not as wives, but as special daughters. Observers speak of the great affection and understanding that develops between a boy and girl who are reared together in this way and who then marry.

While many rules of endogamy seem quite provincial, there is little doubt that most of them exist to perpetuate the tranquility of an existing society. Some of them seek to keep a family or a racial line intact, some to retain wealth and possessions within a particular group, and some to ensure the continuity of a religion. Whatever the reason, it is obvious that the choice of whom to court usually involves a great deal more than the beauty of a woman's face and form.

COURTSHIP

Even after one's society has considerably narrowed the field of eligible mates, there are generally several choices still available. This makes desirable various get-acquainted activities among young men and women, followed in most cases by a courtship period during which two persons begin to think of each other as potential mates. When we consider the great range of behavior adopted as proper by

SYMBOLS OF THE UNMARRIED

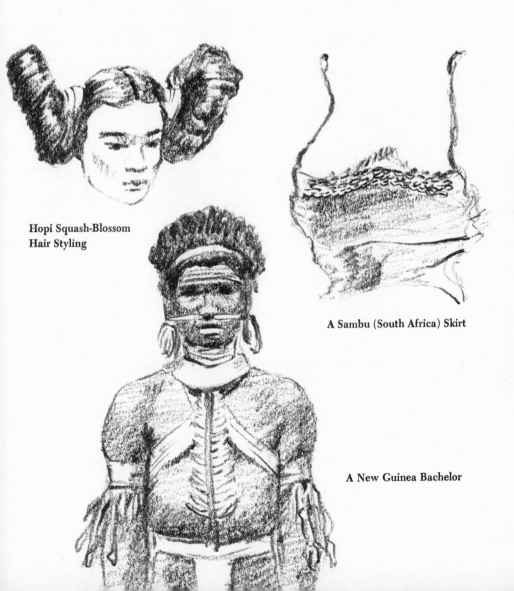

Hopi Squash-Blossom
Hair Styling

A Sambu (South Africa) Skirt

A New Guinea Bachelor

various societies during courtship, few generalizations emerge. We find that African Bushmen and Siberian Chuckchee young people do a great deal of sexual changing about until a compatible mate is found. The Manus of Melanesia, in contrast, are quite strict about pre-marital sexual experience and use chaperons and elaborate restrictions in an effort to prevent it. Strictness among the Samoans and the Ifugao of the Philippines, as with us, is related to social rank. The higher the social position, in general, the less premarital sexual activity.

Some early observers of primitive societies reported widespread sexual promiscuity either before or after marriage or both. The fact that several native vocabularies have no word for "virgin" further convinced many persons that primitive man had made no attempt to bridle his lust and engaged in all manner of sexual excesses. For the most part these reports mirror the reactions of untrained observers, reared in a puritanical tradition, to cultural patterns which failed to correlate shame with a pleasant and normal activity. These people were shocked to learn that Trobriander children play sexual games together and that the courtship period of adolescence is considered an ideal time to get acquainted through sexual experimentation. The additional fact that, once married, Trobrianders are remarkably faith-ful did not impress them, if indeed they bothered to find this out. Moreover, although the boys and girls may have appeared to be promiscuous, a great many social regulations were in force all along—rules which prohibited brother-and-sister, parallel-cousin and one type of cross-cousin play, as well as rules that concerned age differences and various status symbols. Indeed, we may say that, although ideas vary from society to society about the desirability of premarital sexual activity, there is no completely promiscuous society. All groups have an array of rules and regulations and, should it appear otherwise, it is because we do not know enough about the society under observa-tion.

MARRIAGE

It seems safe to assume that man was mating and rearing families long before he decided to make it legal by inventing the marriage ceremony. Even so, the origin of marital rites is apparently quite re-mote since the first written evidence comes from ancient Sumeria and Egypt, where marriage already followed a formal, elaborate, and ongoing pattern. In Sumerian times, when the engagement was an-nounced, the young man made a gift of money to his prospective

A Sambu (South Africa) Skirt

Hopi Squash-Vine Hair Styling

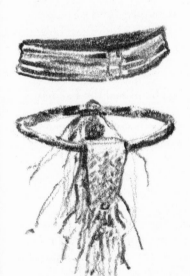

A Buka (Solomon Islands) Belt and Girdle

The lip plug of a Suyá (Brazil) man.

father-in-law. If he subsequently broke the engagement, he forfeited the money. If the girl broke the engagement, the money was returned to the youth together with an equal amount from the girl's father. If things went smoothly and the marriage was consummated, the bride's father matched the groom's money, and the entire amount was turned over to the girl as a dowry. The marriage itself involved a written contract in which the rights and duties of both parties were precisely outlined, along with the legal causes for divorce. It should be added that the practice of paying alimony was also an established custom during this time. Ralph Linton has said that the legal position of married women in ancient Sumeria was much better than that of English women until very recent times. By Babylonian days, however, some changes appear to have occurred, since in a section of the Code of Hammurabi we find that "If a woman gads about, speaks disrespectfully of her husband, and neglects his house, she shall be drowned."

Not all marriage rites in ancient times were as involved as those of Sumeria. We may be sure that men had a great variety of ideas about the actions and words and objects necessary to symbolize the creation of a new marital unit. Contemporary societies, not unexpectedly, vary a great deal in terms of what constitutes a marriage. Perhaps the least involved marital arrangement is simply the decision of a man and woman to live together with no preceding rites or symbols. This is the so-called "common law" marriage and, in many areas of the world, including sections of our country, is considered to be sufficient evidence of the existence of a marriage. Other arrangements, such as those approved by the Wadaba of Somaliland and the Eskimo Aleuts, have a similar "It should be obvious that we're married" aspect. Among these groups no one is considered married until the woman involved is pregnant. Then she is manifestly married to the man she is currently sleeping with. In old China and elsewhere before the marriage was considered binding, ritual defloration was required and public evidence presented that the woman was a virgin.

Our own ceremonies vary from the simple to the complex, from the primarily secular to the primarily sacred. The average girl seems to dream of a church wedding, but will often settle for a justice of the peace. Some couples extend courtship over months and even years; others meet and head for the state line in a few hours. And while the length of the ceremony may vary from minutes to hours, the event is duly recorded in the proper documents. In India the nature of a Hindu wedding may also vary substantially, depending on the caste and circumstances of the families involved. Marriage between Brahmans, however, is one of the world's most prolonged and complex ceremonies, frequently requiring several days to complete. During this time both bride and groom change costumes several times, hear lengthy recitations and chants, participate in symbolic rituals, bathe, anoint one another with various oils and milks, and eat specially prepared foods, but are not allowed to be alone together until the final night of the celebration.

In most societies including our own, there is an exchange of gifts before, during, or after the marriage ceremony. The Sumerian practice discussed above was a good example of this. In the United States the boy usually gives the girl a ring, which she may theoretically keep if the boy breaks the engagement and which she is supposed to return if she ends the affair. If the couple goes ahead with marriage plans, it becomes the focus of a gift flow, beginning with engagement showers and ending with wedding presents. All these gifts belong to the couple, they are kept and used, returned to the store for cash, or occasionally—if they are quite useless—packed away and given to someone else as a wedding present at a later time.

In many societies the flow of gifts and wealth is from the groom and his family to the bride's family. Often this giving is so substantial and one-directional that it is termed a "bride price." However, since almost no society puts its eligible girls up for actual sale, "price" is not an accurate word. More often than not the payment is a good-will present and symbolizes the groom's ability to provide for the girl, his affection for her, and his good intentions. As a rule the more desirable the girl the more wealth the man is willing to part with to get her, and of course the more her parents will expect. But the matter is never just an auction. Usually the families involved must be close and the couple well matched. Also, if there is genuine revulsion on the part of the girl, she can usually refuse to marry no matter how well qualified the suitor may otherwise be. Among the Yurok Indians, men are proud of how much they are obliged to give the girl's father in order to gain his permission to marry her. The higher the cost the more desirable the girl is. By Yurok standards this means she is pretty, small, and trim, has good teeth, and can work hard; emphatically she is not a glutton. Since the ideal couple is also supposed to be in love, the girl may reject a number of suitors even though they may have enough wealth to meet her father's demands. In Yurok society as in many others, all the early phases of the relationship with the family of the prospective bride are handled by a friend of the suitor. It is the responsibility of the go-between to present his friend in the best possible light, state his case convincingly, and try to arrange a fair transaction. After marriage the husband begins to get a substantial return on his investment. Among the Yuroks a man's social rank is measured not by what he has but by what he is willing to spend, give away, or destroy. Obviously then, if he has used a great deal of his wealth

The Manus bride of the Admiralty Islands wears part of her dowry, a delicate apron. Since shells, like dogs' teeth, provide an important medium of exchange among the islanders, the strings of shells woven together for these aprons have particular value beyond the fine craftsmanship evident in the design.

to acquire a wife, his status rises accordingly. For the rest of his life he is allowed to boast about what a valuable wife he has. This situation also discourages premarital sexual experience, since pregnancy out of wedlock greatly lowers the value of a girl.

Occasionally we find societies where the marital payment comes not from the groom but from the bride and her family. Thus in the Moslem world only the groom receives gifts. More frequently, gifts are exchanged in both directions as an expression of good will and accord between all concerned. In any case it seems clear that any exchange, gift, or payment between families involved in a wedding tends to make the union more difficult to dissolve. For in the event the couple cannot make a go of it, it is often required that all gifts be returned. Since much of the exchanged wealth may be in the form of food, clothing, and animals, or objects that have long since been given away, some of the problems of re-exchange may be visualized. In consequence, the families of the young couple generally exert a good deal of pressure on them to stick together and work out their problems. It can be seen that this use of gifts is a definite force making for marriage stability. Our own pattern, which routes all gifts from parents and friends to the young couple, has little, if any, such effect. When problems arise among newlyweds, the last thing they will normally resolve is "Let's both try a little harder to make it work. After all, how will we ever be able to return all that reception champagne?" Think of your own shock if, as the uncle of one of a divorced pair, you should get your gift of a monogrammed tea service back. Or think of your reaction if you lived in a society where uncles received presents at weddings, and you suddenly had to produce that hog you'd been eating all winter!

FAMILY

The question of how many mates one may have has been answered by all societies, but in several different ways. Our solution is a monogamous relationship—the union of one man and one woman. A majority of the world's societies, however, prefer several mates. Polygamy, as this is called, is of two varieties: polygyny and polyandry. The former is most common and is the practice of one man marrying two or more women. Polyandry is the marriage of one woman to two or more men and is found only among the Toda of southern India, the Marquesans of Polynesia, and the Tibetans. Dramatic differences of this type intrigued early social theorists and a variety of explanations were offered by them. One of the most popular guesses advanced the idea that family types had evolved through history and that present-day variation indicates the incomplete evolution of the family within a particular group. Thus conceived, the earliest family was characterized by complete promiscuity. As society progressed, several males began to share the same female (polyandry). This arrangement gave way when dominant males refused to share their females and began instead to add to their collection (polygyny). Finally, as man became increasingly civilized, he saw the error of his ways and began the monogamous family. This very comfortable back-patting theory for the Western world could only have arisen here. It puts us at the top of the heap with the "most highly evolved" family form; all others are still on their way up. The only difficulty is that all the scientific evidence we have stands against this theory rather than for it. It provides another example of the human tendency to consider the differences of others as marks of inferiority—to pass judgment rather than to seek understanding.

Monogamous Americans have great difficulty believing that polygynous Africans feel pity rather than envy when they learn of our family form. Likewise, published interviews with happily married Moslem women fail to dissuade us from our view that "they just don't know any better." It is, of course, natural for us to prefer our own arrangement. But to insist that our system is superior to all others not only denies others the right to differing values, but also conveniently ignores our own closetful of family skeletons. If our family system were at the apex of human evolutionary development, would there be a more-than-one-in-three divorce rate? And would there be such a high incidence of neurosis and juvenile delinquency, both of which are now known to have at least part of their genesis in the family? The fact is, there can be no universally best family form any more than there can be a worldwide standard of beauty, set of courtship practices, sexual mores, or marriage rites. The marital beliefs and practices of each society have allowed it to solve effectively the basic problems of mating and reproduction or it would not now exist.

Families vary in a great many ways other than the number of mates. There are different rules concerning where the new couple should live, how they should trace their ancestry, and what one mate should do if the other dies. A brief sketch of some of the intriguing variations will be offered here, along with the hope that by now you will have begun to think of such human differences as contributing to a rich, not a threadbare cultural tapestry.

Generally speaking, young American couples are free to settle down anywhere they please, except in the same house with their parents. Occasionally they may do so on a temporary basis, but few wish to turn it into a permanent arrangement. Other groups, on the contrary, believe that newlyweds should live in the same village and often the same house with one line of their parents. Thus the Arunta and the Toda require the bride to live among the people of the groom, whereas the Haida and Navaho Indians require the reverse. Where lineage is concerned, we trace ancestry on both sides of the family. Other societies choose to ignore one side or the other, tracing ancestry and bequeathing property either patrilineally or matrilineally. The Crow Indians and the Hottentots of South Africa trace relations through the male side of the family. The Haida Indians and the Melanesian Dobu, in contrast, work backward through the female line. Interestingly enough, some groups, such as the Crow, establish residence with one side of the family and trace ancestry through the other.

Many societies take cognizance of the fact that one of the mates may die prematurely, leaving the other with small children and perhaps no means of support. Two practices have been developed to cope with this problem. When a man's brother dies among groups like the Samoans and the Navaho, he is obligated to marry the brother's widow, if she so wishes. This is called the "levirate," by virtue of its practice among the ancient Jews; in effect it provides the woman with an insurance policy should she need it. Groups such as the Crow and Cheyenne Indians practice the "sororate," which requires a woman to marry the husband of her deceased sister. Here the man is afforded a spare wife if he needs one to rear his children and care for his home. If the woman is already married, the rule does not apply. In actual detail these two practices vary somewhat from group to group, depending to a large extent upon other existing marital relationships.

When men and women marry they usually want and expect to have children. The fact that barrenness has been one of man's most common historical reasons for divorce is an adequate testament to this. For all his interest, however, until very recently he has had little understanding of the process of reproduction. Although Old Stone Age man was living in families and enjoying a continuous sex life, there is no evidence that he understood the male role in procreation. Seemingly only when he was learning to domesticate animals in the New Stone Age did it occur to him. Some societies, out of the cultural mainstream, never learned these basic facts of life. The Arunta, for example, are sure that it is ancestral spirits, not human

males, who are responsible for pregnancy in females. The Trobriand Islanders also ridiculed the facts when they first heard them. One Trobriander husband, when told that intercourse could result in a child nine months later, rebutted with the fact that his wife bore him a child, even though he had not seen her for well over a year. Even in civilized societies, some confusion still exists; it is not unusual to find American young people who believe that deep kissing causes pregnancy.

When man finally learned that he was involved in conception, he still had little real idea of what took place. He seems first to have conceived of fertility as a force of some sort that could be caused to enter and leave animals, plants, and women. If an animal did not conceive, or a field was infertile, or a woman was barren, no one appears to have considered that the seed could have been sterile. The fault lay in the earth or in the womb. Man's task was somehow to induce fertility into the female so that she could properly nourish his seed. The idea of the woman as merely the fertile field which man plows and plants has been widely accepted and still exists in much of the world. Its pervasiveness is exemplified in the belief of imaginative seventeenth-century microscopists that they saw complete little men in human sperm cells. Although Hartsoker and Dalempatius each "saw" a miniature human in these cells, they described them as being in opposite positions—a fact that did little to build confidence in their observations. A theory nearly the reverse of this "sperm-centered" one is held by the Dobu. To them the sperm is simply voided coconut milk, whose sole function is to coagulate the menstrual blood in a woman's womb, from which the infant is formed. As empirical "proof" they offer the fact that menstruation ceases when a woman becomes pregnant.

One approach to barrenness is to enlist supernatural support. Men of the ancient Near East appear to have been among the first to think of this. There survive numerous hymns, prayers, and descriptions of rituals which indicate their faith in this method. Other peoples have also been attracted to the idea. Today virtually every known society has a substantial number of prayers or magical rites through which pregnancy may be induced. From a biological point of view, we know that rites and potions cannot directly cause fertility any more than they can prevent conception if a healthy sperm penetrates a mature egg. But recent evidence indicates that some of this fertility hocus-pocus may have helped many emotionally disturbed women to conceive. Anxiety frequently causes infertility by creating an intrauterine

Sharing the universal desire for an easy delivery and a perfect child, Ashanti women of Ghana carry fertility dolls. This wooden Akua'ba stands 10¾ inches high and is decorated with beads.

environment toxic to spermatazoa. When anxiety is relieved through magic, prayer, or psychotherapy, impregnation often becomes possible.

In matters like conception and pregnancy, of course, we are no longer dealing in areas where one society's opinion is as good as another's. Here science can make objective statements. The biological facts of reproduction are obviously very important knowledge to have. Knowing how children are conceived and how they develop in the uterus, we can plan families, and produce healthy children. Because these facts are valuable to all men, we may be sure that eventually the Dobu and the Arunta will accept them along with much additional technological information. In the long run we are sure that such scientific knowledge will serve man better than his old myths, yet the myths have been of incalculable value in man's struggle to endure and to prevail. Bad guesses, like good guesses, have given him a sense of understanding his world, of belonging in it, and of having at least some capacity to control it. This is no trifling asset. Society itself endures because a group of people derive a sense of unity from facing similar problems and sharing solutions. For survival, it mattered very little in man's history that some of these solutions about where he came from can now be shown to be nonscientific and even irrational. The important thing is that they have answered questions, given social cohesion and direction, and enabled man to plan and dream and predict within an "explained" universe.

PERSONALITY DEVELOPMENT

Once children are born they are immediately immersed in an ongoing social system, full of specific do's and don't's, rewards and punishments, preferences and aversions. The Alorese boy and the Comanche boy, for example, learn the skills and customs of their groups by doing over and over again the things their elders do. All the activities necessary to the survival of their society are learned in this way, by watching, listening, and finally doing in the prescribed social manner. In addition to learning all this information, the Alorese and Comanche boys are also developing definite conceptions of their world, of the people in it, and of themselves, as well as consistent behavior patterns based on these conceptions. The Alorese youth is reared by a mother who feeds him sporadically at her convenience. She teases him a great deal and thinks his temper tantrums are amusing. She does not physically punish him in any way, but she gives him no sense of control over what happens to him, since there are no regular times for doing anything and since his parents do as they please, not as he wishes. In fact the boy is teased and ridiculed whenever he attempts to have his own way. Slowly but surely he grows into a suspicious, mistrustful, anxious, and deeply insecure young man. He has little self-confidence or self-esteem; though intensely greedy, he will do anything to avoid a fight. The Comanche boy, on the other hand, gets consistent, noncontradictory care from his mother. His feeding is warm, loving, and unhurried. While he is given no premature responsibilities, he receives high praise when he emulates his parents. He is teased very little and seldom punished. Gradually he develops high self-esteem and much self-confidence. He is basically secure, friendly, and cooperative. He has few inhibitions, shows great enterprise, and above all is bold and daring with virtually no anxiety about injury and death.

Thus it is that every society teaches its children along two dimensions simultaneously. We learn the techniques, the skills, the customs of our group, and we also develop their loves and hates, their fears and anxieties. The discovery of this second dimension of cultural learning has opened up a fabulous new area to the scientist of human behavior. Through cross-cultural study the scientist has been able to correlate a great many patterns of child rearing with specific features of adult personality. This kind of knowledge has tremendous practical value. In the span of only a few years, we have learned the answers to many of the questions about which man has speculated for millennia. We now have much basic information about how societies create unique personality types. We know many of the constellations of family activities that are responsible for these differences. In thus learning which social factors produce an anxious and rebellious person or an enterprising and cooperative one, for the first time in human history it is becoming possible to develop the traits we want in children.

Much of our rapidly growing fund of information in this area has come from the intensive study of neurotic and psychotic individuals in our own society. To treat personality deviation successfully it is helpful to know how and why it developed. In tracing the histories of mentally ill patients, psychologists found over and over that family conditions were of critical significance in the disorder. Yet, important as these findings were, they were often criticized as applicable only to neurotic persons and consequently of little value to a general theory of personality formation. However, with the cross-cultural investigations by anthropologists of groups such as the Alorese and Comanche, it has been demonstrated once and for all that a great variety of personality traits, desirable and undesirable, have their roots in the family situation. The existence of different systems of child rearing around the world has significantly advanced our understanding of the development of personality. Once again it is the capacity to vary, to produce different cultural solutions, that has given man this new and precious key to his universe. It is possible that this is the most valuable one of all, since it allows man to look within himself and to learn the nature of human nature.

DIVORCE

Because marriage involves two or more individuals, each with varying temperaments, likes, dislikes, and sensitivities, no one expects all marriages to succeed. Provision for a man and woman to terminate an unsuccessful marriage by separating is very common. Acceptable causes range from adultery to bad cooking, from barrenness to bad temper. The remarkable thing is that, although separation is an extremely widespread human practice, the majority of the world's marriages endure until they are broken by death, not divorce. The dramatic suddenness of divorce tends to obscure the quiet but far more socially significant drama of the successful lifelong marriage.

Barrenness is an ancient and widespread reason for a man to divorce his wife or to take another. In early Sumeria there were special rules related to this marital problem. To begin with, divorce on this ground was not possible unless the wife consented and was given a money compensation. If she refused, her husband could take an additional wife. The most common solution seems to have been for the first wife to buy her husband a slave concubine. All children resulting from this arrangement were considered to be the wife's legal offspring.

In the Western world, adultery is one of the most common grounds for divorce, partly because it is often the only reason approved in a particular area. Thus it must be legally shown to have occurred even if it did not. Our attitude toward true adultery is better indicated by the mild punishment for murder motivated by witnessed sexual infidelity. Ancient Assyrians likewise frowned on adultery and associated actions. Their penalty for manhandling another man's wife was the loss of a finger; for kissing another man's wife, the loss of a lip by means of a poisoned dagger. Rape carried the death penalty. The Hittite code, while not as severe as the Assyrian law in most sexual matters, allowed a husband to kill without penalty both his wife and her lover if he discovered them in an adulterous situation. Both legal systems, however, allowed local men great freedom in the sexual exploitation of foreign women whether they were married or not.

FAMILY POTENTIALS

The various differences of marital belief and practice with which we have been concerned in this chapter fall into two major categories. One involves variations between societies in levels of scientific knowledge: the facts known about conception, pregnancy, childbirth, and child rearing. We may expect all societies eventually to have access to this valuable knowledge, although their use of it may vary considerably. As information concerning adequate child-rearing methods is increasingly diffused, we can hope that man will use it wisely to help produce individuals who are personally secure, who are enterprising yet cooperative, and who welcome human variation. But like much scientific knowledge, the potential of these facts is double-edged. As man acquires the power to create emotionally stable children, free to develop their full creative capacities, there exists also the possibility of deliberately rearing insecure, dependent, unthinking, and even willing human slaves. As with nuclear fission, however, the problem lies not in the possession of the knowledge but in its ultimate use.

The other category of familial differences considered above deals with customs and preferences that lie outside the realm of scientific evaluation. Among these are standards that determine physical beauty, whom one may court, how one should court, how one may marry, how many mates one should have, and where one should live. These are differences that man should seek to preserve and to cultivate rather than to destroy. We may not approve of a Chuckchee "wedding," but it would be a sterile world indeed if all brides everywhere wanted to wear white, listen to Mendelssohn, and have rice thrown at them. Sameness here is impoverishment, not enrichment, of mankind, because it limits human creativity in areas where there can be no best way. Variety, on the other hand, is to give free expression to man's imaginative resources and to add to the texture and richness of his family life. Ultimately it is only by cherishing variations in the human family that we can escape the standardized Hatchery and Conditioning Centre so frighteningly predicted by Aldous Huxley in *Brave New World*.

CHAPTER 9

Law and Order

Liberty is the practical recognition
of human polymorphism.

J. B. S. HALDANE

LIVING SPACE AND HOME BASE

All creatures living today have developed unique characteristics
that fit them into some particular geographical niche. A number of
animals have gone further. They make their homes in definite territories and aggressively defend them against the intrusion of other
creatures. Their defense is especially vigorous toward members of
their own species who seek to occupy the same space. You can watch
this contest for spatial position at dusk anywhere pigeons roost, and
you will already have seen enraged dogs and cats "protecting" their
territories against others of their kind. Man, too, vies for space. Zoologist Heini Hediger states it well when he writes that "Just as do
reptiles and birds, man wants to define his living space, mostly for
recognition by his own fellow beings and not so much for the information of different species. A cat in our garden or pigeons on our roof
disturb us little, but our feelings as owners of a territory are most
violently activated if we encounter a fellow being unannounced at
night in our living space." It might be added that some creatures,
including man, extend their defense range to include other species as
well. Nesting mockingbirds, for example, not only fight among themselves, but also begin aggressively to assault cats that they have pre-

viously ignored. A fighting bull, of course, will go after almost anything sizable that moves. However, in a *corrida,* unless he is skillfully
kept in action, he will often fix himself to a particular section of the
ring and refuse to leave it. Having taken such a *querencia* the bull is
far more dangerous than he was before, since the matador must then
come to him.

Territoriality, as this behavior is called, may be temporary or
relatively permanent. The nests of birds and the houses of man reflect some of the variation possible. Whether permanent or not, territories must be demarcated, and animals use a variety of methods to
accomplish this. Some of the lower primates, such as the lemur, the
loris, and the galago, use specific olfactory techniques. For example,
Hediger tells us that the slow loris will "walk importantly around
its freshly cleaned territory (*i.e.,* cage) thoroughly wetting it with
urine." Similarly, to establish their boundaries, galago will "urinate
on their hands and then moisten the branches below them." Some
lower primates like *Lemur catta* construct their olfactory fences with
a secretion from the perineal gland. Among simian primates, however, such as gibbons, orangutans, chimpanzees, and gorillas, sound
rather than smell is the more important territory marker. If you refer
back to Carpenter's observations concerning gibbon vocalizations in
Chapter 6, you will find that six of their nine basic sounds are concerned with group localization or area defense. The other great apes
also have a variety of territory-oriented sounds.

When we consider human territoriality, on the other hand, we
find that man uses three methods to draw property lines—smell,
sound, and sight. Of the group, smell is least important. Detectives
may still link perfumed handkerchiefs with their owners, and the
Berbers hang odorous stuffed sheep gut in the corners of their houses
to discourage evil spirits, but for the most part human territory is
rarely established by its scent. Sound, on the other hand, is much
more useful, especially in a variety of human interactions. A shouted
"Out of my way!" or "Get off my property!" may immediately establish
territory claims or rights. Most of man's boundaries, however, are
delineated by sight. Deeds, boundary markers, fences, and such signs
as "Posted, Keep Out" are typical symbols of territory. Through vision, man is able to control property permanently as well as *in ab-
sentia.*

A great deal of boundary marking by lower animals follows a
fixed, inherited pattern. An animal exists in a given geographical
context, and its actions are triggered in predictable ways by specific

157

stimuli. Introduce a cat into a tree containing an occupied bird's nest, and you know what the behavior of the adult birds will be. Place several chickens in an area without adequate roosting space, and a pecking contest will ensue until an exact line-up has been determined. Once established, the fowl space priorities will vary little, if any, from that time onward. Some learning is involved in all of these actions. Birds learn much about assaulting cats by trial and error. And chickens have to learn how their pecking aptitudes compare with others in the flock. Even so the underlying behavior in both cases is instinctive and invariable.

Man, to the contrary, inherits no specific territorial-centered behavior. While we mark areas in almost every conceivable way—"the old home place," our current address, our section of town, our city or village, our county and state, our region, and of course our nation —it is never an automatic process. In each case our loyalty extends far beyond a mere sense of territory and envelops many dimensions of an area. Landmarks, people, speech characteristics, typical foods, and unique customs are blended in our minds with remembered personal experiences in a place, and the total resultant feeling is usually one of warmth and familiarity. Human territoriality, then, is far more than a blind and instinctive devotion to a section of the world. Man has the potential to be and to feel at home wherever he is. Our loyalty to a particular area is a highly complex, learned attachment—much more than a homing pigeon's instinct. Just because you feel at home only in Capistrano does not mean that you and the swallows have the same reasons. A brief glance at the origins of human territoriality will demonstrate this.

In the earliest days of human prehistory, when our ancestors first began to eat meat and to develop the rudiments of culture, it was necessary for them to change drastically many of their relationships to the territory in which they lived. In the trees, their food supply had been relatively fixed and the spatial range of their activities was consequently limited. But successful hunting on the ground required far-ranging and flexible movement in the search for and pursuit of game. Such activities necessitated a number of cultural adjustments. As we have seen, some of the resulting innovations were in the realm of better weapons and traps. Others involved new social arrangements in which the necessary work was divided along the lines of age and sex. Concurrently, man also developed a conception of how best to fit the members of his group into his new living space—the idea of a "home base." The importance of this idea is especially well described

This pueblo in Mesa Verde, Colorado, illustrates one way that people have marked out the limits of their territory. In early times, these stone and adobe villages were often built in hard-to-reach canyons or under mesa walls as a protection against hostile strangers. The lower floors had no windows or doors and were reached by ladders through hatchways in the roofs. The roof terraces provided outdoor living space. Pueblos are large, averaging three to four stories high and accommodating about two hundred people. Community living on this scale means that dwellers must subordinate much individualism for the harmony of the group.

by anthropologists Sherwood Washburn and Irven DeVore in *Social Life of Early Man:*

All human societies have bases where the weak may stay and from which various combinations of individuals may move out to gather, hunt, or fight. In this location are tools, food, and normally some sort of shelter. Implicit in the idea of the home base (whether relatively permanent or temporary) is the idea that some of the group may stay there while others move out. No such "base" exists among the baboons, other monkeys, or apes. When the troop moves out on the daily round, *all* members must move with it or be deserted. We have seen sick and wounded animals making great efforts to keep up with the troop, and finally falling behind. At least five or six of these were killed, and the only protection for a baboon is to stay with the troop, no matter how injured or sick he may be. In wild primates injuries are common . . . and animals that are so sick that they can be spotted by a relatively distant human observer are numerous. For a wild primate a fatal sickness is one that separates it from the troop, but for man it is one from which he cannot recover even while protected and fed at the home base. The whole evolutionary impact of disease and accident on the human species was changed when it became possible for an individual to stay in one place and not have to take part in the daily round of the troop. Certainly one of the reasons why it has been possible for man to migrate without building immunity to local diseases is that his way of life allows him to be far sicker than a baboon and still recover. Injuries to the legs are common and far more serious, of course, for a biped than for a quadruped. It is the home base that changes sprained ankles and fevers from fatal diseases to minor ailments.

From the outset this tie to home base was probably augmented by man's growing and deepening sense of family responsibility. And as he began increasingly to value blood relationships, it is easy to see how his feelings for his territory and his loved ones were inextricably fused. Home base became infinitely more than a stockpile of supplies and a place to rest; it was a refuge of comparative safety where one loved and had children, played, and listened to the stories of the old people. In short, it became a place to cherish and to defend at all costs.

GROUP LIFE: PROBLEMS AND SOLUTIONS

Thus drawn into group life through ties of security and affection, man was not long in learning that living with others required many new cultural adjustments. If sufficient objects and ideas did not exist

to cope adequately with these problems, they had to be invented or
borrowed. Moreover, once there were solutions, group survival demanded that the bulk of these be generally accepted. Since many of
them were the rules and agreements that bound the group together
in the first place, it can be seen that optional behavior would have
led to chaos. In the day-by-day life of any group, however, disputes
were bound to arise, and all societies had to develop techniques for
settling these disagreements with a minimum of social turbulence.
No group can long survive a constant round of unresolved conflicts
among its members. Finally, it was necessary for every enduring
society to have methods for dealing with people from the outside
world. Foreign policies must differentiate between friends and enemies, and preserve the unity of the group regardless of the nature of
the external relationship. Naturally, societies vary a great deal in
their preferred solutions to these problems. As with other cultural
differences, there can, in many cases, be no best and worst way to
work out a social relationship. Such differences mirror the imaginative
use of human intellect and should be valued accordingly. In other
instances, however, it will be obvious that some political systems
abuse certain individuals and cheapen or degrade human life. These
practices are cultural differences that must be called undesirable if
we accept the basic values espoused at the first of this book. Even
here, however, one must exercise caution, since there are many occasions when such a judgment would represent our culturally based
perception rather than the viewpoint of the societies involved.

We have already learned something of the nature of human
creativity and of cultural diffusion. Neither process flourishes unless
a society encourages them. Thus, while all societies allow some individual creativity, each society is unique in the extent to which it
encourages these activities and the way in which it receives the resulting ideas and inventions. It often happens that a society will
applaud creativity in one area and suppress it in another. In the
United States we encourage the inventor of new technology, the
physical engineer, but discourage the inventor of new economic or
political systems, the social engineer. Some societies frown on technological innovation as well. As we know, diffusion is also a highly
selective, nonautomatic process. Different societies vary considerably
in their receptivity toward the culture patterns of other people. Culture may be diffused wholly, in part, or not at all, depending upon
the needs and problems of the borrowing society. Regardless of the
differentials, however, all societies have obviously made room for as

In addition to totem poles, dance masks, and coppers, Northwest Coast Indians are noted for their superb blankets. The finest are Chilcat ceremonial blankets which are worn only by chiefs. At potlatch ceremonies they are destroyed or given away in order to enhance their owner's prestige and to elevate the status of his family.

many cultural solutions to their basic problems—ideas, things, and customs—as they require for survival.

SOCIAL CONTROLS

Psychological Inertia and Public Opinion / Once practices are adopted by a society, they tend to be kept in use. The old solutions, learned early and well, are usually regarded as the best. Moreover, we soon learn that most of the other members of our society' are also using the same ones. In this way there comes to be a double motivation for following the existing customs and laws of the group. Not only does it seem more natural to do and believe the things we have been taught from childhood, but also there is group approval for such conformity. In reality it is a circular system, since the "public opinion" of parents creates the initial psychological inertia of the child, which in turn produces behavior which is usually reinforced by the public opinion of the group. The effect is such that we can speak of traditional behavior being motivated by both inner and outer forces.

It is difficult to overestimate the importance of the desire for the good opinion of other people within our own group as a force making for social conformity. Human beings will do amazing things to gain and keep the

When swung about the head on a string, these devices produce a deep, throbbing sound. In use since Upper Paleolithic times they are employed by a number of societies around the world in religious rites. It is obvious that psychological inertia has kept their form relatively constant for over 25,000 years. To what extent their function has remained unchanged during this time is a matter for speculation.

Paleolithic

BULLROARERS

Melanesian

high regard of others. Our American need to buy a bigger house, drive a new car, wear expensive clothes, and in general live beyond our means is at least partly motivated by our need for group approval. Rich men in the Kwakiutl and other Northwest Coast tribes vie for group prestige by publicly and ceremonially destroying their wealth. In such "potlatches," the aim is to enhance one's own status either by giving more property to an opponent than he can repay, or destroying more than he is able to, thus shaming him before others. These activities, which take conspicuous consumption to its ultimate extreme, show the power of public opinion over the behavior of individuals. Perhaps the clearest example of this power is found in many Asiatic countries where the fear of public ridicule is so strong that "saving one's face" frequently is thought to be more important than saving one's life.

Religion / Religious belief is another force within society which tends to encourage traditional behavior. In fact anthropologists view group stabilization as one of the universal functions of religion. Many people conform to certain customs, mores, and laws because they feel that standards of morality are involved or they fear present or future supernatural punishment. For example, the Ten Commandments of the Old Testament spell out proper moral behavior for many, and the fear of a real Hell often burns in the background. A number of Eskimo tribes will not eat caribou meat at the same meal with seal, since they believe this will offend a goddess who may then punish the people by keeping the seals away. In another connection we have commented upon the Hindu's avoidance of beef; this clearly illustrates the power of a religious belief in the perpetuation of tradition.

Centralized Authority / All societies have the social controls of psychological inertia, public opinion, and religious belief. In addition, a great many, though not all, have decided that a certain person or group should have the formal authority or power to enforce social customs and laws. As a general rule, centralized authority of this sort is a product of a settled way of life, although, occasionally, strong military leaders arise among nomadic groups. Leadership in any case may be determined in a multitude of ways. The most skillful hunter or the most powerful fighter may on occasion be chosen or may choose to make decisions involving the entire group. In other situations, as among the Arunta, the old people may automatically be accorded the highest prestige and authority. Some societies, like the Yurok, believe that the rich should have more rights and power than the poor. In most societies only male members may lead or rule. Throughout man's history, leadership has been hereditary in numer-

Social controls: Public opinion. This magnificent head, indicative of the wide variation in standards of beauty around the world, was cast in the 17th century by one of the gifted artists who worked only for the Obas, or kings, of Benin. While objects of such power appear to be the trappings of a well-established and prospering society, actually at the time of their production the kingdom of Benin was tottering. It seems that the heads served primarily to help maintain the prestige of worried rulers.

Religious activities bind together the members of a society. To the Pawnees of North America, rituals involving a medicine bundle give a sense of unity. Each village collects and wraps together arrows, bones, crystals, herbs, skins, and other sacred objects. At tribal ceremonies these sacred bundles are used by the participants to dramatize the deeds performed for them by the gods.

In New Ireland, rituals and preparations for them keep the group cooperatively at work throughout the year. The most important rites, the *Malagan*, both initiate young men into full manhood and honor the dead. For these occasions, elaborate masks, figures, and panels are made. This mask, a stylized boar's head, has tall sidepieces carved with characters from tribal mythology; these include fish, birds, and warriors. Snakes are also a common motif. After use the masks are hung in a special house and allowed to rot.

Among the Bushongo, each social rank has its own traditional cup for the ceremonial palm wine. The elaborate horned cup is reserved for the chief.

ous societies, including the Egyptian, Roman, Chinese, the Benin of West Africa, and the Incan of Peru. Additionally, in many cases the ruler is supposed to have been divinely appointed. Regardless of its type, the effectiveness of centralized authority in enforcing social tradition depends upon a number of factors which vary from group to group, as well as within the same group over a period of time. Pertinent variables include attitudes toward the traditions and laws of a society, the popularity of the leader, the standard of living, and the amount of external pressure from competing or hostile societies.

By its very nature the entire area of social control is subject to a variety of abuses. A way of life may be "oversold" to the individuals of a society, so that psychological inertia may almost stifle creativity. All new things may be suspect and the traditional view always considered best. In such circumstances children may be taught not only to honor and respect their own group above all, but also to down-

168

grade other groups and their social systems. Achievements by other societies, if known at all, may be minimized, rationalized, or viewed as threats to the established order. In such a context public opinion is also apt to serve as an oppressive social control. Individuals who do not personally feel bound by tradition may be surrounded by those who do. Innovations, regardless of their worth, may then be rejected by the weight of group opinion. The same fate also will normally await new ideas from other societies, so that diffusion becomes negligible. Religion, like centralized authority, is especially likely to exert stringent control of individual behavior. It may offer great rewards to those who support and believe the particular system, but it may also threaten with severe punishment those who renounce it. A man who shakes off a bit of traditional behavior disturbs, for a while at least, only his own thinking or emotions. If he denounces the practices or ideas of others in his group he may be considered peculiar, he may be avoided and isolated, or perhaps reprimanded

Whether with throne or robes or White House, most societies distinguish their leaders with some mark of authority. In West Africa finely carved stools symbolize the power and prestige of the ruler. The Ashanti fought a bitter, bloody war with the British to retain control of the Golden Stool that signified their independence for two hundred years. Here Sir Osei Agyeman Prempeh II sits in state, with the Golden Stool on his right.

GHANA INFORMATION SERVICES

for his novel behavior. But if he challenges the existing law and order, he may find his wealth, his freedom, and even his life taken from him. He may even find that in renouncing his religion he has lost its assurance of a desirable future life.

All social controls have this double possibility. Moderately applied, they give the society its necessary cohesion and predictability; stringently applied, they may make puppets out of men. Today, wide differences exist among societies in how much freedom individuals and groups have to criticize or to change their established customs, laws, and political systems, and in the punishment, if any, exacted from them if they try. There are no easy answers here. To endure, a society must protect its members from criminal actions and itself from being overthrown. But in securing these ends, it may oppress its members and seek to neutralize other societies by interfering in their affairs. While it is true that freedom only exists under law, it may also perish under law. Indeed, our primary quarrel with communism may lie in this area.

A fundamental question arises here. May the social controls of political systems be rated comparatively, and if so on what basis? Any answer must rest upon certain value agreements. We saw that, with family systems, if we value mental health, there are "best" methods of child rearing to produce this result. So with political systems, if we value individual freedom of expression and creativity, then there are "best" social arrangements for encouraging these qualities. As with ideal child-rearing practices, however, there is still much to learn about an ideal system of social controls. Since social controls begin in the home with parental teaching, fundamental family and political research converge at many points. Also, in political as in family research, it is the existence of differences that affords us the priceless opportunity to study their effect upon mankind. Once again it becomes clear that it is only through variation that man is able to learn about himself and the circumstances necessary for his optimum development. Had he not ceaselessly experimented with his political systems in the past, we would, of course, never have had human slavery or now be threatened by the aims of the *Communist Manifesto,* but neither would we have had the Bill of Rights, a republican form of government, and a United Nations.

SOCIAL JUSTICE

Individual Versus Individual / In the day-in, day-out process of living together, disputes naturally arise between the members of a society. All enduring societies, therefore, have made provisions for settling them. Every group allows its members to work out certain minor problems and disputes among themselves. Individuals may talk and argue and try to reach an agreement which is reasonably satisfactory to both parties. We settle problems of this sort every day. Perhaps we were shortchanged at the grocery store or a neighbor's tree endangers our garage or our little girl practices the piano when the baby next door takes its nap. If no agreement can be reached in situations like these, friendships may dissolve, and other more impersonal methods may be used to settle things.

A few groups, however, provide no methods of settling disputes beyond the direct clash of individual against individual. Among the Eskimos, for example, where there is no formal leadership or judicial structure, all disputes are resolved in one of four ways. Let us assume that an Eskimo returns from a hunting expedition and finds that one of his two wives has gone off to live with another man and refuses to return. The offended husband may simply elect to ignore the event and adjust to life with only one wife. To choose this alternative, however, is usually to invite the ridicule of the group and may well encourage someone to try to lure away his remaining wife. Usually the husband will choose to fight his rival in order to settle the affair. Since he is the injured party he is allowed to select the style of fighting. If he is young and agile, he may decide on combat with weapons. If he is strong and has endurance, he may wish to wrestle with his opponent. But if he has passed his physical prime and has seen his strength and skill with weapons decline, he will probably choose to have an insult-singing contest. Such a match always takes place publicly with the rivals taking turns shouting and singing insults at each other. The object is to lash your opponent verbally so thoroughly that he loses his composure and, consequently, his own effectiveness in lashing you. Usually such a contest favors an older man, since he has probably already had some experience of this kind and knows a great many rhymes, subtle taunts, and tricks that may cause the spectators to cheer him on and jeer his increasingly furious and helpless adversary.

Family Versus Family / In a great many societies, members use less individualistic techniques than the Eskimos and bring the weight of an entire family or clan to back up their position in a dispute. Since the bond of kinship is especially strong in primitive societies, this is the level upon which most disputes are settled. Often such settlements are effected by one family making restitution to another. The Yuroks, for example, frequently require the payment of money

Occasionally societies make common cause with others for mutual benefit. In West Africa the Gio, Geh, and Mano tribes of Liberia cooperate with the Mendi of Sierra Leone and other small neighboring tribes. The intertribal secret society, Poro, to a large extent controls the social and religious life of these tribes. At most tribal celebrations the men of this society, wearing appropriate masks and costumes, conduct the ritual. A particular spirit dwells in and gives his name to each mask.

An analogous society trains the women of the cooperating tribes. Bundu members initiate young girls into their woman's role and into society membership. After the initiation, the leaders, wearing these masks and long black cloaks of dyed vegetable fiber, return the girls to their villages.

to the offended person or his family. Even murder can be paid for in this way. There is generally a fair amount of haggling between the families involved before the "worth" of the dead man is established.

Centralized Authority / It should be pointed out that where blood ties are extremely strong, as among the Yurok, there is little likelihood of an impersonal centralized authority having enough power to settle disputes. In most of the world's societies the stronger and more extensive that family ties are found to be, the weaker will be the controls of centralized authority. Although a basic difference between primitive and civilized political systems is in the relative strength of blood ties, it should not be assumed that all nonliterate

Pieces of paper, official seals, and countless other devices symbolize the agreements among different societies. The Pintinjarra of Western Australia carry "passport sticks" which give the bearer safe passage through hostile regions.

COLLECTION OF THE AUTHOR

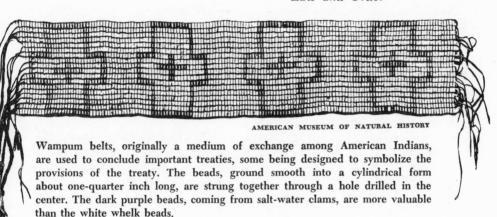

Wampum belts, originally a medium of exchange among American Indians, are used to conclude important treaties, some being designed to symbolize the provisions of the treaty. The beads, ground smooth into a cylindrical form about one-quarter inch long, are strung together through a hole drilled in the center. The dark purple beads, coming from salt-water clams, are more valuable than the white whelk beads.

societies lack the concentration of authority necessary to settle disputes and punish offenders. The Ashanti of West Africa and the Kalinga of the Philippines are good examples of primitive groups with working systems of centralized authority. Often a chief and a council will sit in judgment on serious cases such as murder. This is the practice in the villages of Bali where murder is punished by officially declaring the guilty party "dead" and advising all members of the area to ignore him totally from that time onward. Obviously this is often a virtual death penalty, since no one in his old group will respond to any subsequent need he may have. Some societies use centralized authority on only a temporary basis to settle disputes. The Plains Indians, for example, normally allow the individual great freedom in patching up his interpersonal difficulties. But when an intertribal buffalo hunt is in progress, a special police force is created to resolve disputes and to mete out proper punishment. Individual or family feuds are forced to give way to the more important economic necessity of a highly organized, cooperative hunt for meat.

Justice for All / The process of presenting complaints and disagreements to an impersonal authority for adjudication is well known and much used in modern society. Records of this type of settlement extend as far back into the past as writing itself. In this long history of disputes both with his fellows and with the established law and order, man has produced a great range of cultural innovations—judges, lawyers, juries, trials, rewards, penalties, and countless casebooks filled with the accounts of other disputes. It should be noted, however, that the sheer complexity of a legal structure is no measure

Another example of man's reliance on his gods to aid him in his darkest hours. The fact that one's opponents also seek divine aid in battle has never seemed to deter men ready to fight. These figures are carved by special craftsmen from pine trees that have been struck by lightning.

ZUÑI WAR GOD

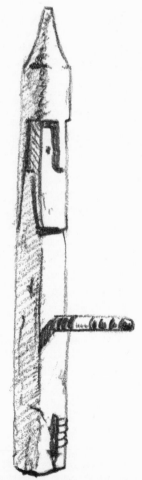

of its adequacy in providing justice for all the members of a social system. As societies increase in size, interpersonal relationships multiply along with the possibilities of law breaking and disagreements. This necessitates a swing toward public rather than private law and an increasingly complex judicial system. Yet fundamentally, the aim of any such system is to settle social disputes in a just manner. Consequently, whatever methods are used may be appraised only in terms of how adequately they serve the ends of justice. On this basis, we can unconditionally reject trial by ordeal, brainwashing, "stacked" juries, and the suppression of evidence. But it would appear to be impossible ever to determine which of several possible systems is most capable of being just. Justice may be achieved through individual arbitration, family settlement, trial by peers, or judge, or council of elders, or by any other person or group who is willing to hear both sides and attempt to be fair. It follows that, although our vast, complex, and impersonal system seems to serve us well, it is not necessarily the most desirable system for the hundreds of smaller societies of the world. In fact the more workable dispute-settling methods man has, the more able he will be to render justice in a world characterized by change and human differences.

WAR AND PEACE

"No *society* is an island unto itself" correctly extends John Donne's statement about man. Every human group has to cope in some fashion with its neighbors or visitors, its friends and foes. Often there is a peaceful relationship characterized by trade and a profitable exchange of ideas. Fortunately for mankind, and in spite of appearances, war is neither a universal nor an inevitable human activity. Modern behavioral science has shown that there is no inborn "pugnacious instinct" in man that causes him to want to fight either as an individual or in groups. Human beings have the potential, but it is a learned tendency, not a biological drive. Children may be reared either to enjoy or to detest fighting and violence. In spite of theological metaphors, man has no wild animal within that is always seeking to escape. Even in Freudian circles, the id forces are usually seen as tamed through sublimation rather than caged through repression. Today, many individuals as well as societies are dedicated to a philosophy of nonviolence or neutrality. This is clearly a learned preference. Even more devastating to the war-instinct theory is the fact that among groups such as the Toda and the Eskimo the concept of war is completely unknown. No matter what the grievance, no one resorts to war, because they have never conceived of the possibility of an entire group fighting another. Nevertheless, peaceful coexistence between interacting societies has been elusive throughout recorded history. Man has obviously found it easier to fight than to live with those who disagree with him.

Even when peaceful relationships prevail between two groups there may be a callous attitude toward the stranger when he is within our gates. Consider, for example, some of the laws of the ancient Assyrians and Hittites as they applied to their own citizens and to foreigners. In the legal codes of both societies fair dealing in business relations was prescribed between members of the same town or area. Dishonest practices were expressly forbidden, and the offender was vigorously punished. The Assyrian judges punished in the following manner anyone who tampered with

Man's provincialism is never more apparent than when he goes to war, for he always has the notion that the gods will help him—not his enemies.

HAWAIIAN WAR GOD

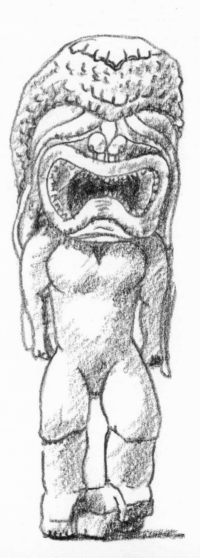

the large boundary markers which separated lands: "One of his fingers they shall cut off, a hundred blows they shall inflict upon him, one month of days shall he do the king's work." The Hittites also stressed honesty and imposed stiff fines upon thieves and those who took liberties with another's property. Stealing a stud horse or bull was punished by fining the thief fifteen horses or bulls; theft of a draft ox or horse required the payment of ten such animals as compensation. In contrast to the relatively stringent controls on commerce within the group, both Assyrians and Hittites had laws which expressly permitted citizens to charge foreigners usurious interest rates and to sell them unclean food. Many a modern traveler, returning home with an empty pocket and an upset stomach, might well believe that such laws still exist. Far from making people more sympathetic toward one another, travel in many circumstances breeds increased contempt and misunderstanding.

Since war and peace are matters that are largely regulated by a society's political system, and since modern weapons are now of such devastating potential, we have arrived at a point in history where man's reactions to political differences may well determine if he is to survive. Today two great nations, with opposing political systems, each armed with fantastic weapons, stand eyeing their differences with cold hostility. A great many wise men from a great many nations believe that a final clash may be averted only by the creation of laws governing the use of force and administered by a world commonwealth. Some suggest that the possession of "ultimate" weapons by both sides makes such an organization a possibility for the first time in history. Be this as it may, if the international control of weapons is accomplished, it will be man's supreme political achievement and one that will release undreamed of potentials for his future development. If we fail and perish, however, it will not be because human political differences are undesirable, but because we were unable to understand their ultimate value.

CHAPTER 10

Man and the Unknown

All faith is false, all faith is true:
Truth is the shattered mirror strewn
In myriad bits; while each believes
His little bit the whole to own.

THE KASIDAH, PART SIX

ANCIENT RELIGIONS

When men face situations that puzzle them or create anxiety, at least four courses of action are possible. They may ignore or retreat from the problem, leaving it unsolved. In this case nothing is answered, and should the problem arise again, there will be no help from the past. Another reaction, usually involuntary, is to become so confused, helpless, and threatened that a psychological defense system rather than a creative impulse is activated. If the threat is severe enough, neurosis or psychosis may result. Fortunately for us, most of our ancestors were both intelligent and audacious, preferring to meet challenges in a third way—head on. We have already examined this kind of response. You will recall that Old Stone Age hunters, faced with survival on the ground among large and hostile animals, and with an acquired taste for meat, developed hand axes, spears, and hunting techniques. Lacking thick fur in a severely cold environment, they mastered fire and discovered how to use skins for clothing. Other problems were solved with equal directness. Distribution techniques were worked out, mating and family systems decided upon, territories delineated.

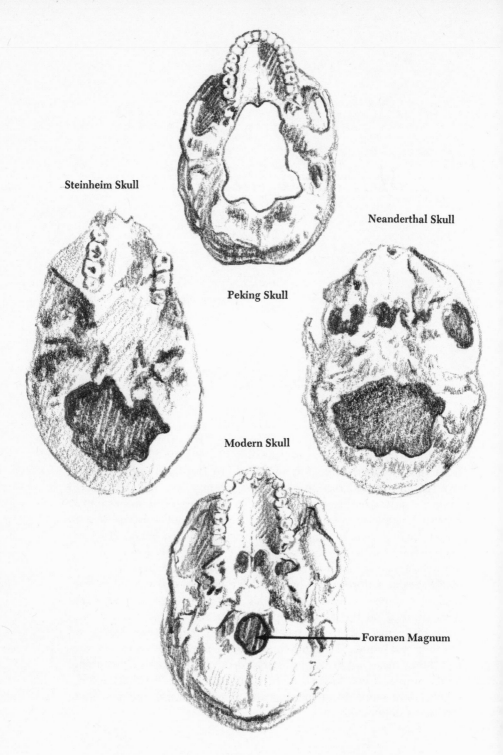

Steinheim Skull

Neanderthal Skull

Peking Skull

Modern Skull

Foramen Magnum

EVIDENCE OF EARLY RELIGIOUS BEHAVIOR

It is likely, however, that from the first, not all of man's cultural solutions followed such neat, rational patterns. Man has probably always found himself confronted with situations that he could neither predict nor explain within the framework of his existing knowledge. Why did game animals suddenly leave a favorite grazing area and how could one get them back? What were sickness and disease and what could be done about them? What were thunder and lightning? How could one explain a dream or a hallucination? What happened in death? Faced with disturbing questions like these, man developed an additional problem-solving method. He conceived of a world of unseen forces and connections between events—a world of supernatural cause and effect that he could manipulate to his advantage once he learned the proper procedures. From the very beginning, this must have been the nature of religion, just as it is now—culture which allays man's fears and explains the unknown through the belief in and utilization of supernatural forces.

Archaeological evidence suggests that religious practices began in the early part of the Old Stone Age, although in some cases the exact meaning of the materials must remain speculative. The earliest find of this nature is an almost complete skull of Peking man assembled by Franz Weidenreich; it is composed of fossil fragments, all from the same site, representing some forty individuals. The striking thing about this skull is that the entire area around the periphery of the *foramen magnum* (where the spinal cord enters the brain case), is missing; not a single bone fragment from this area was found in the cave. Moreover, the outline of the missing section is neat, smooth, and symmetrical, indicating that the skulls were not simply smashed open with a rock or an axe. The reason for getting into the cranial vault seems obvious enough—brains are an excellent food. But to open a braincase carefully, before bringing it to the cave, probably indicates more than a fastidious gourmet. Archaeologist Alberto Blanc and others who have studied the problem intensively are certain that all of this points to ritual cannibalism.

Of course the case for the antiquity of man's religious practices does not stand or fall with the Peking skull, although this is the most

Three early skulls all showing deliberate enlargement of the *foramen magnum* area. The most ancient, that of Peking Man (350,000 years ago), was reconstructed by using all the fragments of skulls discovered. Since no fragment of the white area has ever been found, its ritual mutilation is strongly indicated. The Steinheim skull (250,000 years ago) and the Monte Circeo Neanderthal skull (70,000 years ago) show the persistence of the practice through time.

ancient evidence. A Neanderthal skull from Monte Circeo and a probable Homo sapiens skull from Steinheim have the same general deliberate mutilation around the *foramen magnum.* Commenting on the Circeo skull in the book *Social Life and Early Man,* edited by Sherwood Washburn, Blanc has this to say:

Now, this intentional mutilation is *identical* to the one presently produced by head-hunters of Borneo and Melanesia with the object of extracting the brain and eating it for ritual and social purposes, one of which is the necessity for assigning a name to the newborn. In certain tribes of New Guinea a newborn child receives a name only after the killing and beheading of a man whose name is known. The father or a near relative mutilates the base of the skull of the victim, extracts its brain, bakes it with sago, and eats it, after which the infant may bear the name of the dead one. The mutilated skull is kept as a sacred object in the home until the death of the new bearer of the name.

It would be naive to assume that the Peking, Steinheim, and Monte Circeo skulls were mutilated for the same reasons as those in Borneo and New Guinea. Most anthropologists agree that the behavior of a primitive man does not illustrate that of prehistoric man. Moreover, identical behavior does not necessarily indicate identical purposes. The most we can surmise from the Old Stone Age relics, therefore, is that they indicate some sort of ritualistic use of human skulls and brains and as such seem to be the first evidence of religious activity in man.

Later evidences of religious activity are more plentiful and often appear in a context that makes their functional significance much clearer. Beginning in the latter part of the Old Stone Age we find man deliberately burying his dead, often covering them with red ochre and placing useful objects in the graves beside them. This strongly suggests human concern for the welfare of the deceased and perhaps a belief in some form of survival after death. In this period, many of man's religious practices were designed to assist him in his most important and hazardous activity—the hunting of wild animals.

Confronted by charging animals like this bull painted in a cave at Lascaux, France, Stone Age man survived by using his wits. To aid him in his fight for food, he employed axes, spears, fire, traps, and intimate knowledge of animal habits, and a belief in imitative magic. Apparently he was convinced that if he carefully drew animals being trapped or killed, he improved his chances of achieving the same result in actuality. Directed toward the right foot of this bull, which is ten feet long, is a dart or trap.

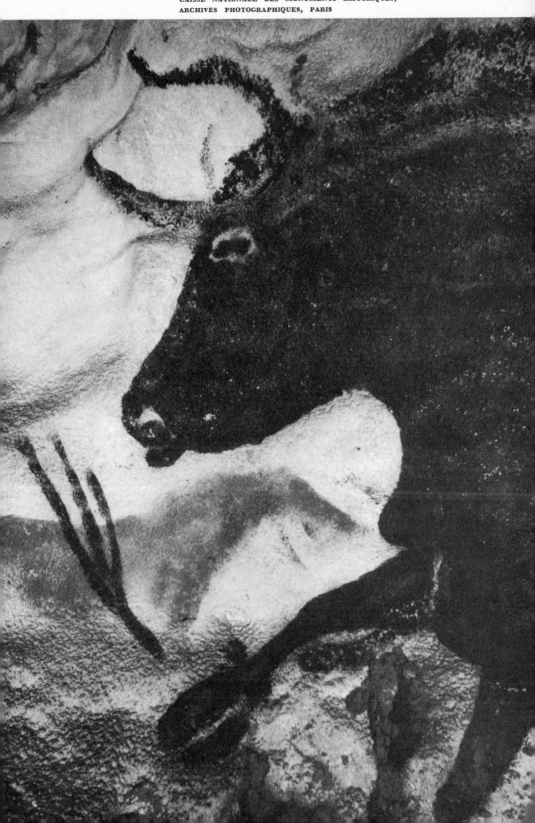

Much of the evidence for this concern is found in the cave art of southern Europe.

Beginning about forty thousand years ago and extending through the Magdalenian culture period, altogether some twenty-five thousand years, ancient men produced an abundance of naturalistic art. They executed most of their art on walls and ceilings deep within huge caves; they used a variety of mediums, techniques, and styles. Yet, although many generations of men made these paintings, their subject matter, with few exceptions, was consistently animals. In cave after cave it is the same—running animals, standing animals, animals with horns and tusks and hoofs, pregnant animals and copulating animals, animals pierced with spears and darts, bloody and disemboweled animals, bulls and bison, cows and horses, mammoths and rhinoceroses, ibexes and deer. The subject matter and the location of the art in the deepest and most inaccessible parts of uninhabited caves have convinced scholars that this was magical art. Not understanding their ability to draw, early men apparently believed that this skill had magical power. By carefully drawing the image of an animal, men gained a degree of control over living animals of the same kind. To depict spears and darts in the side of some creature was to ensure the accuracy of real weapons in an actual chase. Toward this end many drawings were made with spear marks pointing to the region of the heart while others depict the animal as wounded, headless, or dying.

All these discoveries give us a glimpse of some of the first religious practices of man. They indicate a very early belief in supernatural forces and show us something of the cultural innovations related to them. We cannot doubt that there were scores of additional practices and beliefs which left behind no artifactual record. By historic times, man had developed elaborate religious systems, which included beliefs in personal and impersonal supernatural forces, as well as practices of a magical and supplicative nature. Since all religions, primitive or civilized, have some combination of these components, we will consider them in some detail.

SUPERNATURAL FORCES

Impersonal / In a great many societies men conceive of the world about them as being permeated by supernatural forces of an impersonal nature. One such conception, the belief in "mana," is well summarized by the anthropologist William Howells in *The Heathens.*

There is probably no better example of how a basic religious feeling—a sense of the special, the supernatural—takes form as a religious belief than in the idea of mana. The word itself is from the Pacific, being common to many of the languages of Melanesia and Polynesia, but it has other names in other places. Mana means a kind of force or power which can be in anything, and which makes that thing better in its own special qualities, such as they are, perhaps to the point of being marvelous.

A man who has mana is stronger, or smarter, or more graceful, though mana is not strength or brains or agility. That man's spear or, if he has been civilized, his tennis racket, has mana if it does what is expected of it with particular sureness; but mana is something different from the niceness of balance or the workmanship which has gone into it. At the same time, if the pro who made the spear or the racket consistently turns out first-class spears and rackets, then he obviously has mana of his own, or else he has ways of inducing mana into whatever (spears or rackets) he makes. And there is no difference in the mana which is in the tool, or its owner, or its maker; it simply causes each one to excel in his special way.

Mana, then, is an explanation for whatever is powerful, or excellent, or just right. Cole Porter's "You're the Top" reels off a list of things which, if you think of it that way, have mana (Mahatma Gandhi, Napoleon brandy, and cellophane). I need hardly say that if you ever took pains to use a special pen or pencil whenever you wrote a college examination you were thinking along the same lines.

Typically, mana is a sort of essence of nature; it is not a spirit, and it has no will or purpose of its own. It can very well be compared with electricity, which is impersonal but powerful, and which flows from one thing to another, and can be made to do a variety of things, although in itself it remains the same flowing force.

It should be added that many peoples believe that man may not only manipulate and control impersonal supernatural power, but also, with the correct ritual, may actually produce such power. Regardless of its source, people frequently conceive of power as having the potential of both good and evil. Properly controlled and directed, it may bring things such as good crops, victory in battle, or wealth. When misused or approached in a careless manner, it may result in bad luck, disaster, or even death.

Personal / Many societies believe that power may also have a more personalized origin—in a god or a spirit. These beings are often given human attributes of appearance, emotion, thought, or behavior. Like humans, they may be approached through the proper words or actions and may bestow various blessings. However, they usually have a darker side as well and in hate or rage may bring down punishment on those who offend them. Any number of beliefs may surround

185

Gods have appeared to men in many forms. About a foot tall, the figure on this vase from Oaxaca, Mexico, is represented in action. The carved wood adze

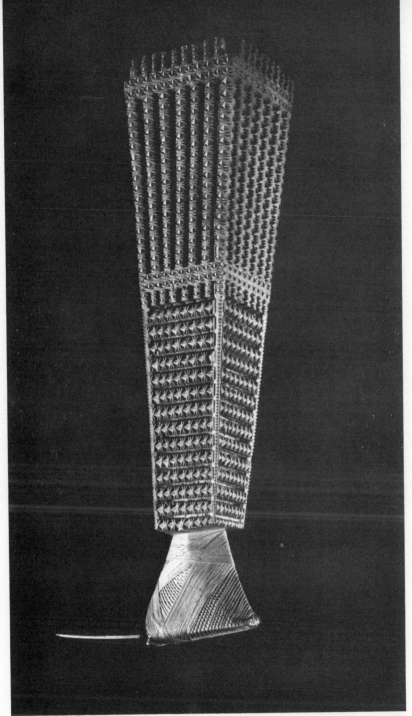

symbolizes to the Cook Islanders their god of carpenters. About three feet tall, it provides an interesting contrast with the Aztec god of song and dance.

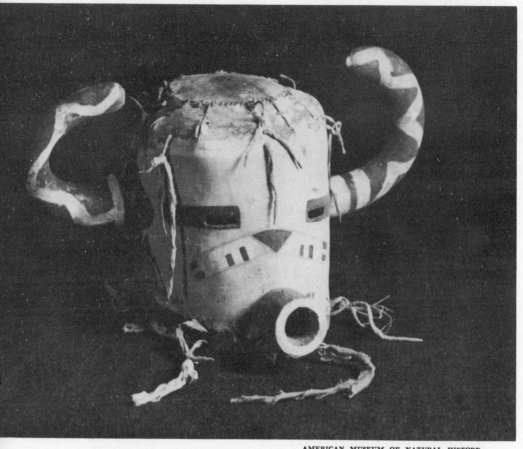

More personal are the spirit masks of the Hopi and other Pueblo Indians. The men of the Kachina cult wear painted masks and costumes representing various ancestral spirits. To please the Kachinas and ensure good crops the Hopi hold elaborate ceremonies several times a year.

the power of gods. It may be thought that they emit power like giant storage batteries, or that they, like humans, tap the great impersonal sources of the world and capture much for themselves. There may be as many types of gods as there are areas about which man is uncertain or anxious. In a few societies all power is believed to be concentrated in a single spirit. However, most societies prefer to take no chances. They feel as did the African tribesman who said, "We in Ashanti dare not worship the Sky God alone, or the Earth Goddess alone, or any one spirit. We have to protect ourselves against, and use when we can, the spirits of all things in the Sky and upon the Earth. . . . If I see four or five Europeans, I do not make much of one alone, and ignore the rest, lest they too may have power and hate me."

APPROACHES TO THE SUPERNATURAL

Believing in supernatural power, man has invested large amounts of creative energy in the production of ideas, objects, and techniques that relate him to its sources. These activities are of two general

Magic gives men confidence in their ability to control unknown forces. To ensure success in the hunt, natives of Northern Australia paint hunting scenes. In this bark painting the artist has shown the kangaroo as it appears inside as well as outside. Other drawings are often highly symbolic designs of tracks, animals, sites, and mythological ancestors.

SOUTH AUSTRALIAN MUSEUM, ADELAIDE

types: magical, or mechanical, and personal, or volitional. Magic, in this connection, includes all practices designed to cause and predict automatically certain events that are otherwise uncontrollable. It is a push-button concept. The believer feels that if he performs the proper ritual, says the correct words, does the right things, he can mechanically compel certain things to happen. Personal religious practices, on the other hand, seek to win the support of the supernatural power, which, it is assumed, can be motivated. The believer emphasizes usually, though not always, his own attitude rather than his specific actions. Personal practices are directed only toward gods and spirits, since there is little sense in attempting to motivate an impersonal force. Magic, while generally reserved for the impersonal supernatural, may also be directed toward the gods, either intentionally or because supplicative acts are performed in a magical fashion. In fact it may be said that magic exists whenever the ritual itself gains paramount importance, and people feel that through its performance they may secure results automatically. You may judge for yourself whether or not magic is the exclusive possession of primitive religions.

Magical Practices / Magic has at least four different forms:

Natives of the Amazon believe that the teeth of a jaguar contain an impersonal supernatural power. This *tsarutama* is contagious if a man wears the teeth properly and treats them ritually.

AMERICAN MUSEUM OF NATURAL HISTORY

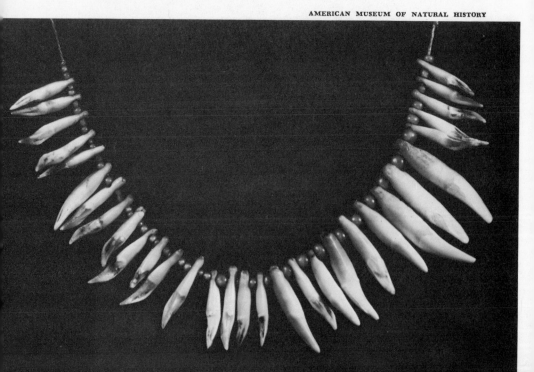

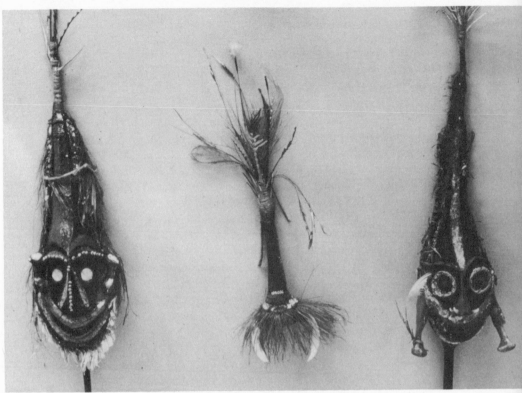

CHICAGO NATURAL HISTORY MUSEUM, PHOTOGRAPH BY THE AUTHOR

In New Britain charms like these produce a deep sleep when waved back and forth over a person. Attached to the wooden handles are pigs' jaws. On two of these charms mashed Parinarium nuts have been molded into faces. Apparently thieves find these charms especially useful.

imitative, contagious, sequential, and divinative. In the practice of imitative magic, man seeks to bring about some event by symbolically causing it to happen. Hunters of the Old Stone Age who drew the pictures of animals and then drew or threw spears in them were imitating the ends they desired. In imitative magic there is the implicit belief that things which are alike are the same.

Contagious magic is based on the idea of association. It is believed that by performing acts on something that is related to or has been in contact with a particular object or being, one may gain control over the original. If you took a bit of hair, some nail parings,

191

clothing, or other objects previously associated with an enemy, enclosed them in wild honey wax and attached them to a spear, as do the natives of western Arnhem Land, Australia, you would be practicing contagious magic. You would be convinced that the actions you directed against these objects would bring harm to their former owner; contagious magic assumes that things which were once related or in contact continue to be connected.

Sequential magic includes most beliefs and actions dealing with supernatural cause and effect which are neither imitative nor contagious in nature. It operates by assuming that when one event occurs after another, the first must have caused the second and will continue to do so. While each such belief has its own unique origin and subsequent history, probably most so-called superstitions had their beginnings in mistaken ideas of cause and effect. Sequential magic establishes that bad luck will follow you if you sleep in room number 13, or see a black cat, or eat milk and meat at the same meal. The conviction that good fortune will come if you carry a buckeye or pick up a pin also belongs to this category of magic.

Unlike imitative, contagious, and sequential magic, the magic of divination is not concerned with causing or preventing the occurrence of various events. Its aim is to predict. Toward this end a large variety of devices and procedures are used. Quite commonly the relative positions of stars and planets may be studied, heads may be carefully scrutinized for lumps and depressions, lines in the palm may be analyzed, the livers or other organs of various animals spread out for interpretation. Not as widespread but certainly as interesting are several additional practices described by anthropologist Edward Norbeck in *Religion in Primitive Society.*

Imagination has soared unfettered in inventing forms of divination. The Zande of Africa, probably the only people who have found a use for termites, make prophecies that depend on whether or not termites eat sticks placed in their nests. The diviner among the Chibcha of Colombia stimulated a flow of mucus from his nose by snuffing irritating powder made from seeds of the Piptadenia tree. Divination rested upon whether the mucus ran straight or crooked down his upper lip, which had been carefully shaved to avoid impeding the flow. The Caingang of South America gave oracular meaning to the belches of a person who had drunk *maté.*

Personal Practices / From the magical paths to supernatural power we turn to the personal. How do men seek to influence their gods? Norbeck points out that personalized religious practices have

In Sierra Leone the high priestess of the Mendi tribe's Yasai society uses divination figures. The large feet indicate kinship with the earth. During cult dances the figure gives in its motions the answers to various questions.

Zulu Shaman

Mandan Shaman

Hindu Siva Nataraja

Buddhist Prayer Wheel

North Carolina Snake Handler

never been systematically classified, but indicates that behavior of this type may be conveniently divided into propitiatory and coercive forms. Of the two, by far the most common is the former, although a surprising number of religions provide means through which man may threaten his gods if they continually fail or ignore him.

One of the most widespread techniques used by man to propitiate and to entreat his gods is prayer. A typical prayer involves a verbal approach to the deity during which one calls on him, perhaps praises him a bit, thanks him for previous blessings, makes certain promises, and then makes an appeal. Occasionally the prayer is quite direct, being little more than a C.O.D. arrangement of the "If thee . . . , then we . . ." variety. While praises are often imbedded in prayers, they also constitute a separate supplicative device as well. Songs, poetry, and prose are all much used for this purpose. In addition to these verbal methods, various actions are believed to be especially well suited for approaching the gods. While personalized supernatural beings enjoy praise, they also like offerings and sacrifices. The more precious the gift, of course, the more inclined the god will be to act in the giver's behalf. Sacrificing yourself or a member of your family is usually considered to be the supreme gift, and is accordingly rare in human society. Devotees may also approach their gods by purifying themselves, or please them by performing good works or ceremonies approved by the gods. Whatever the particular practice, the belief is that it will please the deity, and that his blessings will follow.

Thus far we have examined the basic supernatural forces that man believes in as well as the most used methods by which he approaches these forces. Now we will consider how he employs these beliefs and practices to meet some of the universal problems he faces —the forces of nature, physical and mental health, rules of social conduct, and death. In considering the role religion plays in each of these areas, you will see repeatedly how it allays fears, answers questions, gives a sense of control over the unknown, and provides meaning to human life.

THE FORCES OF NATURE

Among the most ancient and widespread sources of man's anxiety are the forces of nature. The unpredictable and often spectacular events of thunderstorms, earthquakes, fires, eclipses, animal actions, and volcano eruptions have filled him with awe and dread throughout

Powerless before the forces of nature,
man has devised various ways to
control or propitiate them.

In the dry climate of New Mexico, the Zuñis prepare for a rain dance. With the gourds and branches they carry they attempt to attract rain.

Solomon Islanders lash solemn, peering *musumusu* to the bows of their boats.
These protective spirits look out for reefs and other hidden dangers. They may
also ensure the success of dangerous headhunting voyages. The large war
canoes (sometimes ninety feet long) may have mother-of-pearl designs like
these over their entire length, with outlines of black frigate birds on the sides.

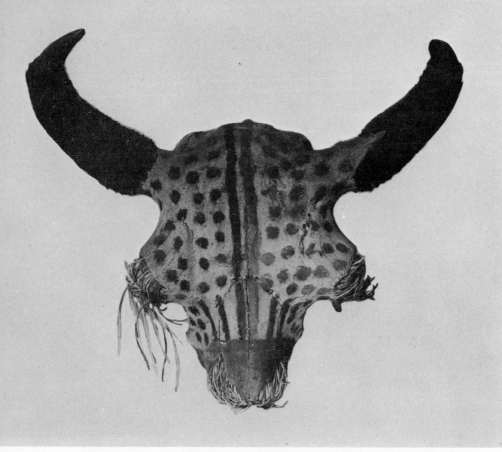

The most important religious ceremony of more than a dozen tribes of the North American plains is the Sun Dance. Held at the summer solstice the ritual reunites the separate groups of the tribe before the great communal buffalo hunt. A perfect buffalo skull, like this one prepared by the Arapahos, is placed on an altar within the ceremonial house. In this rectangular lodge, built around a tall ceremonial pole, the tribe fasts, sings, dances, and drums for four days. Some dancers tie the ends of thongs leading from the top of the pole to skewers in the skin of their chests. Linked to the pole they dance until each becomes unconscious or tears loose. Usually the dancer will experience a vision, giving him special powers and good fortune. The purpose of the Sun Dance, however, is renewal of the land, its plants, and animals.

most of his history. We need not assert, as some do (animatists), that man's reactions to these fears constitute his first religions. It is enough to know that almost every society has oriented at least a part of its ritual toward the manipulation and control of these forces.

Charles Dudley Warner's statement that everybody talks about the weather but no one ever does anything about it may be true. But it is not because of a lack of trying. Plant-gathering and agricultural societies are especially anxious about drought, and their religions are replete with supernatural techniques for controlling the rain. The Nama Hottentot, a nomadic herding people, live in an area of South Africa with a rainfall of less than ten inches a year. They are greatly concerned with securing adequate water, and in *Our Primitive Contemporaries* anthropologist George Murdock tells us that:

The outstanding event in the religious life of the Nama is the great annual rain ceremony, held in November or December when the old men judge that the summer rains are due. The entire tribe gathers on the bank of a watercourse. Each family brings a supply of milk and, if it can afford to do so, a pregnant cow or ewe. The animals are slaughtered and cut up very carefully to preserve the uteri intact. The flesh is cooked and served at a general feast. Later the old men build a special fire on the bank and dig a channel down to the bed of the stream. Then they hold the uteri of the slaughtered animals over the flames and pierce them with sticks, so that the fluid flows through the fire into the trench. Others pour milk and fat on the fire until the liquids flow copiously down the channel and dense clouds of smoke rise on high. Every one now joins in a great tribal dance with prayers to Tsui // Goab for rain and plentiful grass and food. The smoke representing rain clouds, the drenching of the fire, the flowing liquids, the uteri symbolic of fertility—all stamp the ceremony as a rite of imitative magic designed to bring rain and abundance.

You will have noted the twofold nature of the ceremony, involving both mechanistic and personalistic approaches to the supernatural—rituals to trigger the automatic forces and prayers to persuade the personal ones. A similar combination is found among the Masai of East Africa during time of drought. After building a fire of Cordia wood, a special charm is thrown into the flames and the old men sing this prayer:

SOLO. The black god! ho!
CHORUS. God, water us! Oh thee of the uttermost parts of the earth!
SOLO. The black god! ho!
CHORUS. God, water us!

Almost wholly personalized in approach, but still reflecting the ancient Vedic magical use of cows and milk is a modern Hindu rain-inducing ceremony recently reported in the press:

NEW DELHI. Hundreds of cows were brought yesterday by government order to the drought-dried bed of the sacred Bagmati River at Katmandu.

Farmers milked the cows onto the river bed, hoping to appease the Hindu River goddess so that she would ask her husband, the rain god, to end the six-week drought.

Last night it rained.

A good example of a completely personalized supernatural quest for rain is found in the Episcopal Book of Common Prayer.

O God, heavenly Father, who by thy Son Jesus Christ has promised to all those who seek thy kingdom, and the righteousness thereof, all things necessary to their bodily sustenance; Send us, we beseech thee, in this our necessity, such moderate rain and showers, that we may receive the fruits of the earth to our cómfort, and to thy honor; through Jesus Christ our Lord. *Amen.*

The fact that this prayer is for "moderate rain and showers" suggests that its author had a healthy respect for the rain-making capacities of the god who reportedly once inundated the world with water.

These illustrations of man's religious approach to the forces of nature could be extended almost indefinitely. Through the years man has produced a tremendous body of myth and ritual to aid him in understanding and controlling these forces. A few additional examples will show the range of the human imagination.

The Hopi Indians have based their entire way of life on a supernatural concept of rain and the growth of crops. In addition to thirteen major types of ceremonies they have numerous minor ones, so that "throughout the year one rite has scarcely ended before the next one begins." Other groups, not as involved with the weather as the Hopi, nevertheless have rituals to control the elements and myths to explain them. The Ainu of Japan bring rain by sprinkling the ground with water or by dragging a symbolic boat across a garden. Any Haida individual born on a fine day is believed to be able to produce more fine days by loudly forecasting them at night while a slave with a torch stands on a house roof.

Ceremonies to encourage the sun are likewise quite widespread. Many of them, like those of the Navaho, involve the symbolic use of fire and are timed close to the winter solstice. Others, like those of ancient Egypt, include dances in which the paths of the sun are imitated. The earth, too, receives its share of attention in religious rites designed to make it fertile. Human intercourse in the fields at planting time is common, records of this practice extending back to ancient Egypt and Mesopotamia. Many of the ceremonies dealing with the earth are also oriented toward the rain and sun. I have already discussed the extensive cave art of the Old Stone Age and its focus on animals. Quite naturally we find similar concern by other societies whose existence depends upon hunting or fishing. For example, the Manus of Melanesia manipulate the skull of a dead ancestor and believe that this influences his ghost not to drive the fish out to the deep water. After game is killed, the Ainu and the Eskimo propitiate the souls of the slain animals, so that they will return in other bodies to be hunted again. Members of Australian tribes believe that they are actually descended from certain animals and plants. This being the case, they believe that a man related to the kangaroo obviously knows more about that animal than anyone else and is certainly the person to hunt it most successfully. However, he is not allowed to eat its flesh for his own food, but must give it to the other members of the tribe, lest the totem animal be offended. These members, in turn, may not eat the flesh of the animals they are related to but must also distribute it among others. Thus everyone eats what others kill, and no one eats his own relations.

It may have occurred to you by now that most if not all of the foregoing beliefs and practices have no scientific value. By and large they rest on false assumptions, mistaken notions of cause and effect, and erroneous conclusions. While there is yet much to learn about the forces of nature, the boundaries of scientific knowledge have been tremendously advanced in recent years. We know that no amount of magic or prayer or ethical behavior will help the sun to rise, bring the rain clouds, make the game animals plentiful and easily killed, or cause the crops to grow. For those who will see, these things can be shown. But for millions of people even today, to accept scientific explanations for natural phenomena is to go against part of an established religion. And since religious belief usually involves the emotions as well as the intellect, people resist change. Even so, it is probable that science will easily win in this area, since it gives man far more demonstrable control over his environment than even the best supernatural measures. Meanwhile, we should not minimize the great value of the myths and rituals that relate to natural forces. Taken as a whole these beliefs and practices have given man hope where there was none, confidence in the face of great odds, and very probably both the conviction that he could prevail and the will to do so.

SMITHSONIAN INSTITUTION, BUREAU OF AMERICAN ETHNOLOGY

To protect their own bodies against physical harm, people employ various devices. The Arapaho believed that certain shirts had the power to stop bullets. This "ghost shirt" belongs to the brief period in the 1890's when, in anticipation of the coming of their Indian messiah, the return of the buffalo, and the disappearance of the white men, the Plains Indians participated in a Ghost Dance cult.

PERSONAL WELFARE

Man's concern over his physiological and psychological condition is probably as lengthy and as varied as his interest in the natural world about him. Sickness, accidents, anxiety and fear, dreams and hallucinations must have forced him to invent explanations and techniques for their control from the very earliest days of culture. Many volumes in fact have been written about the history of man's attempts to treat himself for his various ailments. An extended review of the varied supernatural beliefs and treatment of disease and accidents is neither possible nor desirable here. Rather we will consider one example from a primitive and one from a civilized society and compare the techniques and functions of the two approaches.

Among primitive societies disease is believed to come from a variety of sources. Causal agents may be enemies, spirits, gods, too much mana, personal sinfulness, natural events, or simply bad luck. Whatever the origin may be thought to be, treatment usually entails a wide mixture of rational, empirical, and supernatural techniques, together with a great deal of faith in the local doctor. Here is an account of the healing practices of the Witoto as described by George Murdock in his book *Our Primitive Contemporaries.*

The Witotos attribute sickness to possession by an evil spirit sent by a hostile sorcerer. The care, which logically consists in the exorcism of the spirit, is the primary function of the medicine man, or shaman. Each clan has one of these practitioners, always a male, whose prestige and authority often exceed those of the chief. . . . The medicine man engages in the ordinary activities of the clan, but distinguishes himself from others by his peculiar food habits, his refusal to depilate, his solitary wanderings in the jungle, and his bizarre attire. His paraphernalia include a rattle, some small magic stones, a jaguar skin, the claws of a condor, and similar objects. He is a skilled conjurer, ventriloquist, and maker of poisons, and is credited with the power of conversing with spirits and assuming the form of a jaguar. Though he can divine the future, warn of impending attacks, and work black magic, his chief function is the cure of disease. When he succeeds, he receives presents for his services. When he fails, he has an impregnable defense: a rival sorcerer used stronger magic.

A shaman lances ulcers, sets fractured bones in splints, applies poultices, and prescribes emetics, narcotics, and herb infusions. That his percentage of cures is large, however, is due less to the efficacy of his remedies than to the implicit faith of his patients. In refractory cases he resorts to extreme methods. In the darkened house at night, stimulated by coca and tobacco, he works himself into a state of wild exaltation, shaking his rattle, beating the floor, and uttering intermittent shrieks and howls, until he summons the spirits with whom he is to converse. Their presence is made manifest to the onlookers by the cries of animals and birds which seem to stream in from all sides—by virtue of his ventriloquistic powers. Eventually, having diagnosed the ailment with supernatural assistance, he collapses with exhaustion. On recovering, a half-hour later, he commences his treatment. He breathes on the affected part, sucks it and spits out a black liquid, and finally produces some object, such as a thorn or a stick, as the material embodiment of the offending spirit.

While this description may pretty well fit our conception of what ought to go on in a primitive healing ritual, it must be said that its wildness is not characteristic of the techniques used by most non-literate societies. Also, in contrast to the Witoto, many groups such as the Nama Hottentots believe that sickness comes from any of several sources rather than only one. As is characteristic of most primitive treatment of disease, however, the Witoto approaches to the supernatural are magical rather than personal. In general they attempt to force a cure by doing something specifically oriented toward the afflicted area or the believed source of sickness.

A number of religions may be said to combine magical and personal techniques in the treatment of disease. This is true of the Hindu approach to disease, for example, and of many Christian revivalists currently on the American scene. The healers in the latter group are deplored by most medical practitioners, but are safe from prosecution because, instead of charging for healing, they take only "free-will" offerings. Most such healers assert that they are simply instruments through which the "healing power of the Lord" is transferred to the patients or that the Lord gave them a "vision" or a "revelation" of how to heal. Since many Americans believe in religious visions and revelations, none of these claims are contested; some may, in fact, appear as full-page newspaper spreads with no danger whatever of a suit for false advertising. Here are a few recent notices from Atlanta and Memphis papers. Each had photographs of the healer in action surrounded by huge crowds, and one had several "Before Prayer" and "After Prayer" healing photographs.

ERICKSON CAMPAIGN SWEEPS INTO SECOND GREAT WEEK!

Faith Memorial Packed with Hundreds to Attend

Revival Healing Campaign

Cancers—Tumors—Blindness—Deafness—Arthritis

Paralysis—And Many Other Afflictions

Have Been Healed the Past Six Nights of This Revival and

Divine Healing Campaign

A noted world-wide evangelist who has preached to millions around the world. A man of faith who has prayed the prayer of deliverance for thousands who have been healed!

Signs! Wonders! Miracles! In Every Service

Healing Cloths Sent on Request

Faith Memorial Church

"Where the Healing Waters Flow"

✦ ✦ ✦

MIRACLE REVIVAL

SIGNS   WONDERS   MIRACLES

According to the Bible

God's Man of Faith and Power!

with the world's greatest miracle revival evangelistic party

A. A. ALLEN

World's Largest Tent

Thousands Filled with the Holy Ghost in a Single Service

Multitudes Saved from Sin in a Single Old Fashion Altar Call

"NO MAN CAN DO THESE MIRACLES EX-
CEPT GOD BE WITH HIM" St. John 3:2

SPECIAL SERVICES!   Holy Ghost Night! Youth Renew Night!

Mass Miracle Night! Liberation Night!

Double Portion Night!

Spiritual Gifts Receiving Service!

Special Miracles Night!

Proxy Night (when you come for another)

Private interviews with A. A. Allen at 2:30 service for those that are desperate and feel they need special help. Prayer cards for healing line given (free) only in afternoon service.

✓ ✓ ✓

AREA WIDE HEALING REVIVAL

Gene Ewing   Coming to Memphis, Tennessee

Hear Miracles as They Happen on Radio KWAM

Coast to Coast, Thousands Are Blessed, Saved and Delivered

Braces, Crutches, Wheelchairs, Glasses

Have Been Discarded After Prayer

Three Services Daily

10:30 A.M.	2:30 P.M.	7:45 P.M.
Rev. Ewing explains Faith and the Sick are prayed for. Some of the greatest things happen in these services.	The Healing Card is issued in this service only. A Great Holy Ghost Service.	Hear Rev. Ewing and entire staff in an old-time camp meeting revival.

Free Ambulance Service and Beds for the Sick to Lie on Waiting Prayer. The Sick that are Emergency Cases are Prayed for in every Service.

✦ ✦ ✦

At services such as these, faith that one will be healed is of paramount importance. To establish this complete belief, songs are sung, prayers offered, emotional sermons delivered, and special healing cards or cloths distributed. Frequently members of the congregation intensify the mood by "speaking in tongues," shouting and chanting things like "Sweet Jesus," "Praise the Lord," and "Hallelujah," waving their arms, and on occasion jumping and flopping about in the aisles in emotional abandon. During the actual healing ceremony there is often a wailing type of prayer accompanied by a "laying on of hands" by the minister. At appropriate intervals his request for supernatural aid may change to sharp commands such as "Heal! Heal! Heal!" or "Now, Lord! Now! Now!" Faith for healing to occur is far more magical than personal in nature because the believer expects an automatic cure if his belief is deep and strong enough. The deity does not suddenly take pity on a person with cerebral palsy or a missing thigh bone (both claimed to have been divinely healed by the evangelist Oral Roberts). The afflicted person must first achieve "perfect faith"; then healing power will flow from God through the minister into him. Supplications, prayers, and thanksgiving, also much used, of course, represent the more personalized aspect of the healing service.

There can be no doubt that the activities of a Christian healer and a Witoto shaman have a great deal in common and that their successes are due primarily to similar psychological states in their patients. All faith healers do well with bodily malfunctions having a psychogenic basis. Blindness, deafness, loss of speech, and the paralysis of various parts of the body are often symptoms of hysteria (a neurosis fully explored by Sigmund Freud and others), and these are the conditions most amenable to Amazon jungle and sawdust trail therapy.

Because the modern psychotherapist can produce "signs, wonders, and miracles" in a more sophisticated way, it is easy to write
off the entire human medicine show that is oriented toward the
supernatural as nonscientific and of no real value. Here again, however, we must accept the enormous value that these myths, magical
rites, and supplications have had and still have to men faced with
the terror of unknown forces that wreck their bodies and minds. Certainly no one defends the Hottentot dung poultice as aseptic or the
injuries that result from a premature throwing away of one's crutches
as desirable. The Witoto bird and animal calls are sheer fakery, and
I have my doubts about the sincerity of the "men of God" who attempt to heal hydrocephaly or claim to create new bones in people.
But none of these healers would flourish if his services were not
needed. People wish to have their organic problems looked after, but
more than this they wish to have their attendant anxieties ministered
to. The modern physician probably fails to do this in spite of his
hospitals, antibiotics, and tranquilizers. In his haste to diagnose and
treat the body, he has largely ignored the mind and emotions. This is

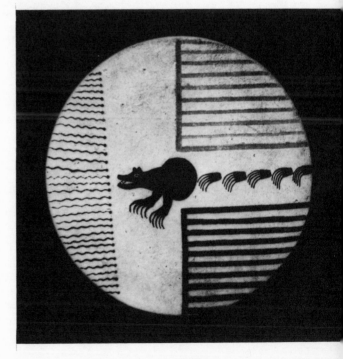

Another Plains tribe made
this buffalo-hide shield to
carry into battle. To the
Kiowa the magical design
rather than the toughness of
the hide affords the real protection. The bear is shown
running toward a line of
flying bullets; he leaves
footprints as he emerges
from the clouds. Other
"medicine shields" may use
the buffalo, also facing bullets, celestial bodies, or abstract designs.

SMITHSONIAN INSTITUTION

207

*To believers
these two masks
have powers
that convey
physical benefits.*

The fertility mask of the Yoruba Gelede Society is worn in ceremonies invoking the cooperation of the spirits of the dead, the purpose being to increase harvests and generally improve the welfare of the people.

The Healing Mask of the Iroquois False Face Society plays an important part in the treatment of disease by spiritual means. One of a number of Iroquois secret societies, this one deals with the horrible bodiless Flying Head demons that haunt the forests and bring disease to the Indians. Both men and women may join the society if they are ill or if they dream that they need to be members.

all the more unusual since physicians are the first to admit that they must have the patient's full confidence if they are to succeed. Thus, while scientific medicine is the basis for the truly effective treatment of disease, healing in human beings is far more than organic therapy. Effective medicine men throughout history have recognized this and, by getting the "full confidence" of the patient, have relieved his anxieties and in general allowed his body to heal itself.

No one who is acquainted with Arunta black magic doubts the power of faith where the health of the body is concerned. Among this group, to be wounded, however superficially, by a spear that has been magically pointed toward the victim and "sung over" is tantamount to death. "No matter how slight the wound," says Murdock, "if the victim suspects magic, he refuses food, pines away, and dies. Nothing can save him, not even European medicine, for faith can kill as well as cure."

ETHICS

The standards by which people conduct themselves form the ethical system of their society. In many societies, such as our own, this system is part of religion. I have commented previously on the contribution of religion to the stability within a society. By supporting the basic social values and goals, prescribing general rules of conduct, and outlining the elements of "the good life," religion may give its adherents a sense of continuity and security. In general we feel that if we perpetuate these traditions, live in this way, do these things, then the supernatural forces will continue to prosper and to protect us. The Ten Commandments illustrate how formalized these ethical controls may be, and the Old Testament accounts of how Jehovah blessed or punished his people show what may be expected when the rules are kept or broken.

Many primitive parallels exist. The Wabena of Bantu South Africa, for example, believe that the ancestral spirits are "the source of all law, the givers of all prosperity and the senders of all misfortune." To live according to the socially accepted rules is to secure the blessings of the ancestral spirits; to break them is to anger the spirits and bring disaster. Knud Rasmussen made similar observations about the Eskimos. He reported them as stating:

We observe our old customs, in order to hold the world up, for the powers must not be offended. . . . If we did not take these precautions, . . . we believe that great masses of snow would slide down and destroy us, that snowstorms would lay us waste, that the sea would rise in violent waves while we are out in our kayaks, or that a flood would sweep our houses out into the sea.

While all societies have many such supernatural prescriptions for social behavior, primitive peoples are more inclined to leave the actual teaching of ethics to their families, not to a formal religious structure. This has convinced some people that nonliterate groups have virtually no ethical standards and that their religions are definitely inferior. Both conclusions are, of course, highly ethnocentric. All societies have ethical systems that carefully delineate approved and disapproved interpersonal behavior. Moreover, the link between religion and ethics is certainly not an inevitable one, and does not indicate anything about the value of the system. Actually, modern psychological research in values indicates that the family is the best place in which to teach ethical behavior to anyone. And lest we think that it requires a religious connection to elevate one's ethics to the proper plane, consider philosopher Richard Brandt's description of the family-taught ethics of the Hopi Indians in his book *Hopi Ethics:*

The Hopi conception of the ideal man has only a few main themes. The good Hopi, in outline, is approximately as follows:

A good family man: is industrious and thrifty, works to provide more material comforts for his family, is concerned for his children and has affection for them, is prudent and cautious.

Agreeable in his social relations: is polite and kind, does not hurt others' feelings, does not get into disputes, does not complain, does not get angry, does not gossip, is not grouchy or mean, heeds valid criticism without taking offense, is cordial, does not cause trouble by having affairs with other men's wives.

Not dangerous: he is peaceable, does not get drunk or into brawls.

Cooperative: helps in community enterprises, does what he is asked to do, gives time and effort for the group and especially for relatives, can be counted on for advice, is reliable.

Generous: is generous with his help and food; is sympathetic, hospitable, and unselfish.

Honest: pays his debts, keeps his promises, respects property rights.

Modest: is not a snob but not bashful.

Quiet and unobtrusive: does not try to be important, has no political ambitions.

Cheerful: does not worry, is not vengeful or jealous, maintains his mental equilibrium, is indifferent to unjust criticism.

Manly and brave: (but on the submissive side in social relations).

A good worker: is persistent, foresighted, and careful.

211

While the Hopi disapproval of any form of aggressive behavior is somewhat unusual among primitive peoples, the rest of their ethical system is not. Many other nonliterate systems are as fully committed to the ideals of love and helpfulness. A further example is provided by anthropologist Paul Radin, who has outlined in his *Primitive Man as Philosopher* the major Winnebago Indian ethical principles as follows:

1. It is always good to be good.
2. What does life consist of but love?
3. Of what value is it to kill?
4. You ought to be of some help to your fellow man.
5. Do not abuse your wife; women are sacred.
6. If you cast off your dress for many people, they will be benefited by your deed.
7. For the good you do every one will love you.
8. Never do any wrong to children.
9. It is not good to gamble.
10. If you see a helpless old man, help him if you have anything at all.
11. If you have a home of your own, see to it that whoever enters it obtains something to eat. Such food will be a source of death to you if withheld.
12. When you are recounting your war deeds on behalf of the departed soul, do not try to add to your honor by claiming more for yourself than you have actually accomplished. If you tell a falsehood then and exaggerate your achievements you will die beforehand. The telling of truth is sacred. Tell less than you did. The old men say it is wiser.
13. Be on friendly terms with everyone and then everyone will love you.
14. Marry only one person at a time.
15. Do not be haughty with your husband. Kindness will be returned to you and he will treat you in the same way in which you treat him.
16. Do not imagine that you are taking your children's part if you just speak about loving them. Let them see it for themselves.
17. Do not show your love for other people so that people notice it. Love them but let your love be different from that for your own.
18. As you travel along life's road, never harm any one or cause any one to feel sad. On the contrary, if at any time you can make a person feel happy do so.

To back up their ethical standards of behavior, many societies utilize the concept of "sin." Since prescribed standards vary enormously from society to society, it is not surprising that the sins of one religion are often the virtues of another. As we know, one of the greatest Hindu sins is to kill and eat a cow. A Maori warrior of New Zealand, on the other hand, receives supernatural blessings and power if he eats the flesh of a bull prior to battle. One of the worst Christian sins is to cohabit with another man's wife. Among the Eskimos, however, a man is ethically required to offer his wife to visiting hunters. Within our own social system, we have competing religions with different ethical requirements. The Jewish Sabbath, which is designated as a day of rest, is a twenty-four hour period beginning Friday night at sundown. This means that every Saturday morning non-Jewish shopkeepers selling their wares or people cutting their lawns violate a part of one of the world's oldest ethical systems. People believing in most of the Protestant faiths, but not the Catholic, may divorce and remain free from sin. A book could be filled with similar examples, each showing that universal ethical principles are difficult to find 'and that any attempt to evaluate ethical systems cross-culturally is largely futile, since acceptable social behavior depends to a large extent on the time, the place, and the situation.

DEATH

Of all creatures on earth, only man has the intelligence to recognize his own existence in time, realize that he cannot live forever, and dread the inevitable end. In view of the great involvement of all religions with death, it is likely that this is the fear that haunts man more than any other. Howells, in *The Heathens*, describes the fear of death and the beliefs it engenders with great insight.

Human beings live a long time, and each one has a personality, a constant combination of the qualities of character and mind, which impresses itself upon the sympathies of all who know the man, and profoundly upon those who know him best or are his relatives. . . . And when he dies, . . . the effect is far more than mere sorrow at his dying; it is a real psychological amputation, . . . and we wish with our whole wills that he may yet live somewhere, if not here. But it is for ourselves as well that we detest death, . . . and we never escape the fear of it. We cannot; we know we must die in the end, and that is everyone's personal hell on earth. . . . Somebody else's death may suggest the existence of souls, and almost make us see one, but the prospect of our own ends would force us to invent souls anyhow. Much as we would like to live forever, we can be willing to relinquish the body if our real inner selves can remain imperishable. The idea of an immortal soul fulfills our wishes, and there is no society, anywhere, that dares to disbelieve it.

Man's imagination has been fully exercised in hypothesizing the nature of his soul and its disposition after death. Few societies, if any, have identical beliefs about the soul, but each is inclined to accept its view as the most probable one. Many Christians think of the soul as a type of personality essence which inhabits a body during its life and is liberated after its death. After this release the soul is believed to be judged for the life the person has led and sent accordingly to Heaven or Hell. The belief in eternal life is central in Christianity and is specifically promised in New Testament passages such as John 5:24: "Verily, verily, I say unto you, He that heareth my word, and believeth on him that sent me, hath everlasting life, and shall not come into condemnation; but is passed from death unto life." Conceptions of the nature of Heaven and Hell vary a great deal among Christians. Some believe that the saved will spend an eternity gathered around the heavenly throne praising God. Others believe that the afterlife will be more like a giant family reunion. Many do not try to guess specifically, but are sure that things will be well set up with no work, hunger, suffering, crime, and the like. Not all Christians believe in Hell, but those who do are sure that it is a fiery punishment which lasts forever. Catholics temper this belief somewhat with the concept of Purgatory, where those just moderately bad in their life on earth may be saved by the prayers and good works of those who still live. While Christians generally are aware that other conceptions of the soul and its destiny exist, they must dismiss them as false, since they believe that their information came from the actual son of God who obviously should know what his own home is like. Yet all societies have excellent credentials for their ideas about life beyond the grave. In fact, the gods themselves often reveal these things to members of some religious systems.

From the anthropological point of view there can be no superior or inferior accounts of phenomena outside the actual experience of man. If you are comforted by the thought of Heaven and behave ethically because of your fear of Hell, then obviously your beliefs benefit both you and your society. But the Maori have the same right to believe that punishment and reward are not features of an afterlife, and that departed souls may choose to live either on earth or in the sky. And who is to say that there are no concubines in Heaven if more than 500 million Mohammedans believe that there are?

The religions of man have served him long and well. Belief in supernatural forces has given him incalculable relief from the great, crushing anxieties of life. In time of heartbreak and desperation, there have been the balm of belief and the reassurance of ritual. Today, however, we are witnessing the tremendous growth of scientific

214

Through masks and figures many societies keep in touch with their dead. Among the most striking of the African funeral masks are those used by the Maw Society of the Ibo tribe in Nigeria. White paint, representing the spirit of the dead, enhances the skeletal features of the mask. Deceased ancestors communicate with the living during the funeral dances in which these masks are used.

knowledge in several of the areas once the exclusive domain of religion. While religion has long given man a sense of control over nature and in the treatment of disease, we cannot doubt that science can handle these things better, and will do so increasingly well in the

215

The Bakota create these figures to act as intermediaries between the living and the gods. Made of copper on wood, they are attached to baskets containing the skeletal remains of departed ancestors. Tribesmen pray and make offerings to the indwelling spirits.

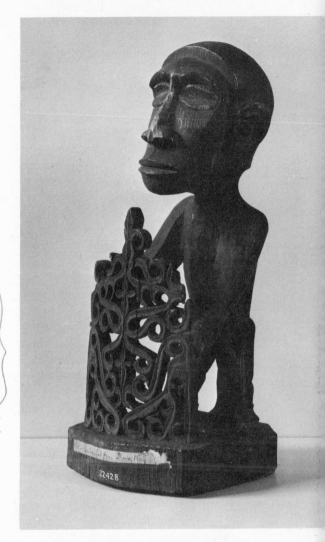

The natives of Dutch New Guinea make sacred mortuary figures to house the spirits of the dead. About a foot tall, the wooden *Korovar* is carved during a man's lifetime so that his spirit may enter at the moment of death. Sometimes the skull of the deceased is placed inside.

UNIVERSITY MUSEUM, PHILADELPHIA

future. Where ethics are concerned, science has little to tell us thus far, although the day will probably come when it will be possible to say, "If these are the values your society wishes, then these are the rules you must live by." In the area of death and beyond, however, the religious approach seems to be unchallenged. Science has no way of establishing the existence or nonexistence of a soul or an afterlife, and

217

may never have. But since this is so, all conceptions of eternity are accurately described as religious guesswork, and one man's faith must obviously be just as good as another's.

"THE TRUE FAITH"

It is interesting that some religions feel that it is their duty to sell their beliefs to members of other faiths. Objectively this process involves a tearing down of differing belief and ritual and the substitution of a new system. Justification for this procedure is usually found in the sacred literature of the religion, from which certain members draw inspiration and go forth as missionaries. For the most part, we must assume that missionaries of any faith are serious and dedicated persons, convinced of the rightness of their cause. Also they are extraordinarily ethnocentric in supernatural matters, for in no other way could they believe that, of the thousands of religious systems in the world, theirs alone is the correct one. As a group they are unable to see that the variety of man's religions is a testament to the greatness of whatever soul he may have, that a world of identical religious belief would mirror the death of the creative imagination that is uniquely human. Somehow a rain dance becomes superstition that needs to be eradicated. Somehow the desperate shaking of a rattle over a dying man is not a magnificent symbol of man's refusal to submit to the terror of the unknown, but is tossed aside as savage magic. Forgotten are their own earnest prayers for rain, their deeply moving entreaties for the life of a loved one, and the fact that it is science, not religion, that has given the world objective knowledge of weather and disease. Certainly no missionary considers himself a destroyer of faith. And yet, unless he truly knows the deep needs and fears of a people, he is apt to tear down far more than he can build. He may in fact destroy a faith and be incapable of filling its place.

The missionary, of course, is a reflection of the ideals of his religion, ideals which taken together contain the noblest thoughts of man. It is all the more ironic therefore that these very religions engage in the same ethnocentric squabbles, proclamations that "this is the true way," and threats of punishment for those who reject them, that characterize the political systems of nations. Somehow, one would expect something a little more charitable from those who preach charity. But since religions are so much a matter of the emotions, it is likely that this will be the final area, rather than the first, where mankind says with Thomas Jefferson, "Blest be God for difference."

CHAPTER 11

Man at Play

Fine Art . . . is by no means bound up
with any one type of human culture.
It is, on the contrary, a hardy plant that
blossoms in all climates and at all seasons.

R. R. MARETT

ANTHROPOLOGY AND ART

All of man's culture is a demonstration of his intellectual powers. Much of it displays another quality as well—the human capacity for feeling. In fact we often categorize culture in terms of the relative amount of emotional expression it contains. The more rational an innovation is, the more it tends to do something obvious and concrete, the more apt we are to term it a technological invention. When, on the other hand, it reflects the emotions of an individual, his moods or fears or fantasies or desires, we are more likely to call it art. There are no hard and fast lines here, however. A great many useful inventions are artfully done, clearly evidencing emotional expression as well as technical skill. It is reasonably simple to make an effective hand axe once you learn how flint fractures and you practice a bit. Rough but efficient and serviceable implements can be turned out with a minimal expenditure of time and effort. But from Old Stone Age times onward man has obviously *enjoyed* working with flint and has seldom been content to settle for utility alone. Any good museum display can make this clear immediately. This affective involvement with materials has resulted in axes and spearpoints and arrowheads of high artistic merit as well as technical worth. Consider the cave art of the Old Stone Age. As we have seen, its primary function was to assist man magically in his hunting. Yet in techniques, mediums, proportion, and realism we see disciplined imagination at work. And we may be sure that in executing these figures artists received basic creative satisfactions in addition to whatever feelings were inspired by the magical rites involved. Thus, much of man's creative work

To make useful objects man must have technical skill. To make these objects art he must inject his own feelings into his work. The Incas of Peru developed the art of pottery to a high degree. Their work shows great subtlety of form and color. On their pots they elaborated animals and various other figures. They also portrayed important people, as on this jar.

AMERICAN MUSEUM OF NATURAL HISTORY

While chiefly noted for their carving of totem poles, houses, and canoes, the Tlingit Indians also ornamented many serviceable objects such as paddles, ladles, and combs. The wooden bear on this comb holds a fish. As with most Tlingit bears, the nostrils are prominent and the tongue protrudes from a mouth full of teeth.

Each of these embellished musical instruments shows great skill in conception and execution. The head of the bull on the Sumerian harp is covered with gold leaf and has a beard of lapis lazuli. The Mangbetu water buffalo drum is of wood carved with geometric patterns in low relief.

In any art form, organization and unity are important. The two South American maté sets show remarkable decorative coherence. Maté is a tealike South American beverage made from the leaves of holly. It is brewed in the gourds, also called maté, and sipped through tubes (*bombilla*).

from early times onward has had this dual aspect—a useful function coupled with an emotional investment. In fact, it is likely that all creative effort by man contains affective as well as intellectual components, but with the arts ranging high in emotional content and technology ranging low.

Art, however, is more than the outpouring of human emotion, although this is doubtless one of its basic ingredients. For emotional expressions to be termed art, it seems necessary that feelings be channeled into some sort of organized format with a reasonable degree of skill. A wild shriek of anger is not art, although an Arunta song of hate probably is; murmured words of affection between lovers are not art, but Elizabeth Browning's "How Do I Love Thee?" is considered to be. The difference in both cases is not in emotional content, but in the organization and skill with which the emotion is made manifest.

Art, like all the great areas of human expression—language, economics, family, politics, and religion—is universal. All men every-

Similarly remarkable is the unified design of the Baluba ceremonial mask. Made of woven fiber, it is completed with shells, bones, and feathers.

where dance, play games, make music, decorate objects, tell stories, and engage in joking. Yet each society has its preferred avenues of emotional expression and its own art forms. Bizarre as some materials, methods, and products of artistic activity by other societies may seem to be, we may be sure that each fits into a meaningful cultural context of shared values and beliefs. None is inherently superior or inferior to any other. There is no objective way to call a bullfight better or worse art than figure skating or temple dancing. Moreover, like other forms of culture, the value of art has nothing to do with whether or not it was produced by a highly civilized society. There is both good and poor primitive art, but it cannot be graded on the basis of how we react to it. In all societies art reflects a number of interrelated factors such as available leisure time, geographical location, relative isolation from other cultures, technology, personality traits, and cultural needs. In considering some of these variables and the art forms directly influenced by them, we shall see something of

Often, art objects from other cultures possess some form or quality that "communicates" to us spontaneously. Other levels of appreciation open up as we learn more about the culture that produced them. The Manus coconut ladle with its wooden handle and gourd bowl appeals to us though our way of life differs from that in the Admiralty Islands. Similarly we do not need to have seen an alpaca to appreciate this silver Incan figure.

AMERICAN MUSEUM OF NATURAL HISTORY

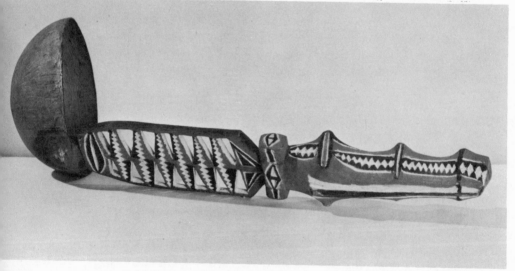

AUETÖ

KARAYÁ

Bats — Wasp Nests

Uluri — Bats

Fish — Rattlesnake Skin

Fish — Snake

Fish — Snake

Young Bees — Snake

Outside of its society of origin, this art would normally be appreciated only for the beauty of its design. This is because it is highly symbolic in nature, and each design stands for something not manifest to the outsider.

the tremendous range of artistic activities engaged in by man and perhaps catch a glimpse of the surge of human emotion that underlies each expressed form.

LEISURE TIME

Many societies lead a very precarious existence, barely able to gather and kill enough food to sustain them. Eskimos, African Bushmen, and native Australians are groups of this type. Life is hard, and much of their creative energy is expended in the day-by-day process of keeping alive. Moreover, they have little time free to express whatever emotional needs remain. It is not surprising that these groups do not produce a large amount of art. Their nomadic existence further limits their artistic output, since there are no permanent villages in which to store materials, tools, and productions. Significantly, the plastic arts are mainly restricted to the ornamentation of useful tools and weapons, while the "portable arts" of singing, dancing, and story-telling are more elaborate. Yet, in spite of their situation, many Australian tribes have produced a permanent art form and have successfully related it to their migratory existence. Flat, oval pieces of stone and wood are beautifully carved and painted with designs of symbolic religious significance. The tribes hide these in various "storehouses" along their route. On returning to the areas from time to time, group members use these *churinga* to aid them magically in hunting, winning wives, and curing diseases.

We may contrast the meager artistic production in these hunting and gathering societies with the all-encompassing artistic life of the agricultural Balinese. On this Indonesian island where food is plentiful and the climate benign, there is much leisure time. Here as nowhere else in the world we find a society devoted to drama, decorative art, music, and dancing. This is not to say that an artistic culture is an automatic consequence of much leisure. Additional factors may encourage a society to use its leisure to elaborate its social organization or religion. But in any case, leisure time is the essential ingredient, and in Bali it is lavished on the arts. Even small children are introduced to musical instruments and dance movements. By six years of age many are playing in the village orchestras and performing intricate dances. In fact, the Balinese say that one of their basic dance forms, the *lègong*, can only be danced well by children. Leisure time in Bali is filled with an almost continual round of dances, dramas, parades, musical events, and the preparations for these activities.

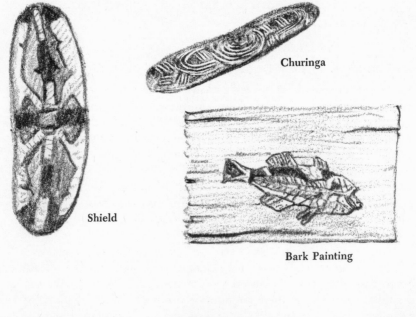

Shield

Churinga

Bark Painting

Dancer

Mask

Pengeta

The difficult hunting existence of Australian natives narrows their art to the relatively simple decoration of weapons, religious objects (*churinga*), and bark. The Balinese are an agricultural people, have little difficulty in securing food, and devote great amounts of leisure time to making elaborate masks and costumes, ornate objects of various types, and to music and dancing.

Neighboring villages compete with one another in composing and playing music, and cash awards are often given to the winners. Perhaps the best indication of how involved the Balinese are with their arts may be found in this description, which originally appeared in 1935 in the journal *Character and Personality*, by anthropologist Jane Belo, who lived with them and knew them well:

Whenever there is a performance of dancing, drama or the shadow-show, the entire village attends. The audience is packed closely around the four sides of the "stage"—an oblong of level ground marked off with bamboos. The first arrivals squat as near as possible, folded up into the least possible space and pressed against each other, the late comers stand in rows eight or ten feet deep at the back, the rearmost able to catch only an occasional glimpse of a performer's headdress. In this tight formation the audience remains from the beginning, which for a play may be anywhere between the hours of nine and midnight, to the end which comes about dawn. The whole temper of the audience is, from the actor's standpoint, ideal—watching, concentrated as one man, happy and pleasantly disposed in the warm contact of a large group of their kind, in festive mood, ready to enjoy themselves to the utmost.

ENVIRONMENTAL RESOURCES

Every society has its acceptable and preferred means of artistic expression. In the plastic arts, at least, some of these preferences are determined by the available resources. On Easter Island, for example, there are no large trees, but there is plenty of volcanic rock. Obviously, if islanders wished to have monumental art, it had to be an art of stone, not of wood. And so it was. Ancient artists found a good supply in the crater of an extinct volcano and set to work on the spot carving giant human figures out of stone. When the images were almost complete, they were cut away from their backgrounds, laboriously lifted out of the pit, hauled away and set on end facing out to the sea. The fact that these figures weigh as much as twenty to thirty tons indicates that some of the artists must have been good engineers as well. Another Easter Island art form that is directly influenced by the treeless environment is jewelry. The only wood of any size that natives see is the driftwood that occasionally washes up on beaches. In fact, wood is so rare that it is treated as we treat precious stones. Just as a diamond cutter will study his material intensely so that when it is cut there will be little waste, so the Easter Island artist studies and treasures his wood. Generally the chance form of the flotsam will dictate what figure is to be carved.

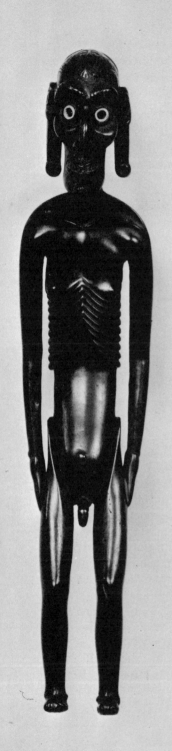

In striking contrast to the Easter Islanders, the Indians of the northwest American coast have a monumental art of wood. Living in a setting of gigantic trees, these tribes produce a great variety of art forms, virtually all from wood. In addition to beautifully carved and painted totem poles ranging from thirty to ninety feet in height, they carve and decorate the corner posts, doorways, interiors, and furniture of their houses. They also make elaborate dance masks, often with hinged sections that reveal a mask within a mask, fashion sixty-foot war canoes, and even use strands of cedar bark for the warp of their ornate and superbly made blankets.

THE CHOICE OF MEDIUMS

Whatever the resources of an area, any material has its limitations as well as its values, and many art forms reflect these qualities. The quantity and quality of colors will vary, depending on available mineral, plant, or synthetic resources. Some rocks may be ground, others must be chipped, and still others cannot be worked well at all. Skill creates the pleasing effect of a finely flaked arrowhead, of course, but it is the natural quality of flint that this skill uncovers. Woods vary a great deal, some lending themselves nicely to cutting, shaping, and boring. Others split and splinter easily, are full of knots, or are too hard or too soft. Metals, too, vary in their malleability, brittleness, and luster. Bronze and copper acquire their best appearance when

On Easter Island where there are no large trees, driftwood has the scarcity value of precious stones in our society. Consequently it is worked with great care and reserved for religious carving or jewelry. Often its original shape dictates the form of the finished object. This is an ancestor figure, *moai kavakava*, and resembles the emaciated appearance of a mummy.

UNIVERSITY MUSEUM, PHILADELPHIA

Geography plays a surprisingly important role in art, not only in determining the materials available but also in influencing the artists' feeling for form. On Easter Island, people pounded and chiseled their monumental figures out of tufa from the craters of extinct volcanoes. This material is quite porous, and hardens when exposed to air. Some of the larger figures stand more than thirty feet high and weigh more than twenty tons.

hammered, brass looks best when polished, scraped, or gouged, and iron is best just as it is cast. There are hundreds of other materials used by man in his arts. A complete listing would probably mention every substance that he has ever encountered, including clay, shells, feathers, hair, skin, blood, bones, and dung. The fact that we approve only of the clay, shells, and feathers in this list has nothing to do with the artistic possibilities of the other materials. Good art is as possible through the skillful and emotional organization of cornflakes and bed lice as it is through the use of burnt umber and egg whites. Each substance on earth has a unique form, color, and texture and, when used properly, may become art.

The Indians of the northwest American coast, unlike the Easter Islanders, have an ample supply of wood. They have transformed many of the region's trees into totem poles thirty to fifty or even ninety feet tall. The poles serve as memorials to the dead and as symbols of family status. They depict family legends or display family crests, but the figures do not follow any general plan or order on the poles. Contrary to popular belief, the poles have no religious significance.

AMERICAN MUSEUM OF NATURAL HISTORY

Like other Northwest Coast tribes the Kwakiutl are renowned for their wood-working. Their dramatic masks, which sometimes may be opened to reveal another mask inside, represent spirits, animals, and mythological ancestors.

The art mediums exploited by man go well beyond the use of the earth's physical materials. Sound may also be artfully made, either by speaking, singing, or manipulating an instrument. Motion may become art through the dance or through a great number of gestures. As with plastic materials, there are no best or worst sounds or motions for the production of art. Few Westerners enjoy Oriental music or the high-pitched, nasalized singing of the Near East, but much of it is excellent art. Moreover, there is no motion of the human body, sexually suggestive or otherwise, that cannot be a part of great art. In all these mediums, however, man often severely limits himself. He selects this small group of materials, that tiny group of sounds, and a minimal set of bodily motions and decides that art must lie within these boundaries. Very occasionally he borrows a form or adds something new. But a generation of psychoanalysts have still not convinced fastidious American mothers that mudpies and fingerpainting are always fun and sometimes art. Nor has there yet been an older generation which approves of the music and the dances of the young.

THE ARTIST

Just as the mediums used in art vary from society to society, so do the temperaments, needs, and personalities of the artists. No two men have identical emotions, perceptions, and skills. Whatever the art form or the material employed, variations in the finished product will come from the artist himself. This may often be seen in the comparative skill of the work. And, unless the individual is simply working a machine or assembling parts, there will be additional differences as well.

Observers who think that all masks from a particular African tribe are identical are as naive as those who think that all African faces look alike. The idea that primitive art is characterized by a dull, gray sameness is pure fiction born of perceptual ethnocentrism. Naturally, some societies insist on more rigid adherence to certain forms than others. But even in these groups control is not complete, and there are usually other artistic areas where relative freedom prevails. In our music we have relatively rigid forms for the symphony, but encourage experimentation in jazz; in painting we are rigid about portraits, less so about landscapes, and fairly liberal about abstractions. The Balinese have the rigid *lègong* dance form and the free and frenzied "trance" dance form. Spanish bullfighting allows maximum individual artistry within a highly formalized, ritualistic framework. Naturally, **to those** who know nothing of *corridas* all matadors look alike, but any *aficionado* can see tremendous variation in the styles and techniques of, say, a Belmonte, a Manolete, and an Arroyo.

A good example of the amazing individual variation possible on a single theme in a single medium may be found in the wooden antelope headdresses of the Bambara people of West Africa. Anyone who browses through a few books on African art can find photographs of these unique figures, which are recognized as some of the world's finest wood sculpture. While most of the headpieces have small antelope statues on them, the figures show endless variation. In his book on African sculpture, Ladislas Segy describes five separate major types but notes that "the variation within each group is so great that none of the known examples are similar." Thus it would seem that, however limited the subject matter and materials may be, creative artists will somehow thrust their individuality into their productions.

SOCIAL VALUES

Thus far we have considered leisure time, available mediums, and individual personalities as factors making for artistic variation among different societies. These things are reflected to some degree in all works of art. Beyond doubt, however, the most important forces behind differences in art forms and emphases are the cultural needs and values of a society. It is customary in the United States to think of the arts and recreation as the meringue on the pie. These activities are considered pluses or bonuses to be enjoyed when the serious work of making a living has been taken care of, and not before. No self-respecting automobile salesman would settle for one less sale per week in order to visit the art gallery or devote an afternoon to landscape painting. He might take off for a round of golf, but here he is forever playing for prospects, as many of us have learned. It would be ludicrous to think that our salesman would ever reverse his work-leisure schedule by selling cars only on Saturdays and Sundays and painting during the rest of the week. Even if he could make a living this way, he would be unhappy, because from boyhood onward he has been convinced that work is sacred. Not working brings him intense feelings of guilt as well as unfavorable public opinion. Our society values work so highly that, after a lifetime at it, people have difficulty retiring. Everyone has heard statements such as "It's great to be back in harness again!" or "His retirement is what killed him." Moreover, for an American male to be extraordinarily interested in the arts often earns him the title of sissy, bohemian, or queer. Flower arranging may be a major art in Japan and a good hobby for American women, but few American men would admit enjoying something like this, even if they did. Along the same line, imagine how this announcement by a college senior would be received by his parents. "Folks, I've decided not to go into medicine after all. I'm going to be a poet."

The Russians have glorified work even more than we, and seek to stimulate it with quotas, awards, penalties, titles, and medals. Three paths lead to the highest Soviet decoration of hero or heroine: many children, great bravery, or hard work. Of the three, the exaltation of work lies closest to the heart of communism. It is no accident that the *Communist Manifesto* begins with the cry "Workers of the world, unite!" The glory-of-work theme runs throughout the communist world and pervades every aspect of their culture. Naturally the arts have been drawn into the net. The best art or literature or music or drama by communist standards must have a theme or message that in one way or another praises the worker or damns the "capitalist" —preferably both.

These two views—that art is strictly for pleasure and should be enjoyed after the real work has been done and that the main value of art is to glorify work—are only two of the scores of views man has in this area. They are significant here because they demonstrate the pervasive role of cultural values in the production and function of art.

THE FUNCTIONS OF ART

Only in the Western world do we find art neatly staked off as something removed from everyday life. This is primarily due to the fact that we generally expect all art to have an aesthetic quality. A common basis for the judgment of artistic merit is how beautiful an object is and how much pleasure it brings. In keeping with this idea is our custom of using art primarily to decorate with, not to do things with. Yet, even our decorative art is for the museum or the wall or the mantelpiece, not for the kitchen sink, the garbage can, or the broom. To most of us, art has become a very narrowly circumscribed area of man's endeavor indeed.

From the cross-cultural point of view, however, art has many functions. Thus, while all art has an aesthetic component in the larger sense of being organized, it does not in the narrower sense of being beautiful. Beautification is one possible function of art, but by no means the dominant one or for that matter an indispensable one. Frequently some other function of a work of art will minimize or ignore whatever aesthetic qualities may exist. An aesthetically superior club or statue may be destroyed in favor of an inferior one, if circumstances convince the user that the latter is a more powerful weapon or instrument of magic. In many cases a single work of art may perform two or more functions simultaneously. An elaborately carved Ashanti or Dahomey stool from West Africa, for example, is aesthetically pleasing, a symbol of power and prestige, and often stands for a household or lineage god as well.

Aesthetic / The art functions mentioned—aesthetic, status, and religion—are products of and vary according to the needs and values of particular societies. Of the three, we are most familiar with the function of beauty, and our initial reaction to art is usually on this basis. Most of us would probably appreciate primitive art that consists primarily of formal design and elaboration of the object. We admire arrowheads, stone axes, Navaho blanket designs, and if we have seen them, the brightly colored feather cloaks of Hawaii. The Bambara antelopes offend no one except sticklers for photographic art, and many of us would be attracted to Polynesian tapa (bark cloth) designs, the mother-of-pearl inlay work from the Solomon Islands, and the intricately carved shell ornaments from New Ireland.

Yet we know how tremendously cultural standards of beauty vary. You will recall that in the Miss Universe contest most of the contestants did not leave their appearance totally to nature, but had artfully aided their cause with paints, scars, binding, tattoos, ornaments, and clothing. The results were anything but universally appealing. In fact it is likely that much of our emotional rejection of primitive art occurs in the area of personal ornamentation. This can be seen if we contrast two types of art regularly done by the Maori of New Zealand. This group is considered to be among the finest wood sculptors in the world, primitive or civilized. They also like to tattoo themselves, and they put many of their best designs on their faces. Here, of course, our aesthetic ideas separate totally. To us a design on a housepost is one thing, but the same design on a human face is another. Our rejection is emotional, so we miss the fact that the facial artist must have immense skill, that any mistake will be permanent, and that the best work is adroitly tied into the natural curves, depressions, projections, and lines of the face. Even if this idea intrigues you, you probably will not like the entire story. For the Maori cut off and save the heads of their deceased loved ones. Naturally they do an artful job here,

Solomon Islanders create many shell ornaments for breast, ears, and forehead. This shell pendant, almost seven inches in diameter, sets off a handsome tortoise-shell ornament.

Looking at the art of other societies, Westerners often judge it on emotional grounds alone. We respond immediately to the appealing design of the Fiji tapa cloth and the Solomon Island pendant but are probably repelled by the Arunta body designs and the New Ireland statue. Tapa, or bark cloth, comes from the inner bark of mulberry, juniper, or similar trees, which has been soaked and pounded together. In Fiji, elaborate designs such as this are usually stamped on the cloth.

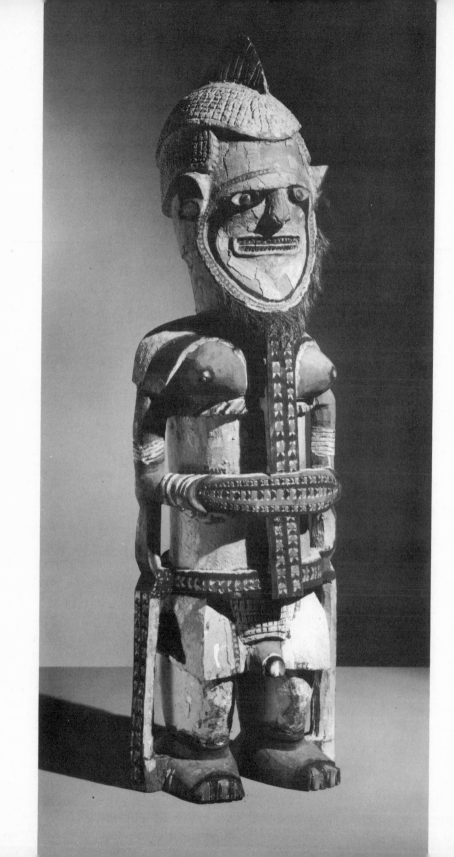

too—removing the brain and smoking the head, but they obviously are more attached to the earthly remains of Uncle George than you or I would be. Before dismissing this as pure savagery, however, remember that in life a Maori is primarily recognized, as any of us, by his facial features. Since his distinctive tattoo is an integral aspect of his face for decades, and one that changes very little, it must come to be considered as natural to him as his nose or eyes or ears. Remember too that in life this beloved visage was never photographed or painted and after death would disappear forever but for the art of head saving. Thus it is by this, to us, ghoulish process that the Maori expresses some of his tenderest sentiments.

Status / The status function of art is much less familiar to us than the aesthetic function. Yet we know of the significance of crowns and thrones although they are alien to our way of life. Art for status' sake is also to be found in hats, gowns, and mansions of the wealthy, who can afford the unique rather than the mass-produced design. In-

The Aruntas of Australia work their ceremonial designs slowly and skillfully. They are made of eagle-hawk down fastened to the skin with human blood.

AMERICAN MUSEUM OF NATURAL HISTORY

The compact, ferocious-looking Uli figure honors a deceased chief in New Ireland society. Bearded, with phallus and breasts, the painted carvings play an important part in ancestor rituals. Following elaborate secret ceremonies, from which women are excluded, the figures are carefully wrapped and stored.

CHICAGO NATURAL HISTORY MUSEUM

terestingly, status may also be had by collecting the works of art which no one else can afford to buy, and perhaps giving them to museums and galleries. American status, however, is largely a matter of wealth and position and has few of the richly imaginative trappings that characterize other societies. Men on their way up in the New Hebrides Islands of Melanesia get this idea across by carving huge figures from the inverted trunks of tree ferns at every major step of their climb. These carvings, often twelve feet high, with painted faces and large round eyes, are set into the ground around the village area as visible proof of one's increasing rank. As we have seen, rank among the Indians of the northwest American coast is determined in great potlatch ceremonies which involve large scale property giveaway and destruction. The intriguing aspect from the standpoint of our present discussion is that virtually every object destroyed in these contests is a fine work of art. Favorite items for burning are blankets woven of mountain goat wool and cedar bark with elaborately conceived and beautifully executed animal designs. Even more valuable are the etched and painted shieldlike forms made of copper; these are frequently smashed to shame a rival. Beautifully executed and worth hundreds of blankets, it is obvious that their aesthetic value is of secondary importance to their status function. There is no question but that both blankets and coppers, in spite of their beauty, are of far more value to their owner destroyed than adorning his house or person.

The highest status among the people of the Amazonian Jivaro goes to the greatest warriors; this is measured by the number of enemies they have killed. Since the locus of a man's power is considered to be in his head, the Jivaro decapitate their victims to gain control of this strength as well as to have visible proof of their prowess in battle. After taking the head, they peel the skin from the skull. Once free of bone, the skin is boiled for several hours, treated with hot stones or sand, smoked for about eight hours, and then polished and decorated. The more shrunken heads or *tsantsas* a man has, the more power he is assumed to control, and the higher his status in the group. The fact that this practice rests upon a way of life devoted to war

t is frequently said that primitive art is far too static and tradition-bound to be reat. While subject categories may be more rigidly prescribed by a primitive ociety, there is frequently unlimited room for individual expression within hese areas. Some of the variations on the Bambara antelope theme, shown ere, demonstrate this.

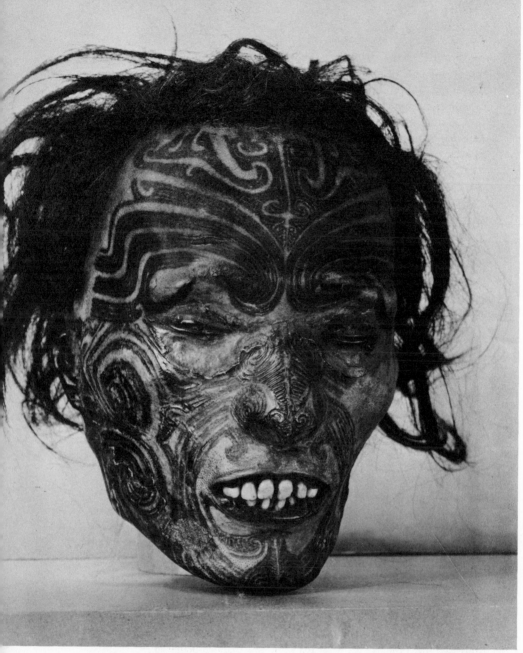

The New Zealand Maori, like the Marquesans, another Polynesian people, decorate their skin by tattooing. Families often preserve the heads of their loved ones. Maori men receive a face, thigh, and upper trunk tattoo; the women usually have only a lip and chin tattoo, with occasional designs between breasts and navel and on thighs, hands, and arms.

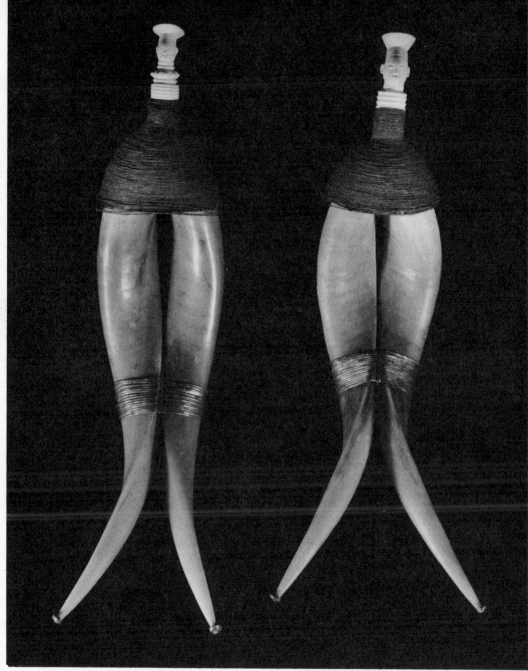

Man's need to shape the world about him artistically is reflected in many ways.
These sensitively conceived Mangbetu bottles are horn. The ivory stoppers
with their elongated heads reflect this tribe's standards of human beauty.

Art often shows the status of its possessor. To make this superb cape the Hawaiian artist needed the feathers of hundreds of birds, preferably red, yellow, and black. The feathers are woven into a meshed net and overlap from top to bottom. These capes are worn in battle or for special ceremonies by the nobility only, the most lavish being designed for the king.

should not obscure the fact that a *tsantsa* is a work of art. We can deplore the endless round of blood feuds and feel shocked by this use of a human head, but the skill, the organization, and the emotion involved all show us art, just as the use of the *tsantsa* shows us its status function. It is interesting how extensively the idea of a shrunken head seems to have appealed to man's imagination. Elman Service tells us in *A Profile of Primitive Culture* that "Tourists in Ecuador and Peru have provided a lively market for *tsantsas,* and thousands of counterfeit Jivaro heads have been sold by enterprising manufacturers during the past 100 years. Most of them are monkey or sloth heads; others are from unclaimed hospital dead." Obviously one does not have to be a Jivaro to collect heads, and not all the motives are for status!

The trophy head or *tsantsa* gives its possessor great prestige and magical power. The Jivaro of Ecuador shrink the head of their enemy as visible proof to ancestral spirits that a wrong has been avenged. Preparation of the head requires both skill and artistry.

AMERICAN MUSEUM OF NATURAL HISTORY

Religious / We have seen that some of the earliest art was magical in nature—oriented toward the procurement of game. In fact, throughout man's history, the religious function has been one of the most important in artistic production. Today in Christian churches several art forms are used to induce a religious mood: architecture, stained glass, pictures, altar trappings, crucifixes, organ music, choirs, and chants. Significantly missing from the list, but found throughout Africa, the Near and Far East, and the Pacific, is religious dancing. Mohammedans exclude all representational art from their lives by a strict interpretation of the Second Commandment: "Thou shalt not make unto thee any graven image, or any likeness of any thing that is in heaven above, or that is in the earth beneath, or that is in the water under the earth." However, they have developed an elaborate art of design, which they employ in frescoes and mosaics in the

In religious observances art has an important function. Sand paintings are a unique form of art employed by the Navaho in healing ceremonies. They are created out of ground clay and rock of different colors. The powders are skillfully sifted by medicine men through their fingers into a bed of sand. This scene is from a rite to heal a child. The figure in the painting shows a benevolent war god—Slayer of Enemy Gods—standing on lightning and with lightning in his hand. At the conclusion of the ceremony the painting is erased.

AMERICAN MUSEUM OF
NATURAL HISTORY

In the *Malagan* ceremonies of New Ireland, participants wear crested helmetlike masks depicting clan ancestors. The crest, which is built up of yellow, blue, red, and white fiber over a wooden frame, follows the old style of wearing the hair during mourning. The masks may also be worn during courtship.

mosques. Hindus probably have the most lavish religious art of the world; their ornate temples are covered with sculpture which illustrates events in their sacred literature. Sculpture abounds within the structures as well, particularly focusing upon images of the generative organs and statues of elephants and bulls. Buddhists have a less ornate religious art, but in addition to the endless statues of the Enlightened One, they devote much time to the arrangement of objects in space to achieve peaks of contemplative and perceptual satisfaction. You may find it rewarding to look at some pictures of Zen gardens.

Most of the arts employed by the major religions are found in their sanctuaries to help instill an aesthetic-religious feeling in the devotee. In primitive religions, however, we find much art produced for a specific ceremonial and with a specific function. Often when the event is over and the object has been used, it is considered to be of no further value and is discarded or destroyed. In such cases, it seems apparent that its primary, if not only, function was religious in nature. Man seldom deliberately destroys objects whose basic use is to give him aesthetic pleasure. For instance, let us look at Navaho dry painting. This art is produced by pouring fine streams of colored earths from the fingers into various designs on the ground. The paintings vary in size from a foot across to some twenty feet in diameter and are used in healing ceremonies. There are over five hundred different traditional designs, each having its own special potency. Service describes the use of the paintings as follows:

For the cure itself, the appropriate painting is made on the floor of the hogan, to the accompaniment of the related song and prayer. The patient is then seated upon the painting in a ritually prescribed way and the treatment begins. First, the singer gives the patient an infusion of herbs to drink; next he touches the feet of a figure in the painting and then the feet of the patient, chanting at the same time, "May his feet be well. His feet restore unto him." The same procedure is followed for the knees, hands, shoulders, breast, back, and head, that each member be restored. When the patient has finally risen, the painting is destroyed bit by bit, following the order in which it was made.

Another example of religious art that is functionally employed and then discarded comes from New Ireland. At an elaborate ceremony in honor of the dead, these people display and use a great number of masks, figures, and reliefs. Even expert carvers require nearly a year to make the large amount of equipment. Yet after only two to four days ceremonial use most of the carvings are discarded and allowed to rot.

Perhaps the best known of all magically related primitive art forms are masks. These always mysterious, often wild and ferocious looking creations have captured the imaginations of civilized men everywhere. Museums and private collectors all over the world have procured masks, and several American manufacturers are busily turning out reproductions for home decorative purposes. While some of them, such as a special variety made by the Eskimos, are for comic use, most primitive masks have a clear-cut religious function. Among the Hopi, they are used in Kachina dances oriented toward securing rain and making crops grow. In the Bundu and Poro secret societies of West Africa, they have a variety of functions ranging from puberty rites and initiations to divining the cause of disease and increasing the harvest. The skull-like masks of the Nigerian Ibo are specifically made for use at funerals and are believed to be the medium through which the ancestors speak to the living. Indians of the northwest American coast make a large variety of masks, most of which are highly abstract animal forms. They are used in ceremonial dances that commemorate the mythical events in the history of the group. Iroquois Indians of a special healing society carve masks out of living trees, embellish them with horsehair, and use them in the curing of disease. If you have already seen some of the masks described above, you will assuredly have reacted to their highly imaginative shapes as well as to the skill with which they were executed. Some of them, such as the Dan masks of West Africa and the Hopi Kachina masks, are attractive even by Western aesthetic standards. Others, like the Ibo funeral masks, the Iroquois healing masks, and the *Malagan* fertility masks of New Ireland, seem grotesque and weird. In museums almost all masks make striking exhibits; in use during religious rituals, with the bonfires, the chants, and the dances, they are art functioning as religion with all the raw, unbridled emotional expression that this makes possible. It should be stressed, however, that the masks themselves are never mistaken by their wearers for the gods they represent. The same is true of the religious figures used by primitive man. Regardless of what you may have heard, the "heathen" does not bow down to "idols" any more than a Christian genuflects to crucifixes.

MAN AS CREATOR

The varied world of art shows the glory of human diversity as no other facet of culture can. For with art, man is expected to let himself go, to exercise his imagination to its utmost. With a world full of different arts, we have the product of this imagination at work within thousands of varied environmental and cultural contexts. If we can rise above our provincialism and objectively behold the vastness of man's existing creative efforts, we will know that art is not optional or petty with the human animal. It is his saving grace. For it is the one area of all his cultural activities where his intellect and his emotions may fuse easily and naturally, where he may become a whole man. Those who are afraid of new artistic expression, whatever it may be, are denying the very nature of being human. For we are both thinkers and feelers, and to create in the arts is to reach for the summit of human experience. Thus conceived, the vastly different arts of other peoples should never be threatening but seen as clear symbols of man's unending effort to express himself through the creative use of his mind and his emotions.

CHAPTER 12

Human Potentialities

So the world must be kept safe for differences.

CLYDE KLUCKHOHN

MAN'S RISE to greatness as an animal has been shown to
be a product of biological variation through time. Mutations have enabled him to adapt to his climate, to disease, and to varying food
supplies. Through genetic change, our line developed dexterous hands,
sharp eyes, upright posture, large brains, and permanent sexuality.
Our present racial varieties show clearly that man, wherever he has
found himself, has had the genetic resources to prevail.

The cumulative product of these biological variations was a creature capable of shaping his own environment—a human being. As he
became increasingly adept at changing his circumstances, man became
decreasingly dependent upon biological adaptations for survival. He
could invent a device or technique to cope with the problems of his
environment; he did not need to wait for a suitable mutation. Moreover, since millions of creative thoughts and acts are possible in the
time required for one adaptive mutation to take hold, the new form
of adaptation was far more rapid and flexible than the old. From pas-
sive autoplastic clay, man became active alloplastic potter.

With culture aiding his survival, man multiplied rapidly and scattered himself about the world. Wherever he went he took with him
the joys and problems inherent in group life. He looked at the world
about him, perceived relationships, and symbolized what he saw into

communicable sounds and gestures and marks. With both brain and brawn the necessities of life were wrested from nature. He made rules concerning mating and family life. He created guidelines for solving internal and external disputes. Nagging questions about the nature of the world, reproduction, disease, and death were answered imaginatively, and practices developed to replace fear with assurance. With increased leisure he employed his creative energy in a variety of activities, including storytelling, dancing, carving, drawing, and play. Man's cultural responses to these areas varied enormously and reflected both the variety of his settings and circumstances, and the versatility of his reason and imagination. That his responses *could* vary widely is the meaning of being human; that they *did* vary widely is the key to human survival.

Naturally, not all man's cultural adjustments to his circumstances and felt needs have been realistic from the standpoint of modern science. Nevertheless, each such creation attests to the fact that man in all times and places has never passively accepted his situation. He has always sought to understand it and explain it. That he has not been afraid to guess, to try, to experiment, is as manifest in his failures as in his successes. In every imaginative failure there was the possibility of success, and man's survival into the present shows that he has succeeded much of the time. Moreover, all man's questioning and probing and answering were destined to lead to his discovery of the scientific method. Without a history full of different questions and answers, it would not have been possible.

Most of man's behavior, past or present, has nothing to do with science but is a matter of group or individual preferences. Day-by-day actions generally may only be rated in terms of the society and the age in which they originate; they cannot be scaled on a universal measuring stick or weighed by changeless standards. Science can tell us nothing about the comparative beauty of nosebones and earrings, nothing about the relative tastiness of fried grasshoppers and pork skins, nothing about the correct way to court a woman, about the just settlement of arguments, the proper worship of god, or the best artistic way to express oneself. These are matters of preference, not of science, and man is the richer for the tremendous range of taste that he has developed.

Unfortunately, in the contemporary world of power states, there is little patience for the bizarre, unstandardized behavior of technologically undeveloped societies. Both the United States and Russia, confident of their own great destinies and the correctness of their views, are, for the most part, supremely callous toward men of different cultures. About all that can be said for us is that our ethnocentrism has been sincere. We have genuinely believed that our way is the best and that we are doing others a favor by giving them a chance to learn it. Our revulsion for the appearance and behavior of primitive peoples has been both genuine and obvious, and we have had noble aspirations to release them from what we have believed to be the darkness and misery of their lives. Only recently have we begun to realize that our approach to other peoples has been all the more obnoxious because of its self-righteousness. When we have encountered people who prefer a loin cloth to a business suit or grubs to a steak, who enjoy competitive orchestra concerts more than competitive business activity, we have ridiculed, despised, pitied, or laughed at them for their "backwardness." They must be wrong, not we—never we— always they. And so, fully convinced that we have the best way of life, we have set about to bestow upon them the blessings of civilization whether they have sought them or not, ever mindful of the fact that our religion urges us to "help" our fellow man.

Toward this end we have usually made certain that these peoples learned that a dark skin or slant eyes are inferior traits, but that to improve them by racial intermarriage is even worse. We have tried to give them a new religion, because they are heathens whom our faith alone can save. We have striven to impose monogamy upon them, since we all know that it is the most advanced family system. We have put clothes on them—tropical comfort and hygiene be damned—and turned them, if possible, into businessmen. We have taught them the value of possessions, competition, and profit. Somewhere along the way we may have taught them a little about modern agriculture, technology, and medicine. But the price has been terribly high— the loss of their cultural integrity and very likely their self-respect as well. If you believe I have stated the case too strongly, I might ask what, if anything, you find objectionable about an unclothed African with five wives, who spends his nights participating in masked cult dances and refuses to work at profitable enterprises during the day?

The Russians, on the other hand, while fully as ethnocentric as we, profess great respect for the cultural traditions of the backward societies. They have portrayed themselves as the true friends of those people who have felt deep fury against the ridicule from the West. Often they have encouraged the folk arts and music of a people, admired their native dress and foods, and participated in their traditional celebrations. However, their true attitude toward cultural variation is reflected in the complete rigidity of basic communistic doctrine. The rich and well-to-do, whether primitive or not, are chastised, since it is obvious that they must have stolen their wealth or unfairly obtained it from the masses. A variety of political systems, be they democratic, hereditary kingship, or divine right, cannot be tolerated, since the only perfect system is communistic. Religion must be discouraged and ultimately eliminated, since it is known to be the opiate of the masses. Everyone must work, because this is man's finest activity. All creative artists, of course, should stick to realism and glorify the most sublime of subjects—the worker, the party, and the revolutionary leaders. It is probable that an honest Russian reaction to our theoretical nonworking African cult dancer would be even more disparaging than our own.

The basic intolerance of the communistic system in Russia, China, and elsewhere has been repeatedly demonstrated in recent years. Armed coups, firing squads, brainwashing, all attest to the fear of differences and their forceful elimination. But communist success with both civilized and primitive peoples has been much more than a matter of guns and strong-arm tactics. For years we have prepared the way for them with our overt intolerance for the diverse peoples and customs of the world, and they have been both clever and ruthless in exploiting this advantage. And so, onto the obliterating rocks of cultural sameness, society after society smashes, lured by the sweet communist songs of bread and respect, and pushed by our own winds of ridicule.

Today we are striving desperately to stem the communist flood with our own deluge of money, technology, and arms. In this struggle for the minds of men, we have failed to see that at bottom we, like they, are working for the same fatal design—worldwide cultural homogeneity. The only difference is that each side wishes to use its own rubber stamp, and that the communists generally stamp with political and military force while we rely on economic power. In either case, humanity is the loser. The strange aspect of all this is that we, a freedom-loving nation with a historical background of respect for individual differences, have had such difficulty in championing the right of whole societies to be different. Perhaps we have never thought about it in precisely this way. We can hope that Ruth Anshen is correct when she says that, "There is in mankind today a counterforce to the sterility and danger of a quantitative, anonymous mass culture, a new, if sometimes imperceptible, spiritual sense of convergence toward world unity on the basis of the sacredness of each human person and respect for the plurality of cultures." If indeed we have begun to treasure the unique society as we do the unique individual, and if we can infuse our statesmen, our representatives abroad, and ultimately all people everywhere with a feeling for the inestimable value of human differences, communism can never prevail. For after man has secured his bread, he must have respect, and he will ultimately cast his lot with a system that provides both. John F. Kennedy knew much of this, and his enthusiasm for the Peace Corps, aid to underdeveloped areas, and the United Nations demonstrated his understanding. He was, in fact, convinced that "The wave of the future is the liberation of the diverse energies of free nations and free men."

Although I have wished to emphasize the sterility of communism, I do not suggest that we should adopt a less ethnocentric attitude toward the world simply in order to "beat the Russians." *The fundamental problem of mankind is not which specific nation state or political and economic system is best. It is a matter of discovering that man is more important than any system—of accepting him in all his diversity, of cherishing his different customs, ideas, and things, of understanding that it is his basic nature to vary creatively, and that this is where all his ultimate hopes lie.* Certainly there is no easy way to do this. An entire nation is unlikely to lose its ethnocentrism in a few years. Indeed a basic level of *esprit de corps* is necessary for group survival. Yet I am convinced that a sincere belief in the right to vary can be man's one great and fundamental weapon against tyranny in any form. The world will not be won with food, or bombs, or Christianity, or communism. Man will either blow himself up or he will finally learn to live with differences, and in so doing reach undreamed of cultural heights. If he prevails, it will be because in the long agony of universal despair he has discovered with Terence that "I am a man; and nothing human is foreign to me," *Homo sum; humani nihil a me alienum puto.*

APPENDIX

Notes

I HAVE TRIED to make this section of the book more than a repository of acknowledgments, sources, and references. Here also are additional facts, doubts, conjectures, lists, and ideas that I believe are of interest, but that would have unduly interrupted my main story.

While the idea of a complete book espousing the value of human differences was my own, anthropologists and biologists have been defending variation in man for decades, and my debt to them is both obvious and profound. I am especially grateful to the late Clyde Kluckhohn, who not only was a germinal source for many of the concepts appearing here, but also took the time to encourage me in writing. To Carleton Coon go my thanks for fruitful discussions and the reassurance that not all physical anthropologists belonged to the "hide-race" school. For helping me to finish the book after a three-year delay, and more importantly for showing me that human choice, though it brings anxiety, is man's only hope for freedom, I owe a permanent debt to Dr. Mary Duwall. Any writer knows that there is an inverse correlation between productivity and the heat, humidity, and noise of one's office; my friend Albert Johnson understood this and generously provided me with an air-conditioned retreat from Memphis summers and child-rearing sounds.

All quotations appear with the kind permission of the publishers concerned, and are acknowledged in the notes that follow. As far as possible reference is made to the edition most easily available.

The "ethnographic present" has been used throughout the book in describing primitive peoples and their customs. This is to say that all practices are described as now existing although, in many cases, the groups have changed a great deal since originally being observed.

CHAPTER 1 / *The Chosen People*

The quotation by Ruth Benedict is from her ground-breaking book on the close interrelations of cultural elements within a society, *Patterns of Culture* (Boston: Houghton Mifflin Company, 1934).

Books with excellent sections on ethnocentrism are: *Cultural Sociology* by John L. Gillin and John P. Gillin (New York: The Macmillan Co., 1948), and *Folkways* by William G. Sumner (Boston: Ginn & Co., 1906).

There are a number of books that have especially fine collections of articles dealing with variations in human society and culture. A leisurely session with any of these will yield rich perspectives on the diversity of human behavior. William I. Thomas, *Source Book for Social Origins* (Boston: The Gorham Press, 1909); Margaret Mead and Nicholas Calas (editors), *Primitive Heritage* (New York: Random House, 1953); A. L. Kroeber and T. T. Waterman (editors), *Source Book in Anthropology* (New York: Harcourt, Brace & World, Inc., 1931); George P. Murdock, *Our Primitive Contemporaries* (New York: The Macmillan Co., 1954); Elman Service, *A Profile of Primitive Culture* (New York: Harper & Row, Pubs., 1958); Carleton S. Coon, *A Reader in General Anthropology* (New York: Holt, Rinehart & Winston, Inc., 1947). *The New Golden Bough* (New York: Criterion Books, 1959) should also be mentioned as very much worth perusing. It is an abridged edition of Sir James G. Frazer's work, edited and with extensive notes by Theodor H. Gaster which nicely update this classic source of exotic information about human behavior.

Of special interest to the general reader and all those new to anthropology are the two record albums *Ways of Mankind,* each of which contains thirteen half-hour dramas which dramatically and effectively present many basic anthropological concepts. The albums were produced by the National Association of Educational Broadcasters under the supervision of anthropologist Walter Goldschmidt.

Also of value to those with a general interest in anthropology is a set of three hundred color slides and a descriptive catalog called *Museum of Man,* which illustrates twelve areas of man's culture with photographs of museum artifacts. I directed the production of this collection under grants by Southwestern College at Memphis and the National Science Foundation. It is now available from the University of Wisconsin.

My use of the concept "value judgment" follows the theoretical position of Dr. Howard Jensen, who taught me some years ago and is now professor emeritus at Duke University. His encyclopedic and brilliant work in this area must one day be published fully, and I can do little more than allude to it here. Jensen differentiates between "value judgments" (areas amenable to scientific proof) on the one hand, and "value preferences" (areas of personal choice) on the other. Value judgments are those truths that have nothing to do with one's personal opinions or preferences but concern the nature of the world and man at large. Value preferences, on the other hand, concern all areas where choices are not related to science, but indicate varied, optional, and imaginative decisions by individuals or groups. Taken as a whole, my book seeks to establish as a value judgment the proposition that variation in (1) man's biology and (2) man's value preferences are two of his greatest assets.

In affirming the value of human variation, I do not oppose similarity of belief and practice *per se,* if such uniformity is voluntarily assumed and the freedom to change still exists. In other words, I am more concerned with the freedom to be different than with the perpetuation of specific differences for their own sake.

My emphasis on the value of cultural differences, and the right to varying ways of life is not meant to imply that each society has a perfect system for its particular situation, that all of its varying parts are necessary, or that they function together as a completely harmonious whole. This is an older anthropological view and one still held by a great many laymen who had their only college course in the area some years ago. We now know better. Societies are organized, of course, some tightly, some loosely. But in every case they contain erroneous beliefs and disruptive practices—in short, dispensable behavior patterns along with the central, necessary, and functional culture core of the group. Even so, I affirm the right of each society to its nonintegrative elements, liabilities though they may be, and I believe that their elimination should come when the group itself decides to change and not before.

CHAPTER 2 / *Creation and Evolution*

Charles Darwin's historic statement is from his *Origin of Species* (New York: Modern Library, N.D.). The Winnebago creation myth comes from a book edited by Paul Radin, *Crashing Thunder: The Autobiography of an American Indian* (New York: Appleton-Century-Crofts, Inc., 1926). The Boonoorong story is told in R. Brough Smyth's *The Aborigines of Victoria,* Vol. I, p. 424 (London: John Ferres, 1878) and in R. B. Dixon's "Oceanic" division of *The Mythology of All Races*, Vol. IX, edited by L. H. Gray (Boston: Marshall Jones Co., 1916). This book also contains a number of the other creation stories described in this chapter. It is part of a fascinating thirteen-volume set. The statement by Dr. John Lightfoot concerning the exact time of man's creation appears in A. D. White's *A History of the Warfare of Science with Theology in Christendom,* Vol. 1 (New York: Appleton-Century-Crofts, Inc., 1929, and George Braziller, Inc., 1955).

Figures concerning the odds against the spontaneous generation of life are from Lecomte du Noüy, *Human Destiny* (New York: Longmans, Green & Co., Inc., 1947). For one of the clearest accounts of current thinking in this area, see George Wald, "The Origin of Life," *Scientific American,* Vol. 191, No. 2 (August, 1954), pp. 44–53. Other sources of general interest used in the chapter include G. L. Jepsen, Ernst Mayr, and G. G. Simpson (editors), *Genetics, Paleontology, and Evolution* (Princeton: Princeton University Press, 1949); Noel Korn and Harry R. Smith (editors), *Human Evolution* (New York: Holt, Rinehart & Winston, Inc., 1959); D. E. Green (editor), *Currents in Biochemical Research* (New York: Interscience Publishers, 1956); Theodosius Dobzhansky, *Evolution, Genetics and Man* (New York: John Wiley & Sons, 1955) and *Mankind Evolving* (New Haven: Yale University Press, 1962). For an excellent summary statement of contemporary perspectives in genetic theory see Theodosius Dobzhansky, "Inside Human Nature," in *Frontiers of Knowledge: In the Study of Man,* edited by Lynn White, Jr. (New York: Harper and Row, 1956).

A common mistake in conceptualizing evolution is to assume that each living creature has a "straight line" history into the past, or conversely that most ancient creatures can be paleontologically traced into the present. Here are Dobzhansky's observations on the subject from *Evolution, Genetics and Man* (New York: John Wiley and Sons, Inc., 1955):

One of the most striking facts of paleontology is that the inhabitants of a given period are descended not from all the inhabitants of prior periods, but from only a part of them. In other words, many creatures leave no descendants at all; their races become extinct. . . . If we examine the fossils of any remote geological age, say Mesozoic or Paleozoic, we find that most of them represent organisms which have no direct descendants living in the present. They have succumbed at some point in time. On the other hand, some few of the denizens of the past have multiplied greatly, and their descendants, usually modified by evolutionary changes, fill the earth today.

Yet this is not to say that there are fewer species now than in the past. In fact there are many more.

For one of the things which the fossil record shows beyond reasonable doubt is that the diversity of life has become greater and greater in the course of time. The dying-out groups of organisms are replaced not only by the surviving ones, but also by quite new organisms, which exploit the environment in novel ways, and are added from time to time.

Since photographs of human babies with tails are not generally available, the name of an easily obtainable book that contains two such pictures may be of interest. It is Lorus and Margery Milne's *The Biotic World and Man,* 2nd edition (Englewood Cliffs, New Jersey: Prentice-Hall, Inc., 1958). See photographs numbered 420 and 421.

In the text I have deliberately stressed the positive role of mutation as a basic force in the evolution of man. In so doing I did not believe it necessary to comment at length on the generally well-known fact that most mutations are deleterious rather than advantageous to the specific organism involved. In his article "Radiation and Human Mutation," which appeared in *Scientific American,* November, 1955, H. J. Muller (Nobel laureate geneticist) says: "In more than 99 per cent of cases the mutation of a gene produces some kind of harmful effect, some disturbance of function." However, such an estimate may not be entirely realistic since, as geneticist James F. Crow points out in "Ionizing Radiation and Evolution," *Scientific American,* September, 1959, "What is advantageous in the short run may be ruinous in the long run. What may be good in one environment may be bad in another. What is good this year may be bad next year. What is good for an individual may be bad for the species." Even so, most mutations are nonadaptive and this is at least partly shown in the fact that, as Dobzhansky puts it in *Evolution, Genetics and Man,* "the most probable fate of any group of animals or plants in the course of time is extinction."

Dramatic evidence of the influence of the prenatal environment on the developing child has recently come to light in the linking of a sleeping pill and tranquilizer containing thalidomide with the production of congenital malformations. According to Dr. Helen Taussig, who was instrumental in keeping the drug off the American market, the condition produced by the drug is "phocomelia, which is characterized by reduction in the length of the long bones of the arms or legs, or both. In extreme cases the appendages are reduced to completely functionless nubbins. Occasionally the external ear is absent,

and in the most severe cases the visceral organs are badly malformed."
(Editorial in *Science*, Vol. 136, 1962, p. 683.)

Other drugs, it is believed, have varying potentials in inducing congenital defects. You are probably aware of the great range of opinion held by scientists about the effects of radioactive fallout on human germ cells. Geneticist Alfred Sturtevant sees the rise in deleterious mutations as already affecting a minimum of 1,800 infants each year ("possibly 100 times greater"), with the figure increasing as nuclear testing continues. Zoologist Curt Stern, on the other hand, feels that the threat is minimal: "In terms of mankind as a whole the biological consequences of controlled test explosions are very small." The outstanding Russian geneticist, N. P. Dubinin, though possibly inspired by political motives, indicates that human genetic material is highly sensitive to radiation damage and that only ten roentgen units will double man's mutation rate. Since recent estimates indicate that the U.S. is receiving about .05 to .1 roentgen annually from fallout alone, it is clear why some geneticists are concerned about increasing man's exposure to radiation.

CHAPTER 3 / *Animals, Apes, and Men*

Weston La Barre made the quoted statement (the italics are his and appropriate) about man the animal in the preface to his fine book *The Human Animal* (Chicago: University of Chicago Press, 1954). This exciting inquiry into the nature of human nature shows that, while man is human, he is also an animal and that many of his deepest problems come from not facing up to both sets of facts. Other quoted sources include W. E. Le Gros Clark's brief but absorbing *A History of the Primates* (Chicago: University of Chicago Press, 1959), and Carleton S. Coon's fascinating *The Story of Man* (New York: Alfred A. Knopf, Inc., 1962). Coon's revised edition convincingly and readably sketches the case for Homo erectus. Most of the figures in the chart showing comparative brain and body weights are from A. L. Kroeber's *Anthropology* (New York: Harcourt, Brace & World, Inc., 1948).

Among the most interesting additional sources for this chapter are William Howells' *Mankind in the Making* (New York: Doubleday & Co., Inc., 1959); E. A. Hooton's *Up From the Ape* (New York: The Macmillan Co., 1946); M. F. Ashley Montagu's *An Introduction to Physical Anthropology*, 2nd edition (Springfield, Illinois: Charles C. Thomas, Pub. 1951; 3rd edition, 1960), and Gabriel Lasker, *The Evolution of Man* (New York: Holt, Rinehart & Winston, Inc., 1961).

As was pointed out in the text, tree dwelling carries a serious risk of falling. Recent studies show clearly that broken bones must have always been a hazard of life in the trees. As anthropologist Adolph Schultz writes:

That crippling accidents are not at all rare in the life of wild monkeys and apes is proved by the many more or less well-repaired fractures one finds in every large series of skeletons. The frequency of fractures, as of diseases of bones and teeth, increases markedly with age. Among 233 wild gibbons, I encountered healed fractures in only some older juveniles, but in 28 per cent of fully grown (but not old) adults and in 50 per cent of the oldest adults, some of which had as many as seven repaired fractures. . . . The many cases of severe and even multiple fractures in skulls, hip bones, clavicles, sternums and ribs that have been recorded in adult wild monkeys and apes must have been caused mostly by falls when animals had misjudged the strength of a branch or mismanaged a hurried leap. . . . As soon as the early hominids had become bipeds and had invaded open country, they were favored by much lower rates of incapacitating or fatal accidents than occur in arboreal life.

This excerpt is from his article "Some Factors Influencing the Social Life of Primates in General and of Early Man in Particular," in *Social Life of Early Man*, edited by Sherwood Washburn (Chicago: Aldine Publishing Co., 1961).

Recent research indicates that elephants are smarter than rhinos and the like because of a vision-related brain with larger and more dense gray-matter cells. See B. Rousch, "The Intelligence of Elephants," *Scientific American*, February, 1957. To keep this in proper perspective with human intelligence, however, one should bear in mind that no pachyderm has yet published a study of a primate.

CHAPTER 4 / *Race: Myth and Fact*

The introductory statement by Theodosius Dobzhansky is from his article "Genetics and Equality," which appeared in *Science*, Vol. 137 (1962), p. 112. Other quotations are from the following sources: The Iroquois story of race formation is told in Robert E. Speer, *Race and Race Relations* (New York: F. H. Revell Co., 1924). This book is somewhat dated and hard to find, but Chapter II, "The Idea of Race Superiority," is well worth the trouble. Carleton Coon's comment about race in an atom-age world concluded his article "Climate and Race," in *Climatic Change*, edited by Harlow Shapley (Cambridge: Harvard University Press, 1954). Color tests among the Balinese are described by Ruth Benedict in *Race: Science and Politics*, rev. edition

(New York: Viking Press, Inc., 1945). Weston La Barre's critique of racial adaptation is from *The Human Animal* (Chicago: University of Chicago Press, 1954).

The chart that shows man's apelike traits is modified from E. A. Hoebel, *Man in the Primitive World,* 2nd edition (New York: Mc-Graw-Hill Book Co., 1958). Racial pathology materials are from A. L. Kroeber, *Anthropology* (New York: Harcourt, Brace & World, Inc., 1948). It is interesting that certain racial pathologies have a positive aspect as well. Thus the high incidence of sickle-cell anemia in the Negroid race has been correlated with a correspondingly high resistance to malarial infection.

Not everyone agrees that culture has replaced biological adaptation in man's evolutionary development. Some scholars see our present condition as one in which men especially suited for culture are being genetically selected. From this point of view, successful sociocultural living is the new condition we are adapting to rather than the older conditions of hostile animals and climatic variations. Moreover, it is said, because we are culture adapted, we are becoming more and more adept at producing culture. Dobzhansky clearly expressed this position in "Anthropology and the Natural Sciences—The Problem of Human Evolution," *Current Anthropology,* Vol. 4, No. 2, April, 1963.

Since the environment in which man lives is in the first place his sociocultural environment, the genetic changes induced by culture must affect man's fitness for culture and hence may affect culture. The process thus becomes self-sustaining. Biological changes increase the fitness for, and the dependence of their carriers on culture, and therefore stimulate cultural developments; cultural developments in turn instigate further genetic changes. This amounts to a positive feedback relationship between the cultural and the biological evolutions. The positive feedback explains the great evolutionary change, so great that it creates the illusion of an unbridgeable gap between our animal ancestors and ourselves. Human evolution is the outstanding example of what Simpson has termed quantum evolution, a rapid change to an entirely new way of life.

Additional books that contain sound and readable information on race are Mischa Titiev, *The Science of Man* (New York: Holt, Rinehart & Winston, Inc., 1954) and Carleton S. Coon, *The Origin of Races* (New York: Alfred A. Knopf, Inc., 1962), which is probably the most comprehensive and authoritative work available on the subject. Of special usefulness in getting a clear, concise, and expert statement concerning the current state of our racial knowledge is the

"Statement on Race," drafted in 1951 by twelve internationally prominent geneticists and physical anthropologists for UNESCO. This has
been reprinted in many places including *Readings in Anthropology*,
Vol. 1, edited by Morton H. Fried (New York: Thomas Y. Crowell
Company, 1959) and is included at the end of this book.

Many of the problems, both settled and unsettled, relating to race
are found in the article "Scientific Racism Again?" by Juan Comas,
Current Anthropology, Vol. 2, No. 4 (October, 1961). Following this
essay there are a number of interesting and often fiery commentaries
by several authorities on the subject. The reader will discover that
much remains unsettled in this area.

In reviewing the current intercultural limitations of intelligence
tests, one should not, of course, discount their value among persons
with similar opportunities and backgrounds in the same society. Under these conditions they provide a reasonably good indication of
intellectual capacity and are especially useful in pointing to extremes
in intellect—to the subnormal and to the supernormal members of
society.

CHAPTER 5 / *Human Society and Culture*

Lawrence K. Frank's observation is from his article "World Order
and Cultural Diversity" which appeared in the magazine *Free World*
(New Brunswick, New Jersey: Rutgers University Press, 1942). The
dedication by Elman Service is from his book *A Profile of Primitive
Culture* (New York: Harper & Row, Pubs., 1958).

The materials relating to the nature of creativity are the product
of highly imaginative and fruitful research by the Institute of Personality Assessment and Research of the University of California, Berkeley.

Ellsworth Huntington's *Civilization and Climate*, 3rd edition
(New Haven: Yale University Press, 1924) shows us the point of view
of a geographical determinist; W. H. Sheldon's *The Varieties of
Temperament* (New York: Harper & Row, Pubs., 1942), biological
determinism; Leslie A. White's *The Science of Culture* (New York:
Farrar, Straus, & Co., Inc., 1949), cultural determinism. Books of
greater value in assessing the forces producing cultural differences
are Sherwood Washburn (editor), *Social Life of Early Man* (Chicago: Aldine Publishing Co., 1961); Ralph Linton, *The Tree of Culture* (New York: Alfred A. Knopf, Inc., 1955); H. G. Barnett, *Innovation* (New York: McGraw-Hill Book Co., 1953).

Appendix

As Freud and others have pointed out, the pressures and demands of society often produce repression and neurosis. Yet were it not for society, we could not be human. Some of the case studies that affirm this position are found in J. A. L. Singh and R. M. Zingg, *Wolf-Children and Feral Man* (New York: Harper & Row, Pubs., 1942), and Kingsley Davis, "Final Note on a Case of Extreme Isolation," *American Journal of Sociology*, Vol. LII, No. 5 (March, 1947).

One of my students was so intrigued by the attitude of the Ona toward their environment that she was moved to poetry:

ODE TO AN ONA

Oh, thou Ona, cold and naked,
Thou dost wander unbedeckèd.
Unlike the Yahgan to the south
You simply won't in furs go forth.
Faces smeared with fat and ochre,
'Round the fires you vainly polka.
Always hating icy water,
Never bathing like you oughter.
Smiling through a count'nance greasy,
Often times it's mighty breezy.
We know you've ankles fat as flues,
And high metabolism too,
But with only your caps furry,
Little wonder why you scurry!

CONNIE WHITE

In recent years many highly intelligent and well-educated persons have made judgments about racial creativity by comparing the civilizations and achievements of the white race with those of the yellow and black. One of their favorite quotations is from Arnold Toynbee: "The only one of the primary races which has not made a creative contribution to any one of twenty-one civilizations is the black race." Those who like this statement are also pleased that the Mongoloids rank numerically well below the Caucasoids when we finish our civilization counting. The appeal of this exercise is in its dramatic simplicity. It even seems scientific, since a given race either did or did not establish a civilization; to establish a civilization obviously takes intelligence, imagination, and creativity. A basic flaw in this approach is the difficulty of obtaining scholarly agreement about what constitutes a civilization or a "creative contribution" to one. Anthropologists generally agree some West African peoples created civilizations, for example, the ancient kingdom of Benin, which flourished for several hundred years; but some historians such as Toynbee use different qualifying criteria and exclude such societies from their lists. My own position is that civilization-counting gets you nowhere. At best it shows in a general way which groups were most isolated in history and which were able to borrow most heavily from their neighbors. At worst it vastly oversimplifies what is shown in the text to be a very complex problem.

CHAPTER 6 / *Symbol Systems*

Edward Sapir's comment is from his pioneering book in anthropological linguistics, *Language: An Introduction to the Study of Speech* (New York: Harcourt, Brace & World, Inc., 1921). The chart on gibbon vocalizations is taken from a more comprehensive one in Clarence R. Carpenter's "Field Study in Siam of the Behavior and Social Relations of the Gibbon (Hylobates Lar)," *Comparative Psychology Monographs*, Vol. 16, No. 5 (December, 1940); reprinted in Carleton S. Coon, *A Reader in General Anthropology* (New York: Holt, Rinehart & Winston, Inc., 1948). Harry Hoijer's three groups of evidence for the antiquity of language as well as the quotation are from "Language and Writing" in *Man, Culture, and Society* edited by Harry L. Shapiro (New York: Oxford University Press, 1956). Illustrations of contemporary American "jive-talk" were selected from a longer list that appeared in an August, 1960, news column written by Brook Benton and copyrighted by King Features Syndicate. Clyde Kluckhohn's statement about the relation between language and reality is from his *Mirror for Man* (New York: McGraw-Hill Book Co., 1949).

Additional background sources for this chapter include Dorothy Lee, "Being and Value in a Primitive Culture," *The Journal of Philosophy*, Vol. 46, No. 13 (1949), reprinted in E. A. Hoebel, J. D. Jennings, and E. R. Smith (editors), *Readings in Anthropology* (New York: McGraw-Hill Book Co., 1955); Benjamin Lee Whorf, *Language, Thought, and Reality*, John B. Carroll, editor (Cambridge, Massachusetts: The Technology Press, and New York: John Wiley & Sons, 1956); Harry Hoijer (editor), *Language in Culture*, American Anthropological Association, Memoir No. 79 (1954). A general review of recent research in language and culture is Clyde Kluckhohn's "Notes on Some Anthropological Aspects of Communication," *American Anthropologist*, Vol. 63 (1961), pp. 895–910.

The position described in the text concerning the importance of language in the perception and assessment of reality is known as the

Sapir-Whorf hypothesis. It has been extensively investigated by empirical study in recent years. Most of these studies tend to support the basic hypothesis, although researchers have broadened the original concept to include other forms of symbolic behavior in addition to language. This is to say that a child's perceptions, thoughts, and emotions are shaped by much behavior other than linguistic, and that all these factors should be recognized as contributing to his ultimate world view.

Words and parts of words that have meaning are called morphemes. They are of two types, bound and free. Free morphemes are noncomposite words that stand alone, *i.e.*, are meaningful in themselves. Words such as "dog," "two," "man," "red," "happy," are free morphemes. Bound morphemes are always found attached to free morphemes. They have meaning but are never used alone. Thus various prefixes and suffixes such as "-s," "un-," "-er," "re-," are bound morphemes in English since "-s" means "several," "un-" means "the opposite," "-er" means "one who," and "re-" means "to do again."

The four consonantal click sounds of Hottentot have been symbolized as follows: dental (/), alveolar ($\neq$), cerebral (!), lateral (//).

Our main discussion in this chapter dealt with only the symbolic world of spoken language. There are several other symbolic systems which man's fertile mind has produced, such as gestures and writing. While there was no need to treat these additional systems individually in the text, I consider the differences among them to be of similar importance to variations in spoken language. While I do not insist that the Dyak gesture for "no" (slight contraction of the eyebrows) gets him any closer to reality than we are, I am confident that his gesture is as good as ours and that it fits into a total system, some aspects of which may well provide insights into the nature of things that we cannot fathom with our own symbol system. Since I am realistic enough to know that the Dyaks will ultimately be either westernized or easternized, I hope sincerely that we may learn their way of life as completely as possible before it disappears.

CHAPTER 7 / *Man at Work*

The introductory statement by Ralph Linton as well as his original version of the American debt to diffusion are from his classic *The Study of Man* (New York: Appleton-Century-Crofts, 1936). I have used his longer essay on culture borrowing, which appeared as "One Hundred Per Cent American" in *The American Mercury*, Vol. 40 (1937).

Kenneth Oakley's view on early tool using and making are from "On Man's Use of Fire, With Comments on Tool-making and Hunting" in Sherwood Washburn (editor), *Social Life of Early Man* (Chicago: Aldine Publishing Co., 1961). The anthropological menu was compounded by Lister Sinclair under the direction of Walter Goldschmidt for the "Museum of Man" record in *Ways of Mankind* album No. 1, produced by the National Association of Educational Broadcasters, University of Illinois, Urbana, Illinois. Daryll Forde's comment on the correlation between low technology and high solidarity appears in "Primitive Economics" in Harry Shapiro (editor), *Man, Culture, and Society* (New York: Oxford University Press, 1956). The quotation by Felix M. Keesing is from his *Cultural Anthropology* (New York: Holt, Rinehart & Winston, 1958). Of special interest in this general area is the magnificent five-volume set edited by Charles Singer, E. J. Holmyard, A. R. Hall, and T. L. Williams, *A History of Technology* (London: Oxford University Press, 1954–1958) which is filled with authoritative articles about man's technological development from prehistory to the present century. Also useful in appraising the formative forces of civilization are books by V. Gordon Childe, such as *Man Makes Himself* (New York: New American Library, 1952). The best anthropological analysis of man at work is Melville J. Herskovits, *Economic Anthropology* (New York: Alfred A. Knopf, 1952).

In teaching courses in general anthropology over the past several years, I have been impressed that so few students know anything about the most fundamental aspects of man's technology. Even the knowledge picked up by Boy Scouts has little to do with the simplest and yet most essential information that man has accumulated. But students are not alone in their ignorance. It is actually the normal condition of our society. Our civilization has become so fantastically complex, so microscopically specialized, that few if any of us could exist for more than a few days on our own, unsupported by the groups in which we live. We have reached such tremendous cultural heights that we have no knowledge of the foundations upon which this culture rests. We are in the ironic position of having perhaps the best mass technology but the worst individual know-how on earth.

CHAPTER 8 / *Man and His Mate*

The introductory quotation is from William Kenkel's *The Family in Perspective* (New York: Appleton-Century-Crofts, 1960).

Henry Pratt Fairchild's description of the international beauty contest is from his book *Race and Nationality* (New York: Ronald Press, 1947). Like Coon, Fairchild is not afraid to face the fact that races *are* different, and that the acceptance of this fact may lead in many directions other than bigotry. I have placed Dr. Fairchild's description of the American beauty contestant in the notes rather than in the text because I believe it, in contrast to his other portraits, is a little severe. Of course he did this to make a point. But, in fairness, if the American girl's painted lips are caricatured as resembling over-ripe beefsteak and her fingernails bloody claws, then Miss Africa's cicatrizations should be described as looking like whiplash welts and Miss Samoa's color the result of a fall into a vat of lemon juice. Here is his description:

Finally comes Miss United States, one of the few blondes on parade, her fair hair artificially curled according to the latest pattern of the beauty parlors, her eyebrows darkened and plucked to a sharply arched pencil line, her lips painted until they resemble over-ripe beefsteak, rings in her ears, around her neck, and on her wrists, like Miss China freed by her modernity from the hourglass waist that her mother was so proud of, the tips of her fingers looking like bloody claws, toenails of the same hue peeking out from high-heeled shoes, which not only give their wearer an awkward mincing gait but also throw her whole skeleton out of kilter with variegated unhappy consequences—but beautiful, oh! so beautiful, in the eyes of her admiring fans in the audience.

There are a variety of excellent books dealing with courtship, marriage, and child rearing. C. S. Ford and F. A. Beach's *Patterns of Sexual Behavior* (New York: Harper & Row, Pubs., 1951) is a broad and scholarly treatment of sex, drawing on a wealth of cross-cultural materials. For perspective, it is vastly superior to the studies made by Alfred Kinsey and his associates. A good discussion of the relationship of permanent sexuality to the development of the human family is found in Weston La Barre, *The Human Animal* (Chicago: University of Chicago Press, 1954). John J. Honigmann's *Culture and Personality* (New York: Harper & Row, Pubs., 1954) still provides the best general summary and bibliography of the fascinating area of culture and personality development. The literature in this area is mushrooming, but basic works still must include Ralph Linton, *The Cultural Background of Personality* (New York: Appleton-Century-Crofts, 1945); Abram Kardiner, *The Individual and His Society* (New York: Columbia University Press, 1944); Abram Kardiner, *The Psychological Frontiers of Society* (New York: Columbia University Press, 1945); Clyde Kluckhohn, H. A. Murray, and D. M. Schneider (editors), *Personality in Nature, Society, and Culture,* 2nd revised edition (New York: Alfred A. Knopf, Inc., 1953); Douglas Haring (editor), *Personal Character and Cultural Milieu,* 3rd revised edition (Syracuse, New York: Syracuse University Press, 1956). A very useful and readable book that compares the family systems of a number of different societies is S. A. Queen and J. B. Adams, *The Family in Various Cultures* (New York: J. B. Lippincott, 1952). Several approaches to the study of the human family are successfully combined by William Kenkel in *The Family in Perspective* (New York: Appleton-Century-Crofts, 1960). René Spitz has given us the basic study of the close correlation between love and infant survival and development in "The Role of Ecological Factors in Emotional Development in Infancy," *Child Development,* Vol. 20 (1949).

CHAPTER 9 / *Law and Order*

J. B. S. Haldane made the introductory point in an address delivered in January, 1947, and subsequently published in the *Atlantic Monthly,* March, 1947. It was later reprinted in G. L. Jepsen, Ernst Mayr, and G. G. Simpson (editors), *Genetics, Paleontology, and Evolution* (Princeton: Princeton University Press, 1949). He elaborates on this point as follows:

That society enjoys the greatest amount of liberty in which the greatest number of human genotypes can develop their peculiar abilities. It is generally admitted that liberty demands equality of opportunity. It is not equally realized that it demands a variety of opportunities, and a tolerance of those who fail to conform to standards which may be culturally desirable but are not essential for the functioning of society.

The observations by Heini Hediger on living space are from his article "The Evolution of Territorial Behavior" in Sherwood Washburn (editor), *Social Life of Early Man* (Chicago: Aldine Publishing Co., 1961). In the same publication, Sherwood Washburn and Irven DeVore explore the concept of "home base" in their essay, "Social Behavior of Baboons and Early Man."

Franz Boas described the potlatch ceremonies at length in "The Social Organization and the Secret Societies of the Kwakiutl Indians," *U.S. National Museum, Annual Report, 1894–1895* (Washington, 1897). Portions of his account have been reprinted in a number of readers including Margaret Mead and Nicholas Calas, *Primitive Heritage* (New York: Random House, 1953).

Several books show the intimate relationship between family structure, child rearing, and political systems, among them Geoffrey Gorer, *The American People* (New York: W. W. Norton & Co., Inc., 1948); Erich Fromm, *Escape From Freedom* (New York: Holt, Rinehart & Winston, Inc., 1941); and Erik H. Erikson, *Childhood and Society* (New York: W. W. Norton & Co., Inc., 1950).

Six of the half-hour recordings in the *Ways of Mankind*, Album No. 2, deal with law and justice in a cross-cultural perspective. An excellent book in the general area is E. Adamson Hoebel, *The Law of Primitive Man: A Study in Comparative Legal Dynamics* (Cambridge: Harvard University Press, 1954).

Many people believe that our own trial by jury, while sound in principle, flounders in allowing virtually anyone to serve. Now that a science of human behavior exists, some think a panel of clinical psychologists, criminologists, and legal experts could render better verdicts in serious and complex cases than the butcher, the baker, and the electric-light maker.

CHAPTER 10 / *Man and the Unknown*

The statement by Alberto Blanc is from "Some Evidence for the Ideologies of Early Man" in Sherwood Washburn (editor), *Social Life of Early Man* (Chicago: Aldine Publishing Co., 1961). William Howells' description of "mana" appears in his book *The Heathens* (New York: Doubleday & Co., Inc., 1948), as do his quoted ideas concerning death and souls. The Ashanti justification for worshiping several gods is found in R. S. Rattray, *Ashanti Proverbs* (Oxford: The Clarendon Press, 1916). Edward Norbeck's discussion of divination is from *Religion in Primitive Society* (New York: Harper & Row, Pubs., 1961). I have followed his classification of magic in this chapter. The materials on the rain ceremonial of the Nama come from George P. Murdock, *Our Primitive Contemporaries* (New York: The Macmillan Co., 1934). The name of the Nama deity "Tsui // Goab," mentioned in the quotation, contains a lateral click which is indicated by the two slanting lines (see page 274). Murdock's description of the Witoto shaman is also from this classic book which summarizes the way of life of a number of primitive societies.

A. C. Hollis recorded the Masai prayer for rain in his book *The Masai, Their Language and Folklore* (Oxford: The Clarendon Press, 1905). The news item concerning the Hindu rain-oriented ritual was an Associated Press release. An early and sensitive chronicler of the

Eskimo, Knud Rasmussen, described their need to observe old customs in *The People of the Polar North,* edited by G. Herring (London: K. Paul, Trench, Trübner, 1908). Richard Brandt's materials on ethics are from his book *Hopi Ethics: A Theoretical Analysis* (Chicago: University of Chicago Press, 1954). Winnebago ethical attitudes are taken from Paul Radin's *Primitive Man as Philosopher* (New York: Appleton-Century-Crofts, 1927).

For a comprehensive cultural history of the religious origins of the Spanish bullfight, see my book *The Horn and the Sword* (New York: E. P. Dutton & Co., Inc., 1957).

The impersonal supernatural force described as "mana" appears with various modifications as a belief in "orenda" by the Iroquois, "manitou" by the Algonquins, and "wakan" or "wakonda" among the Sioux and other Indians of the Plains.

Oral Roberts' claim about the nonsurgical restoration of a missing bone is somewhat extreme even for American healers. Yet it and others were made in a healing service, recorded on tapes by one of my students who studied some of the healing cults as a primitive-religion course project.

It is no secret that American and Russian scientists are currently attempting to invade one of the last areas to which religion has previously laid sole claim—the nature of death. Experiments concerned with long-term human deep-freezing are in progress, and obviously raise both technical and theological problems.

CHAPTER 11 / *Man at Play*

The comment by R. R. Marett is from his foreword to the first edition of Leonhard Adam's *Primitive Art* (London: Penguin Books, 1954). The description of a Balinese crowd at a theatrical performance is found in Jane Belo's article "The Balinese Temper" in *Character and Personality,* Vol. 4, 1935. Her entire article is conveniently reprinted in Douglas Haring (editor), *Personal Character and Cultural Milieu,* 3rd revised edition (Syracuse: Syracuse University Press, 1956). Ladislas Segy's statement comes from his extensively illustrated *African Sculpture Speaks* (New York: Lawrence Hill & Co., 1955). Jivaro *tsantsas* as well as Navaho dry paintings are described in Elman Service, *A Profile of Primitive Culture* (New York: Harper & Row, Pubs., 1958).

A number of interesting and beautifully illustrated books are available on primitive art. The most comprehensive is Erwin Christensen's *Primitive Art* (New York: Viking Press, 1955), although the text is more for the artist than the anthropologist. Douglas Fraser's *Primitive Art* (New York: Doubleday & Co., Inc., 1962) is a visual delight, and though its scope is perhaps too broad for its length, it is a fine book by an art historian for the general reader. Perhaps the best anthropological approach to the area is Paul Wingert's *Primitive Art* (New York: Oxford University Press, 1962). The text is highly competent and well illustrated, but has no color plates. Franz Boas' book *Primitive Art* (New York: Dover Publications, 1955) is an anthropological classic, but is quite limited in its range of illustrative materials. Originally published some 35 years ago, it does not include the newer "functional" interpretations of art. In this book, however, Boas convincingly relates leisure time to artistic production, and clearly delineates the nature of formal, representational, and symbolic art. Books devoted to special regions of primitive art include Ralph Linton and Paul Wingert, *Arts of the South Seas* (New York: Museum of Modern Art, 1946); Frederick Dockstader, *Indian Art in America* (Greenwich, Connecticut: New York Graphic Society, 1960); Frederic Douglas, *Indian Art of the United States* (New York: Museum of Modern Art, 1941); and Robert Inverarity, *Art of the Northwest Coast Indians* (Berkeley: University of California Press, 1950). These books are scholarly in content and well illustrated. Also useful for their excellent drawings and photographs are Miguel Covarrubias, *The Eagle, The Jaguar, and the Serpent* (New York: Alfred A. Knopf, 1954), and *Indian Art of Mexico and Central America* (New York: Alfred A. Knopf, 1957). Of basically pictorial interest are Eliot Elisofon, *The Sculpture of Africa* (New York: Frederick A. Praeger, Inc., 1958), and Warner and W. L. Muensterberger, *Sculpture of Primitive Man* (New York: H. N. Abrams, 1955).

CHAPTER 12 / *Human Potentialities*

I could not resist using the title of Gardner Murphy's fine book *Human Potentialities* (New York: Basic Books, 1958) to head my chapter summarizing the major thesis of the book: that human potentialities are as great as human variation—no more and no less.

The introductory quote comes, appropriately, from Clyde Kluckhohn's *Mirror for Man* (New York: McGraw-Hill Book Co., Inc., 1949). This book has received justified praise from professional and layman alike. Kluckhohn's Chapter 10, "An Anthropologist Looks at the World," is one of the finest declarations of our time. Ruth

Anshen's statement is from her introductory essay "World Perspective" in Erich Fromm's *The Art of Loving* (New York: Harper & Row, Pubs., 1956).

The first two chapters of Ruth Benedict's *Patterns of Culture* (Boston: Houghton Mifflin Co., 1934) are stirring prose that clearly enunciates the anthropological position on cultural variation.

Margaret Mead, Carleton Coon, Weston La Barre, Melville Herskovits and a host of other professional anthropologists have also written in defense of various cultural differences, and I have made liberal use of their ideas both in this chapter and throughout the book.

Some Symbolic Gestures

LANGUAGE includes far more than spoken sounds. Gestures can be very expressive. And as you may expect, the same gesture means different things in different parts of the world. Here are a few samples.

How to say "yes" and "no" with gestures.

WESTERN
> Yes = Nod head.
> No = Shake head.

AINU (no head motions for yes and no)
> Yes = Hands together, palms upward. Bring gracefully up to chest and wave gracefully downward.
> No = Right hand at chest level, moved from right to left and back.

SEMANG (pygmy Negroes of interior Malaya)
> Yes = Thrust head sharply forward.
> No = Cast eyes down.

ABYSSINIANS
> Yes = Throw head back and raise eyebrows.
> No = Jerk head to the right shoulder.

DYAKS (Borneo)
> Yes = Raise eyebrows.
> No = Contract eyebrows slightly.

MAORI (New Zealand)
> Yes = Raise head and chin.

SICILIANS
> No = Raise head and chin.

282

How to greet someone with gestures.

COPPER ESKIMOS
> Welcome strangers with a buffet on the head or shoulders with the fist.

NORTHWEST AMAZONIANS
> Slap one another's backs in greeting.

POLYNESIAN MEN
> Embrace and rub each other's back in greeting.

TORRES STRAITS ISLANDERS (old form of greeting)
> Hook fingers of right hand into those of person greeted and draw away so as to scratch the palm. Repeat several times.

AINU (man meeting sister)
> Holds her hands for a few seconds. Suddenly releases her hands, grasps her by both ears and utters a cry. Then each strokes one another on the face and shoulders.

ANDAMAN ISLANDERS (two friends or relatives meeting after a separation of several weeks or longer)
> Greeting: Sit down, one on the lap of the other, arms around each other's neck, weeping and wailing for some two or three minutes. (Husband sits in wife's lap on such occasions.)
> Parting: One lifts the hand of the other toward his mouth and gently blows on it.

The symbolic significance of some common gestures.

HISSING
> England and USA: Disapproval of actor or speaker.
> Japan: Polite deference to social superiors.
> Basuto (South Africa): Applause.

SPITTING
> Western world: Contempt.
> Masai (Africa): Sign of affection and benediction.
> American Indian medicine man spitting on sick person: A healing practice.

RISING AND SITTING
> Western world: Stand in presence of superiors.
> Fijians and Tongans: Sit in presence of superiors.

KISSING
> Western world: A demonstration of affection, always ap-

proved as private love play and under certain conditions in public as well.

Orient: Highly erotic, for private pleasure only. Arouses disgust when done in public. In Japan, love scenes in American movies are generally censored.

Tapuya (South America): Men kiss as a sign of peace. Men do not kiss women since the latter wear labrets or lip plugs.

Eskimo and Polynesians: Do not kiss. Nuzzle faces together, noses, cheeks, etc.

STAMPING THE FEET

Western world: Impatience.

Tasmanians: Expression of surprise or pleasure.

DANCING

Western world: A recreation, or a skilled sequence of motions complete and meaningless in themselves, that one watches (minor exceptions in classical ballet).

Orient: Also a recreation, but the skilled sequence of motions (the natya dancing of India, Ceylon, China theatrics) have meaning, semantic content. Dance forms and sequences have articulate, literary meanings.

THUMBING THE NOSE

Europeans and Americans: Somewhat obscene or at least disrespectful.

Toda (South India): Expresses respect.

STICKING OUT THE TONGUE

Europeans and Americans: Expression of mocking contempt used by children . . . or between friends in fun.

South China: To express embarrassment at a faux pas.

Maya: Probably some religious significance.

STICKING OUT THE LOWER LIP

America: Pouting.

Kiowa (Apache): Direction pointing.

Culture and Survival Test

C O U L D Y O U S U R V I V E alone in the jungle? The desert? The Arctic? Most Americans are so highly "civilized" they know almost nothing of the natural lore that is essential to the life of many "primitive" peoples. The brief true-false test given below always amuses my students—because they do so badly on it. If you can answer more than forty of the questions correctly, you are good. Remember, however, that only one incorrect answer in a real situation might easily result in your death! The answers are printed at the end.

JUNGLE

____ 1. The chances of being bitten by a poisonous snake in the jungle are about as remote as being struck by lightning.

____ 2. While food is plentiful in the jungle, good water is extremely difficult to obtain.

____ 3. Contrary to popular opinion, a good wool shirt is cooler in the humid jungle heat and more resistant to fungus rot than one of cotton.

____ 4. A jungle-wise man knows that by leaving his sweat-drenched clothing on after a vigorous hike he is "cashing in" on nature's air conditioning.

____ 5. One can frequently get fresh water in the jungle by locating a depression in the earth and digging a hole about 3 or 4 feet deep.

____ 6. Tincture of iodine can be used as an emergency water purifier.

___ 7. Should one stumble upon a deserted native village, he may be sure that a good water hole is in the area.

___ 8. All jungle animals, with few exceptions, travel toward water at dawn and dusk.

___ 9. If one attempts river travel in the jungle, he should know that rapids are apt to be most common in relatively flat terrain.

___ 10. In hilly jungle country, the ridges are easier to follow than the valleys.

___ 11. It is extremely inadvisable to follow elephant trails in spite of their firmness and width.

___ 12. Since the heavy growth of jungle foliage generally ends about a foot above the ground, one can generally see much further by lying on one's stomach than by standing up.

___ 13. The bulk of distance walking should be done in the jungle in late afternoon and during the long, cool twilight.

___ 14. One should seldom if ever follow a direct compass line in the jungle.

___ 15. A good jungle camp site would be half-way up a small hill from a stream with jungle growth between you and the water.

___ 16. Good tinder for a fire may be obtained by scraping the fuzz from the bottom sides of palm leaves.

___ 17. A particular quality of burning bamboo will clear most animals away from your camp site.

___ 18. Anything that you see monkeys eat, you can eat.

___ 19. A good jungle rule is to avoid all plants with a clear sap or sweet taste.

___ 20. Green cashew nuts cause a rash similar to poison ivy.

___ 21. Most ferns growing along swift streams are edible.

___ 22. The number of poisonous plants is not great and few are common in the jungle.

___ 23. One of the most plentiful and tasty jungle staples is the breadfruit, which resembles a small pumpkin, being green when unripe and brown when ripe.

___ 24. The Mamey is a jungle peach with brown skin, yellow or reddish meat, and edible either raw or cooked.

___ 25. If one knows the Sandbox, the Manzanillo, the Cowitch and the Strychnos, he is not apt to eat a poisonous plant in the jungle.

___ 26. Man's worst enemy in the jungle is the mosquito.

___ 27. A good coating of spit will cause ticks to release themselves; a lighted cigarette will cause leeches to drop off; and a coating of oil will bring botfly maggots to the surface of the skin.

DESERT

___ 1. In the desert on very hot days, it is very important for one to wear a woolen band around the stomach.

___ 2. When walking in the desert, it is highly desirable to wear two pairs of socks.

___ 3. If one lies down to escape the force of a sandstorm, he should move around frequently.

___ 4. Salt tablets should only be taken if plenty of water is available.

___ 5. Chewing gum increases thirst.

___ 6. Because of the dry air, food spoilage is not a serious problem in the desert.

___ 7. As long as you stay under cover, there is no danger of heatstroke in the desert.

___ 8. Heatstroke is best treated by removing most of a person's clothing, placing him in the shade, pouring water over his body and fanning him.

___ 9. A good desert rule is where there is water, there is food.

ARCTIC

___ 1. In late August, 80 percent of all land north of the Arctic Circle is free of snow; most of the remaining 20 percent being in Greenland.

___ 2. Very little snow falls in the Arctic during the winter.

___ 3. In the Arctic, cloud formations are fairly dependable indicators of the terrain beneath.

___ 4. If a polar bear is killed, its liver should be cooked and eaten immediately for its rich concentration of food elements.

___ 5. Snow blindness can occur during a bright overcast as quickly as during sunny weather.

___ 6. To protect the eyes against snow glare, goggles can be made by cutting inch-wide slits into a scrap of metal or wood.

_____ 7. It should be remembered that one good heavy layer of clothing provides more warmth than several layers of light clothing.

_____ 8. Loose clothing generally leads to frostbite.

_____ 9. A heavy beard is good protection against frostbite.

_____ 10. In the Arctic, few if any clothes should be worn inside a sleeping bag.

_____ 11. In some areas of the Arctic, chunks of coal can be found on the beaches and in river valleys.

_____ 12. Carbon monoxide poisoning is one of the greatest dangers of the Arctic.

_____ 13. Seal blubber and animal hides may be burned to provide light, but do not provide enough heat for cooking purposes.

_____ 14. Polar bear meat is usually tough and stringy when cooked and is considerably more tender if eaten raw or frozen.

_____ 15. There are no poisonous flowering plants or grasses in the Arctic.

_____ 16. Generally speaking, the coastline of the Arctic is more friendly than the interior.

_____ 17. Although boiling is the best way to prepare food in the Arctic from a nutritional standpoint, it is highly wasteful from the standpoint of fuel.

_____ 18. Sea ice two or three years old is blue in color and actually fresher than average river or spring water.

_____ 19. One should not scoop up handfuls of snow to eat from time to time while traveling overland in the Arctic.

_____ 20. Where there is a choice, snow should be melted rather than ice for drinking water, since it requires less heat and takes less time.

_____ 21. Valleys are always warmer than slopes and ridges in the Arctic and should be used for camp sites.

_____ 22. A real problem in the Arctic is to keep from freezing to death while one sleeps.

_____ 23. Simple frostbite is best treated by gently rubbing snow or ice over the affected spot.

_____ 24. The worst Arctic pest is the mosquito, but it is not a disease carrier.

Correct answers to test:

14T, 15T, 16T, 17T, 18T, 19F, 20T, 21T, 22T, 23T, 24F, 25T, 26T, 27T.

DESERT: 1T, 2T, 3T, 4T, 5F, 6T, 7F, 8T, 9T.

ARCTIC: 1T, 2T, 3T, 4F, 5T, 6F, 7F, 8F, 9F, 10T, 11T, 12T, 13F, 14T, 15T, 16T, 17F, 18T, 19F, 20F, 21F, 22F, 23F, 24T.

Statement on Race

FROM UNESCO

1. Scientists are generally agreed that all men living today belong to a single species, Homo sapiens, and are derived from a common stock, even though there is some dispute as to when and how different human groups diverged from this common stock.

The concept of race is unanimously regarded by anthropologists as a classificatory device providing a zoological frame within which the various groups of mankind may be arranged and by means of which studies of evolutionary processes can be facilitated. In its anthropological sense, the word "race" should be reserved for groups of mankind possessing well-developed and primarily heritable physical differences from other groups. Many populations can be so classified but, because of the complexity of human history, there are also many populations which cannot easily be fitted into a racial classification.

2. Some of the physical differences between human groups are due to differences in hereditary constitution and some to differences in the environments in which they have been brought up. In most cases, both influences have been at work. The science of genetics suggests that the hereditary differences among populations of a single species are the results of the action of two sets of processes. On the one hand, the genetic composition of isolated populations is constantly but gradually being altered by natural selection and by occasional changes (mutations) in the material particles (genes) which control heredity. Populations are also affected by fortuitous changes in gene frequency and by marriage customs. On the other

hand, crossing is constantly breaking down the differentiations so set up. The new mixed populations, in so far as they, in turn, become isolated, are subject to the same processes, and these may lead to further changes. Existing races are merely the result, considered at a particular moment in time, of the total effect of such processes on the human species. The hereditary characters to be used in the classification of human groups, the limits of their variation within these groups, and thus the extent of the classificatory sub-divisions adopted may legitimately differ according to the scientific purpose in view.

3. National, religious, geographical, linguistic and cultural groups do not necessarily coincide with racial groups; and the cultural traits of such groups have no demonstrated connection with racial traits. Americans are not a race, nor are Frenchmen, nor Germans; nor *ipso facto* is any other national group. Muslims and Jews are no more races than are Roman Catholics and Protestants; nor are people who live in Iceland or Britain or India, or who speak English or any other language, or who are culturally Turkish or Chinese and the like, thereby describable as races. The use of the term "race" in speaking of such groups may be a serious error, but it is one which is habitually committed.

4. Human races can be, and have been classified in different ways by different anthropologists. Most of them agree in classifying the greater part of existing mankind into at least three large units, which may be called major groups (in French *grand'races*, in German *Hauptrassen*). Such a classification does not depend on any single physical character, nor does, for example, skin color by itself necessarily distinguish one major group from another. Furthermore, so far as it has been possible to analyze them, the differences in physical structure which distinguish one major group from another give no support to popular notions of any general "superiority" or "inferiority" which are sometimes implied in referring to these groups.

Broadly speaking, individuals belonging to different major groups of mankind are distinguishable by virtue of their physical characters, but individual members, or small groups, belonging to different races within the same major group are usually not so distinguishable. Even the major groups grade into each other, and the physical traits by which they and the races within them are characterized overlap considerably. With respect to most, if not all, measurable characters, the differences among individuals belonging to the same race are greater than the differences that occur between the observed averages for two or more races within the same major group.

5. Most anthropologists do not include mental characteristics in their classification of human races. Studies within a single race have shown that both innate capacity and environmental opportunity determine the results of tests of intelligence and temperament, though their relative importance is disputed.

When intelligence tests, even non-verbal, are made on a group of non-literate people, their scores are usually lower than those of more civilized people. It has been recorded that different groups of the same race occupying similarly high levels of civilization may yield considerable differences in intelligence tests. When, however, the two groups have been brought up from childhood in similar environments, the differences are usually very slight. Moreover, there is good evidence that, given similar opportunities, the average performance (that is to say, the performance of the individual who is representative because he is surpassed by as many as he surpasses), and the variation round it, do not differ appreciably from one race to another.

Even those psychologists who claim to have found the greatest differences in intelligence between groups of different racial origin, and have contended that they are hereditary, always report that some members of the group of inferior performance surpass not merely the lowest ranking member of the superior group, but also the average of its members. In any case, it has never been possible to separate members of two groups on the basis of mental capacity, as they can often be separated on a basis of religion, skin color, hair form or language. It is possible, though not proved, that some types of innate capacity for intellectual and emotional responses are commoner in one human group than in another, but it is certain that, within a single group, innate capacities vary as much as, if not more than, they do between different groups.

The study of the heredity of psychological characteristics is beset with difficulties. We know that certain mental diseases and defects are transmitted from one generation to the next, but we are less familiar with the part played by heredity in the mental life of normal individuals. The normal individual, irrespective of race, is essentially educable. It follows that his intellectual and moral life is largely conditioned by his training and by his physical and social environment.

It often happens that a national group may appear to be characterized by particular psychological attributes. The superficial view would be that this is due to race. Scientifically, however, we realize that any common psychological attribute is more likely to be due to a common historical and social background, and that such attributes may obscure the fact that, within different populations consisting of many human types, one will find approximately the same range of temperament and intelligence.

6. The scientific material available to us at present does not justify the conclusion that inherited genetic differences are a major factor in producing the differences between the cultures and cultural achievements of different people or groups. It does indicate, on the contrary, that a major factor in explaining such differences is the cultural experience which each group has undergone.

7. There is no evidence for the existence of so-called "pure" races. Skeletal remains provide the basis of our limited knowledge about earlier races. In regard to race mixture, the evidence points to the fact that human hybridization has been going on for an indefinite but considerable time. Indeed, one of the processes of race formation and race extinction or absorption is by means of hybridization between races. As there is no reliable evidence that disadvantageous effects are produced thereby, no biological justification exists for prohibiting inter-marriage between persons of different races.

8. We now have to consider the bearing of these statements on the problem of human equality. We wish to emphasize that equality of opportunity and equality in law in no way depend, as ethical principles, upon the assertion that human beings are in fact equal in endowment.

9. We have thought it worth while to set out in a formal manner what is at present scientifically established concerning individual and group differences.

(a) In matters of race, the only characteristics which anthropologists have so far been able to use effectively as a basis for classification are physical (anatomical and physiological).

(b) Available scientific knowledge provides no basis for believing that the groups of mankind differ in their innate capacity for intellectual and emotional development.

(c) Some biological differences between human beings within a single race may be as great as or greater than the same biological differences between races.

(d) Vast social changes have occurred that have not been connected in any way with changes in racial type. Historical and sociological studies thus support the view that genetic differences are of little significance in determining the social and cultural differences between different groups of men.

(e) There is no evidence that race mixture produces disadvantageous results from a biological point of view. The social results of race mixture, whether for good or ill, can generally be traced to social factors.

Text drafted for UNESCO, June 1951, by the following scientists:

PHYSICAL ANTHROPOLOGISTS

Professor R. A. M. Bergman, Netherlands Anthropological Society, Amsterdam

Professor Ashley Montagu, Rutgers University, New Brunswick, New Jersey

Dr. Eugene Schreider, Laboratoire d'Anthropologie Physique, Institut de Paléontologie humaine, Paris

Dr. Harry L. Shapiro, Chairman, Department of Anthropology, American Museum of Natural History, New York

Dr. J. C. Trevor, University Lecturer in Anthropology, Faculty of Archaeology and Anthropology, Cambridge (U.K.)

Dr. Henri V. Vallois, Professeur au Muséum d'Histoire naturelle, Directeur du Musée de l'Homme, Paris

Professor S. Zuckerman, Department of Anatomy, Medical School, University of Birmingham

GENETICISTS

Professor Gunnar Dahlberg, Director, State Institute for Human Genetics and Race Biology, University of Uppsala, Sweden

Professor L. C. Dunn, Department of Zoology, Columbia University, New York

Professor J. B. S. Haldane, Department of Biometry, University College, London

Professor Hans Nachtsheim, Institut für Genetik, Freie Universität, Berlin

SEROLOGICAL ANTHROPOLOGIST

Dr. A. E. Mourant, Director, Blood Group Reference Laboratory, Lister Institute, London

Index

Index

Index

divorce, 149, 154–155
Dixon, R. B., 265
Dobuans, 114, 149, 151
Dobzhansky, Theodosius, 19, 39, 266–267, 269, 270
Dockstader, Frederick, 280
Douglas, Frederic, 280
Dravidians, 48, 90, 140
Dubinin, N. P., 268
Dunn, L. C., 294
Dyaks, 13, 14, 274, 282

Easter Island, 231–233
economic systems:
  bibliography of, 274–275
  and diffusion, 120–124
  and distribution methods, 124–130
  and division of labor, 109–111
  early technology, 105–109
  necessities of life, 111–120
Egyptians, ancient, 14, 200–201
  ethnocentric attitudes of, 2, 4, 39–40
Elisofon, Eliot, 280
endogamy, rules of, 139–140
English language, 89, 92, 95, 97, 98, 99, 101, 103
environment:
  cultural adaptation to, 71–72
  influence of, 290, 292
  prenatal, 19, 267–268
  and racial adaptation, 51–56, 270
  resources of, for art, 231–234
Episcopal Book of Common Prayer, 200
equality, human, 293
Erikson, Erik H., 278
Eskimoan language group, 90, 95–96
Eskimos, 57, 117, 119, 124, 144, 164, 201, 253, 279
  creation myths of, 39–40
  cultural shaping of, 74, 75, 78
  dispute settlement by, 171, 177
  ethics of, 210–211, 213
  ethnocentric attitudes of, 2, 4
  gestures of, 283, 284
ethical systems (see also values), 164, 210–213, 217

ethnocentrism, 1–5, 40–41, 256–259
  literature on, 262
  religious, 218
European racial varieties, 48
evolution:
  cultural, 51–53, 270
  and development of man, 24–38
  evidences of, 15–18
  process of, 18–23, 266–267
exogamy, rules of, 139
eyes, in evolution, 27, 34

Fairchild, Henry Pratt, 133, 275–276
family systems, 147–155, 160, 170, 211, 276
  bibliography of, 273–275
  biology and, 131–132
  courtship and, 141–142
  and dispute settlement, 171, 174
  marriage and, 144–147
  mate selection and, 132–140
fathers, role of, 131–132
fertility, 150–152
fertility rites, for earth, 201
Fijians, 241, 283
Finno-Ugric language group, 90
fire, discovery of, 107–108
fish, and evolution, 25–26, 28
food, 105–107, 123–124
  and cultural variation, 111–114, 265
  distribution of, 124, 126
  and religious belief, 164
Ford, C. S., 276
Ford, Daryll, 126, 275
Forest Negro racial variety, 48
fossils, 15–17, 266–267
Frank, Lawrence K., 64, 271
Fraser, Douglas, 280
Frazer, James G., Sir, 264
freedom, of variation, 7, 170, 277
French, 98–99, 114
Freud, Sigmund, 206, 272
Fried, Morton H., 271
Fromm, Erich, 278, 281
funeral masks, 253

Gaster, Theodor H., 264
genes, 18–21, 267–268

Index

Index

Nootka Indians, 103
Norbeck, Edward, 192, 278
Nordic racial variety, 46, 48
North American Colored racial variety, 48
North Carolina snake handler, 194
North Chinese racial variety, 48
Noüy, Lecomte du, 8–9, 266

Oakley, Kenneth, 106, 107, 275
Old Stone Age, 38, 149, 179, 219–220
    inventions of, 106–108
    religious practices of, 180–183
Ona, of Tierra del Fuego, 77, 78, 272
Orient:
    food variations in, 112, 114
    gestures of, 282, 283
    and westernization, 79
ornamentation, 117–120, 239, 243, 246
ownership, concept of, 129–130

Paleo-Asiatic language group, 90
Paleolithic, see Old Stone Age
paleontology, 15–17, 266
Pawnee Indians, 166
Peking man, 50, 68, 180–182
pelvis, 30, 32, 35
Penutian language group, 90
personality development, 152–154, 155
    and racial comparisons, 60–61
Peruvians, 55, 96
Philippines, 142, 175
phonemes, 92–95
physical appearance:
    and beauty concepts, 2, 118, 133–138, 275–276
    and racial classification, 44–50
physical differences, see biological variation
Pindal, Spain, 70
Pintinjarra "passport stick," 174
Pithecanthropus erectus, 34, 36, 37
Pithecanthropus pekinensis, see Peking man
Plains Indians, 118, 175, 279
Pleistocene epoch, 30–31

political systems:
    bibliography of, 277–278
    and cultural differences, 161
    and social controls, 170
    and social justice, 170–176
    territoriality and, 156–160
    and war concept, 178
polygamy, 147–148
Polynesians, 139, 147, 283, 284
    language of, 83, 98
    as racial variety, 48
Poro masks, 172, 253
Porteous, Stanley, 58
potlatches, 128, 164, 245, 277
pregnancy, 144, 147, 149–152
primates, evolution of, 26–38, 269
primitive groups, and intergroup relations, 82–83
psychological characteristics (see also personality), 54, 75, 292–293
psychological inertia, 79, 163–164, 168
public opinion, 163–164, 169
Pueblo Indians, 77–78, 188
punishment, 171–178
Pygmies, 118, 138

Quechumaran language group, 90
Queen, S. A., 277

races:
    bibliography of, 269–271
    classification of, 44–50
    comparison of, 53–62
    and cultural variation, 75, 272
    definition of, 45
    myths of, 38, 39–44
    origin of, 50–53
    UNESCO statement on, 271, 290–294
racial discrimination, rationalization of, 41–43
racial fusion, 46–47, 61–63, 139, 293, 294
racists, 47, 62
Radin, Paul, 10, 212, 265, 279
radioactive fallout, 266
rain ceremonies, 196, 199–200, 278
Rasmussen, Knud, 210, 279

302

Index